*This volume is dedicated
by its editor to*
REGGIE GRENFELL
*and to the joyous memory
of his darling wife*
JOYCE

INTRODUCTION

This penultimate volume will need no introduction to the faithful, but new readers may demand a little guidance.

In 1926 I had been taught by George at Eton, where he was an outstanding teacher and housemaster. In my last year he started an English course, and it was then that I fell under the spell of his infectious enthusiasm for literature. After I left Eton our ways parted. George taught for a further twenty years before retiring to Suffolk. We met again in 1949 and thereafter saw and wrote to each other occasionally, but the origin of this correspondence was a dinner-party in 1955, during which George complained that no one wrote to him in Suffolk, and I accepted his challenge.

To avoid repetitive footnotes I should say that Comfort was my wife; Bridget, Duff, and Adam my children. Ruth Simon had been my beloved prop and stay since 1946.

As before, in the first letters I have retained the opening and signature, which are afterwards omitted, since they are almost always the same: any variation is printed. Similarly I have given our full home addresses in the early letters and then abbreviated them. From Monday to Friday I lived in a flat above my publishing office at 36 Soho Square. At the beginning of this volume George was almost seventy-seven and I was fifty-two.

RUPERT HART-DAVIS

Marske-in-Swaledale
December 1982

My dear George

I can see that it's going to be another week before this correspondence resumes its normal level. Towards the end of last week I was
submerged by what you and Shakespeare would call a whoreson cold,
and was obliged to cancel my week-end plans and stay here streaming
—but greatly cherished by Ruth. Today I am nearing normal again,
and your letter has been forwarded from Bromsden.

So glad you approve of Adam, who, as you may have guessed, is
the apple of his mother's eye—and indeed of his father's. I now find
that you can't put a boy up for the M.C.C. till he's *seventeen*, so I shall
hang on to the form and submit it for your signature in June. What a
gay time you examiners have in Cambridge—movies every night
indeed! I have finished *Coningsby* and enjoyed it all, though I'm sure
Sybil is a better book. I long to know the name of the don who told you
I was doing wonders for the London Library, but perhaps you never
knew it.

Ruth and I are both sad to know that you won't be at the Lit. Soc.
And who will protect me from the Knight of the Rueful Countenance?[1] Your visit to Bromsden was enormously popular with all ranks,
and I rejoiced to see Pamela looking so well.

I expect you saw Raymond Mortimer on Hotson[2] in the *Sunday
Times*. Priestley in *Reynolds News* (but who reads it?) was much more
forthcoming and pronounced himself entirely converted. I shall
eagerly await your opinion. As always, vested interests will be massing
on the other side: if Hotson could be proved right, all their damned
text-books would have to be rewritten. We ran into John Wain to-day,

---

[1] Cuthbert Headlam.
[2] *Shakespeare's Wooden O* by Leslie Hotson (1960), in which he sought to
prove that the London theatres of Shakespeare's time were literally 'in the
round'.

just married again and very cheerful—no sign of the Angry Young Man about him except that he wore no tie.

Now I must do some of the mass of work which Xmas and my cold have caused to pile up. You shall get a proper letter from Bromsden next week.

Ruth sends her love.

Yours ever
Rupert

The Timbralls
Eton

6 January 1960 (77th birthday!)

My dear Rupert

I did not know of the new M.C.C. rule about entry, but anyway my support of Adam remains, whatever vagaries the Committee may indulge in.

My three days at Cambridge were oddly busy, partly because what you regard as my masochistic instincts made me go to two films; one, *Great Expectations*, excellent, the other—My God! It was called *Expresso Bongo*,[1] all din and glitter and semi-nudity, and acrobatic dancing, and prestissimo dialogue, mostly to me inaudible, but, they told me, crackling with wit and satire—which made it particularly unfortunate that all the w. and s. I did hear was insipid beyond words. I felt 150 years old. My colleagues—intelligent young-middle-aged men—were as pleased with it as Mr Peter Magnus said his friends were when he signed himself 'Afternoon'.[2] Have you or has Ruth seen it? If either of you didn't think it dreadful rubbish, I shall give up trying to keep up.

The don who spoke of you and the London Library was *either* Duff of Trinity (son of T.D. Duff) or Denis Robertson (eminent economist) or Stanley Bennett (bibliographer, Chaucerian, fellow of Emmanuel), a genial friendly chap, commonly known in charitable Cambridge circles as 'Backstairs Bennett'—they all pull strings, but apparently he does it more successfully than most. All three are men who do not talk nonsense, and never talked less than when they praised R.H-D.

[1] The film of a musical play by Wolf Mankowitz (1958).
[2] In *Pickwick Papers*, chapter xxii.

I haven't yet got round to Leslie Hotson, as I have been tackling *The Owl of Minerva*[1] which is not a short book. What a grim and disillusioning series of experiences! Why, I wonder, though always interested, did I feel vaguely unsatisfied? Is it that his experiences are somehow not digested—or that the style, when at all elaborated, often misses the target? I don't know. I am in fact a hopeless critic. Amis would know, Leavis would know. The sop to my humiliation is my confident certainty that both, in their separate ways, would know wrong, as Dizzy said was the defect of great thinkers. I must try *Coningsby* again.

At Cambridge I always find Trollope best for bedtime reading, after reading third-rate manuscripts all day. And shall I be lynched if I say how awfully bad *The Warden* seems to me? All its issues go below its surface—the whole business of John Bold and Eleanor left in the air, and he does not succeed in persuading me, at least, that the Archdeacon is not essentially a man of four letters, which he appears to want to do. I forget whether you are a Trollope fan—or share perhaps Gosse's distaste for 'the listless amble' of Trollope's style? I wonder if anyone in England has *all* his novels. I have read scores, it seems, but am always coming across the names of many I haven't. No secondhand bookshop ever has any beyond the Barchester lot. Odd.

I am sorry to miss the Lit. Soc. (though perhaps it is no bad thing not to attend *all* the dinners). I met a lady at tea with Christopher Stone—do you know him?—who asked if Sir Cuthbert was still (a) very handsome, and (b) carping, as he was when she knew him thirty years ago. My answer was yes and no (to which adjectives do you think?).

We go back on Friday, and a day or two later shall be housing my youngest, Mary, and her family. You would like her. The Lord Cranworth—*aetat* eighty-two—thinks she is the most fascinating young woman he has ever seen, to the frank amusement of M. and her husband. How the Ancient of Days does like making fools of us.

Do you ever do things quite wrong, misquote etc, as I am always doing, e.g. in a crib supplied to examiners in the G.C.E. Because here is the perfect defence: 'What is obvious is not always known, what is known is not always present. Sudden fits of inadvertency will surprise

[1] The autobiography of Gustav Regler (1959).

3

vigilance; slight avocations will seduce attention, and casual eclipses of the mind will darken learning.' Isn't it perfect? Johnson of course. I do hope it isn't too familiar to you. But even if it is you won't mind turning it over your tongue in the new year. Best love to Ruth. See you both in Feb—and even the wolf-month doesn't last for ever. But don't forget it is apt to show its teeth round about the 20th. *Verb. sap.*

Yours ever
G.W.L.

9 January 1960   Bromsden Farm
Henley-on-Thames
Oxon

Your excellent letter, written on your birthday, makes me fear you never got my birthday card. When I asked the girl in the shop whether she had any special ones for 77th birthdays she seemed amazed, so I had to make do with an ordinary one embellished with an apt quotation. Perhaps it will catch up with you.

I'm happy to say my whoreson cold has departed, and I am almost fit for what at Cambridge should clearly be called Examiners' Licence. *Expresso Bongo* indeed! It'll be strip-tease next, mark my words. I certainly haven't seen *E.B.*, nor has Ruth: we call for sterner stuff. I am not a Trollope fan, but only perhaps through lack of leisure. I mean, I'm all *for* him but haven't read many. Certainly I'm not in any way *anti*, and the professional hardheadedness of his writing habits, which so scandalised the readers of his *excellent Autobiography*, endears him to me. The Ivory Tower is not necessary for the production of literature, as I'm sure you'll agree. Where exactly does that splendid bit of Johnson come from ('What is obvious is not always known' etc)? It's a splendid Editor's Defence and I should like to have it by me, with chapter and verse.

Yesterday I, as they say, 'took delivery' of a new car—a Morris station-waggon, like our old one but seven years more up-to-date. Heinemann's[1] have bought it for me, and we are all delighted with it. Never before have we enjoyed a car with a *heater* in it, and today, in

[1] My publishing firm had been taken over by William Heinemann Ltd.

glorious sunshine, we drove snugly through the cold, at the sedate speed which 'running-in' demands, to the Cotswolds to lunch with Comfort's darling old stepmother. On the way I snatched half an hour in the antiquarian department of Blackwell's and emerged with five good books. Next Wednesday I am to spend the night with Sparrow at All Souls and attend a Christ Church gaudy as the guest of J.I.M. Stewart (the Michael Innes of detective story fame): you shall hear of it all next week, and of Tuesday's Lit. Soc.

Yesterday morning I took Diana Cooper to the crypt of St Paul's for a private view of Duff's memorial tablet (carved by Reynolds Stone), which is to be unveiled later this year. All the cathedral's heating is in the crypt, which is always warm and to me full of beauty and romance—with Nelson and Wellington sleeping out eternity side by side in vast hideous sarcophagi—though Wellington's battle-flags are wonderfully romantic and threadbare. Upstairs in the Cathedral proper the huge hanging Epstein strikes me as a fine thing in the wrong place. The surroundings are altogether too classical for such savage individuality.

Arthur Ransome, whom I visited on Tuesday, has had to give up chess, which he has played all his life, because at seventy-five he says it gives him a blinding headache. He is proposing to give all his chess books to Adam, much to A's delight.

Did I ever mention my friend Christopher Devlin? He is a Jesuit priest, brother of Patrick Devlin the judge and William Devlin the actor, and a charming person. He helped me a lot with the Gerard Manley Hopkins papers which were left unfinished when Humphry House died, and soon afterwards he (C.D.) was sent out to South Africa as a missionary. At first he hated it but gradually became reconciled. I have sent him books and occasional letters. Just before Christmas I got a scrawled note to say he was being flown home for a serious operation. Poor creature, he had cancer of the rectum: can you imagine anything more agonising? He had the operation just after Christmas and is apparently going on all right. His sister-in-law (the judge's wife) rang up to say he could have visitors, so I'm going to see him on Monday: he's at Cheam in Surrey. He's about my age: isn't it awful! I suppose one ought to be grateful every moment that one is well and without pain, but one never thinks of such things until someone one knows is involved. I suppose Christopher will somehow re-concile this appalling event with God's infinite mercy, but it will take some doing.

To end on a lighter note, Duff has discovered a new restaurant in Leicester Square called 'Guinea and Piggy'. You pay a guinea each as you go in, and you can eat as much as you like of over a hundred dishes hot and cold. Duff and his girl ate two kinds of fish, roast chicken, Boeuf Stroganoff, casserole of pheasant and two sweets—ah, youth, youth! I fear they'd make money on me.

14 January 1960   *Finndale House*
                                                 Grundisburgh
                                                      Suffolk

Your admirable birthday card arrived all right, many thanks, but at least two days late—after I had written. Never have I known the Xmas post so haywire. It was a very good quotation—dreadfully true. My Johnson sentence for you was from the magnificent preface to his Dictionary. Was ever a defence so complete—and every noun and adjective and verb is exactly the right one. I remember a large majestic youth called Keele giving it at the Fourth of June speeches on J's bicentenary, and the sight of Augustine Birrell's rich enjoyment of it in the audience. Keele spoke it beautifully, and I can still hear the final sentence: 'I therefore dismiss it with frigid tranquillity, having nothing to fear or to hope from censure or from praise.' Keele was killed in the first war. He was a fine chap. The preface is bound to be in the Johnson book which you published.

Exciting about your new car. I hope it means Heinemann has seen the light and is no longer tiresome. We too find the heater a great boon at the moment. The great frosts and snows are ten days early, damn them. Tyres have no real grip, and I walk to the post-box like Agag. The answer to Shelley's optimistic question 'Can Spring etc.' is 'Yes, a devilish long way.'

You must be, at the moment of writing, dining with John Sparrow and Michael Innes. Alington always put his detective stories at the very top. I liked some (viz *Hamlet, Revenge!*) but found some *too* ingenious, and one, *Stop Press* was it, curiously dull. You will have good company. I have a feeling that at All Souls talk flows more freely than at the Trinity high table, where the ghost of A.E. Housman still seems to exercise its costive sway. Do you remember his frigid comment on Wilfrid Blunt's saying in his diary that he thought A.E.H. would much prefer to remain silent. 'He was quite right.'

I like your remark about Epstein in the Abbey—nail on the head. You remember Johnson on the point 'A cow is a very good animal in a field, but we turn her out of a garden.' Things, high and low, must be in the right environment.

'Guinea and Piggy' sounds delicious. I can remember a dozen friends of sixty years ago who would have bust the restaurant in a week—but that, no doubt, is why *all* of them are no longer alive. How long did Mr Woodhouse[1] live on his gruel—'thin but not too thin', and his not very strong belief that 'an egg, lightly boiled, is not unwholesome'? I feel inclined to echo Marlow's 'Ah youth, youth'[2] at my youngest daughter and son-in-law who are going off on grossly unsafe roads this evening six miles to see Danny Kaye. They find the Suffolk climate a bit grim after Malaya, though frankly admitting that you *can* get tired of feeling sticky every day.

The three children regard their grandfather as an old funny. 'Out of the mouth of babes and sucklings' etc but they are great fun. Not that I share *all* their tastes. I suspect you too have outgrown your enthusiasm for snowballing or even making a snow-man. I hate the stuff more every winter.

By the way, I hope that grand Alpine book you sent me is selling well—oh yes *The White Spider* by name.[3] It has had very good reviews. I re-read bits of it and the pictures still give me a delicious shudder. Sleeping on a four-inch ledge half way up a precipice with the thermometer at zero—riotous fun it must be! Mountaineers must resemble chess-champions, possessing something in their make-up which others not only don't have but cannot even understand.

Tell me of your visit to Devlin. What awful things Fate can and daily does do. A cousin, whose memorial service I attended last week,

[1] In Jane Austen's *Emma*.
[2] In Conrad's 'Youth'.
[3] An account of climbing the Eiger by Heinrich Harrer (1959).

had had several years of absolute immobility from arthritis, and for the last year had been stone-blind. 'Fatherlike he tends and spares us!'

I have a pain in the chest—probably some form of dyspepsia. My family cheerfully suggest angina pectoris. How scored off they would feel if they turned out right! Was it not Walter de la Mare who said what splendid names for heroine and villain Lady Angina Pectoris and Sir Rheumatoid Arthritis would be?

To-morrow I stay a night with one XYZ, who wants to find out what exactly Eton has that no other school has, with a view to articles in the *Evening Standard* or *Daily Express* (which hates Eton). But how can it be put into words?

16 *January 1960*   *Bromsden Farm*

Almost as soon as I'd written to you last week I realised that the Johnson quotation must come from the preface to the Dictionary, and found it there. What a splendid piece of writing it is: perhaps I shall persuade Adam to recite it at Speeches when he's in Sixth Form.

The new car has survived its baptism of snow, though yesterday Comfort had to employ spade and sacks on her way to school. Heine-mann's paying for it is, I fear, more like hush-money than anything more encouraging—but we shall see. I'm sure you'd be wise to put in central heating: I'd do it here if I had the money. As it is I hug the library fire, whence I can watch the nuthatch bullying the tits on the bird-table.

Yes, *The White Spider* is selling well. This week I shall be sending you a brief memoir called *The Witch*,[1] which delighted me. The author was an émigrée Russian princess, and is now married to Edward Hulton, the newspaper tycoon.

Last week began with my visit to poor Christopher Devlin: it took me three hours, though I was with him for only twenty minutes. He is in a Catholic hospital at Cheam—an endlessly sprawling and flat section of what I believe is now called Subtopia. I took him some flowers and books, and I think he was pleased to see me, though he was clearly in pain: I shall try to go again next week.

[1] By Nika Hulton (1960).

On Wednesday I lunched with a beautiful and intelligent woman called Margaret Lane (when she writes) and Lady Huntingdon in private life. With her I went to my second meeting of the General Advisory Council of the B.B.C. (again quite amusing) and then caught a train to Oxford, where the arrangements for getting taxis at the station are barbaric and involved standing for ages in the snow with F.C. Francis, the Director of the British Museum, whom I ran into there. There were 101 diners in the festal lights of Christ Church hall, but I spoke only to my host, Michael Innes, a very shy Canon on my other side, and Masterman, the Provost of Worcester. I saw at once that, as regards the menu, it was all or nothing, so I went doggedly through the seven courses and six wines, all excellent (list enclosed), and was no whit the worse. M. Innes is a most civilised and amusing chap: he has written all those thrillers to educate his five children. I think the two best are *Lament for a Maker* and *The Journeying Boy*— but I daresay I've said so before. At about eleven I walked back through the snow to All Souls, where I found the Warden sound asleep by his study fire in the Lodging. He woke refreshed and kept me up till one, showing me all his latest book-acquisitions. The house is thoroughly comfortable, with a cherishing old manservant. I hadn't had a bath run for me since I left the army in 1945. Next morning Sparrow nobly drove me to catch the 9 a.m. train. I enjoyed it all.

Sparrow has promised to read all my Oscar proofs, and will probably review the book in *The Times Literary Supplement*, if his enthusiasm conquers his procrastination.

Meanwhile the plans for the London Library sale at Christie's go forward: I have a meeting about it on Monday, and *three* meetings on Monday and Tuesday about the Phoenix Trust. Adam is coming up for the night on Tuesday (the last of his holidays) and Ruth and I are taking him to *The Importance of Being Earnest* at the Old Vic. I feel that a few grains of general culture must be added to his strictly scientific diet.

Have you ever read anything so drearily turgid as Eden's memoirs? They're like chunks of the day-before-yesterday's newspapers written by a civil service clerk. I've always thought him a weak dull mediocrity (although he was at my tutor's) and here is proof positive. He deserves to have these tedious pages read back to him at dictation-speed by a Foreign Office Spokesman.

This is really the dead vast and middle of the winter—when, according to M.D. Hill[1], all the great frosts of the past century have begun. But all our six inches of a week ago are no more, save for a patch or two, and the usual sulky rawness, child of the East wind, has taken its place. The neighbourhood is stricken with fowl-pest and an obscure hepatic complaint is wiping out all the foxes. Not that I was ever a hunting-man. To sing 'John Peel' in my bath was as near as I ever got to being one. It was a kindly dispensation of Providence to see that I weighed thirteen stone when I was sixteen, so that my economical father would not run to what would practically have been a shire horse—certainly by the time I was eighteen and weighed fifteen stone I should have needed one whose neck was clothed with thunder, like the great Suffolk punch, Naunton Prince, over whose demise his late Majesty and I shed tears together.

I like your idea that Adam should speak the Johnson preface; it should certainly recur every fifty years. I suppose A. will be in Sixth Form about 1962. A great moment. I have told the library to get *The World of Paul Slickey*.[2] How you will jeer! I am having a row with them at the moment, as they are hesitant about getting *The Rainbow Bridge* by R.W. Livingstone.[3] They probably think it is a *San Luis Rey* whimsy whereas it is educational, and he is about the best writer on the subject. I have gently suggested that it would find more readers than *Biscay Harbourages and Anchorages*, *Hors d'oeuvres and Cold Table*, *A Concise Textbook of Midwifery*, *Asparagus*, *The History of Grocery*, and *Your Poodle*, all of which are recent acquisitions. The pretence that many human beings—especially officials—are sane must surely soon be abandoned.

Thank you for your Oxford menu. Very toothsome. Did I tell you about *my* lunch at the Ecu de France with XYZ, a nice journalist? All out of the Beaver's[4] pocket, I am glad to say. The peas and beans we ordered were shown to us beforehand in their pods. No deception,

[1] Eton master.

[2] A play by John Osborne (1959).

[3] Classical scholar (1880–1960). President of Corpus Christi College, Oxford 1933–1950. Knighted 1931.   [4] Lord Beaverbrook.

12/6 a helping (no, sorry, no such thing at the E. de F.—*a portion*). And after seeing the Beaver's face in this week's *Radio Times*, I wish I had asked for asparagus (15/-). I am sorry to see old C.H. Wilkinson of Worcester is dead.

All Michael Innes's whodunits are in the Ipswich library (with *Your Poodle*) and at the moment *not one* is on the shelves. Popularity!

I cannot agree with you about Eden's memoirs, for the simplest of reasons. I read half the first one and was too crushingly bored to read another line—for my line is Johnson's 'If I pick up a skein and find it packthread, I do not expect on going further to find it silk.' He must be the driest of sticks; I couldn't see a gleam of interest. Surely *The Times* will drop a packet over the stuff.

I had got to here yesterday, and this morning *The Witch* was on the breakfast-table, from the best and kindest of men, whose good deeds shine ever more brightly as the world grows naughtier—and sillier. Pamela instantly pounced upon it, saying she had nothing to read, so what will you. I am *pro tem.* up-to-date with my R.H-D. books, so got yesterday from the library Coleridge's Letters Vol IV, but they look a little daunting. You know of course Carlyle's perfect picture of C. in *John Sterling* 'Glorious islets too I have seen rise out of the haze (of C's talk)—islands of the blest and the intelligible'. Ten per cent genius and ninety per cent bore—an uncomfortable blend, but perhaps not a very uncommon one, e.g. daddy Wordsworth too—in his poetry as well as (I expect) his conversation.

I must go and hew wood.

23 *January 1960*   *Bromsden Farm*

Adam is due to leave Eton in July 1961, so he'll have to reach Sixth Form before then—perhaps this September. He went back cheerfully on Wednesday with an enormous stack of kit and rations. The night before, Ruth and I took him to dine in Soho (whitebait, steak, Beaujolais, cream cake) and on to the Old Vic, where we all three thoroughly enjoyed Oscar's masterpiece. The production wasn't frightfully good and Fay Compton couldn't get anywhere near Lady Bracknell, but the words and jokes are good enough to survive almost any acting (have you read the play lately?). Edith Evans was the Lady B of all time, and, as John Gielgud once said to me, any perfect performance spoils a part for a generation. E. Evans has similarly spoiled Millamant, and the Nurse in *Romeo*, but her Cleopatra was an agonising disaster.

Your lunch at the Ecu de France sounds pretty shameful: do you realise that all those restaurants would close down in a week if no one were allowed to eat on expense-accounts? Still, I'm glad you ate your way through a helping of beans at Lord Beaverbrook's expense.

Preparations for the London Library sale at Christie's are going forward, and since everything must be assembled *eight weeks* before the sale (which we hope will be at the end of April or beginning of May) I've got to try and collect it all by the end of February. My secretary (nice but stupid and oh so *slow*) is mercifully leaving on Feb 15, and I have hired a new one who promises much better, but she will not arrive in time to be much help with the sale.

Ruth and I were going down to Worthing on Monday to spend the day with the Eliots, but they can't bear it (Worthing—not the thought of us) any more and are returning to London on their way to Tangier. Like Jonah, T.S.E. suffers from breathlessness.

Last week we had a meeting of the Phoenix Trust, which, considering there was no progress to report, took an unconscionable time. I've told them that until the London Library's plight is dealt with, I can't give much time to the P.T.

I am going to include FitzGerald in my Reynard Library series. Except for *Omar* and a few oddments, the volume will consist entirely of letters—and jolly good ones too. There is no edition in Everyman or World's Classics. You will have to do your best to promote the sale in Suffolk. The editor is a nice woman called Joanna Richardson: I hope she won't make a mess of it.

I am deep in a 700-page-typescript history of the Franco-Prussian War (which I shall publish) and other manuscripts await my pleasure —or disgust. I have had specimen pages of Oscar, but as yet no date for first proofs: I rather long to get back to it and finish it off.

I see Diana's baby is safely christened, with Roger at the font: I trust he will take his duties seriously and in due course lead the boy to the Bishop. Every grinning press-photograph of your old chum

Cantuar confirms my dislike of the canting old sadist. He may be a good chairman, but that means nothing, as I know full well.

And now back to Moltke and the Siege of Paris—

I read *The Importance* a few years ago, when with a spurt of imbecility, unusual even for them, the Oxford and Cambridge Board set it in the Higher Cert. And Harrow, if you please, had to have a special paper, and I had to set it, when there were quite simply no more questions to ask. I suggested that we should ask for a suggested comment by Oscar on his play being set for examination; they grinned but wouldn't have it; they (rightly) feared reflections on the Board. Of course Edith Evans made any other Lady B. impossible. And I often read how the other parts are spoilt by the performers' obvious consciousness that they are being funny. They often strike me as very stupid people in the way they force things. E.g. *Hassan*[1] was nearly ruined by some farcical over-playing. But, as you say, the language of the play is unspoilable. Don't our sillier young critics object to any attempt to use words with grace and point, or is that fatuous little fashion on the way out? I am dubious. The hosts of Philistia, constantly changing their uniforms, seem to me to grow pretty steadily. But then I am frequently charged with pessimism. Well, I don't know. It depends on how far you look. I am not one, as regards friends and family etc., but I suppose that fundamentally anyone who has no belief whatever in a future life may or must be called a pessimist. Do you know that magnificent paragraph of Arthur Balfour's about the almost contemptible brevity of the human race's sojourn on the earth, which some day, 'tideless and inert, will no longer tolerate the race which has for a moment disturbed its solitude'?[2] Nowhere that I know is the stark factuality of science so majestically garbed in language. Bertrand Russell has a similar passage somewhere, but, as that old devil Logan Pearsall Smith noted, it is vitiated by a slight self-con-

---

[1] By James Elroy Flecker. First published 1922, produced at His Majesty's Theatre 1923.

[2] From *The Foundations of Belief* (1895).

sciousness; he quotes it in *Trivia* and adds 'By jove, that's a stunt!' The old lynx-eye!

I have just heard from the library that *Paul Slickey* is waiting for me, so by next week I shall have given it the minute attention that 'so great a work of art' (Alan Brien etc) deserves. But I am afraid you never went to see it. Pamela has *The Witch*, but as you might guess is so full of household chores that she is asleep before reading at night and up too early to do so in the morning. Hotson is tough but rewarding—like mountaineering.

Odd people, journalists. XYZ wanted to know all about Eton, and expressed great admiration etc. A very pleasant and civilised man. I told him plenty, but as I was fifteen years out of date, referred him to Oliver Van Oss[1]. I wrote to V.O. and told XYZ all was well. XYZ saw him and a few minutes later his articles appeared (though he had told me he would show them to me before they did). And all through this he has not sent me a line of thanks, information, or the articles in proof or print. I suppose when a journalist has got what he wants from A. that is the end of A. as regards courtesies etc. Or am I oversensitive? Very likely. They don't much like the articles at Eton. Perhaps his professed love for E was bogus; perhaps he is all bogus. He was once on the *Daily Express*. 'Shameful' is the right word for the Ecu de France luncheon. Easily overpowering the savours of rich viands and vegetables, the stink of money pervaded the place. Jowls, dewlaps and paunches were much in evidence. If, as I believe, some lunch there every day, have I not, as Wordsworth wrote, reason to lament what man has made of man?

I remember liking one or two Gerhardi novels, one of which was certainly *The Polyglots*. Is G. dead? Probably you know him quite well. What a mysterious job is yours. How *do* you spot a best—or even a good-seller? That page in *The Times* has a positive genius for dealing with books that I, at least, feel no desire to read. Do you find that?

I will do all I can for your Reynard FitzGerald. Isn't it time his letters were properly edited, or am I out of date? I have only Aldis Wright's two vols, which aren't really edited at all. Nobody and nothing alluded to ever have an explanatory note. A.W. was an old humbug. I remember him at Trinity—one of those absurdly formid-

[1] Eton master, later Headmaster of Charterhouse.

able-looking old dons, grim, rigid, incurably 1850. 'Sound your alarum, sir' was his angry injunction to an undergraduate on a bicycle who nearly ran him down (or have I told you that?). F. was a crusty, humorous old homo, almost forgotten in Woodbridge. He died the year I was born, but I have spoken to a man at whom F. aimed a mild blow with his stick when he got in his way. This man was ninety-eight.

Must I read Coleridge's letters? I opened a vol recently in the library and read 'So beautiful a countenance [Byron's] I scarcely ever saw, his teeth so many stationary smiles, his eyes the open portals of the sun.' Of course I read on, but soon lost my way in the purple fog of his English. But perhaps I should have persevered?

Love to Ruth. See you both on Feb 9.

30 January 1960   *Bromsden Farm*

The only thing Adam left behind this half was his electric torch, which is two foot long, made of rubber, and contains *five* batteries: a very jolly thing to pack. He is now in First Hundred and starting English Extra Studies (nowadays lowlier specialists don't do any E.S.).

I thought your Mr XYZ's articles were some of the worst (or rather, most pointless) of all time. What was the *reason* for them? Or didn't he know?

On Thursday Ruth and I had drinks with the Eliots in their flat. He is terribly breathless, poor old boy, but very amusing and nice. We talked of Max Beerbohm, whom he loved and admired, and he read me Ezra Pound's lines on Max, remarking on E.P.'s vision of Max's Jewishness. The lines run:

> The sky-like limpid eyes,
> The circular infant's face,
> The stiffness from spats to collar
> Never relaxing into grace;
>
> The heavy memories of Horeb, Sinai and the forty years,
> Showed only when the daylight fell
> Level across the face
> Of Brennbaum 'The Impeccable'.

Whatever one may think of Ezra (and I don't think much), these lines are rather fine, don't you think? And they start new trains of thought. The Eliots have now flown to Morocco, where they stay till March.

You will be disappointed to hear that I *don't* know William Gerhardi, though he is undoubtedly alive, and I imagine pretty hard up. It's usually impossible to forecast what books are going to sell, unless the author already has a steady public. I always assume that anything I particularly like will not sell at all, but publish it nevertheless. If one abandons one's own opinion in an attempt to gauge the market, one is lost indeed. It's a mug's game.

I loved the Aldis Wright anecdote: it now looks as though my Reynard FitzGerald may not materialise, since the American who has been editing the Letters for twenty years, and seemed to have died on them three years ago, has now announced that his labours are almost completed.

The only way to tackle Coleridge's letters is one or two at a time, skipping: otherwise you'll assuredly get bogged down.

A very sprightly letter from Edmund Blunden in Hong Kong contains two brief epigrams, *viz*:

ON CERTAIN MEMOIRS
Does EDEN call to mind *Paradise Lost*?
One thing was not in Eden—well, a Frost.

K. LEAR continues
Let them anatomise Eden. My fierce daughter
Poured poison on me, this boss pours cold water.

When are you coming up to London next week? If I don't hear to the contrary I'll post on Sunday to Grundisburgh, and in any case we shall expect you at six at Soho Square on the Tuesday. I shall have had a London Library meeting in the afternoon. Dear old Masefield has offered a set of all his books in print (about twenty), with something specially written in each. Tomorrow morning I am driving round to John Piper and Osbert Lancaster to collect their contributions to the sale. It all takes a lot of time and work.

Last week Ruth and I went to *two* entertainments—the film of *Our Man in Havana*, which was enjoyable if not frightfully good, and the Eugene O'Neill play *A Moon for the Misbegotten* at the Arts Theatre, which is gripping and excellently acted.

I found I hadn't got the first volume of Froude's *Carlyle* here, so I've started the *Life of Sterling* instead, and am finding it most enjoyable.

Estimates on Oscar show that it will make 850 *large* pages, and if I can't somehow manage to print more than 3000 copies the price will have to be *five guineas*. (The setting up of the type will cost £1500, and the more copies one can spread this over, the cheaper each copy will be.) My chief hope is that the American publishers will agree to my printing their edition at the same time as mine. If they do, and I can print a total of 10,000 copies, I can publish at *three* guineas, which is a little better. See with what mundane considerations the purity of scholarship is beset!

We have some aconites in flower, and a few tiny snowdrops, but there is water, water everywhere. Take care you don't go under.

4 February 1960 (the day Carlyle died)   *Grundisburgh*

I wonder who does English Extra Studies now. It is very important. Only Macnaghten of my colleagues knew that it was a more exacting job than nearly any other. He used delightfully to say 'Anyone can teach Latin and Greek', which of course isn't quite true, or why do so few manage to do it? But he did realise what a razor's edge one is on, rousing interest in Eng. Lit. And among *my* bouts of melancholy, which all old men have, one of the worst is 'how much better I could do that job now!' An old story of course. My successor was H.K. Prescot, a man I always found rather gloomy. He was apt to talk about Chekov (spelling?) and on one occasion took them through 'The Turn of the Screw', which to me verges on the outlandish as a set study for adolescents. Tell me how Adam gets on. I suspect that he will get more light on Eng. Lit. from his father than from anybody else.

Those are good lines of Ezra P's (a tremendous ass, by his comments on other and better men—and of course the war). *Was* M.B. a Jew? I miss the allusion to Brennbaum ('That's it!' cried Michael Finsbury, 'Very stupid!').[1]

[1] In *The Wrong Box* by R.L. Stevenson and Lloyd Osbourne.

I am sorry about your FitzGerald. I had already been preparing the Woodbridge library for its reception and dissemination. And those two admirable epigrams of E.B. He is wasted at Hong Kong.

You might be amused to hear the story of XYZ. He rang me up at Eton, saying he was about to write four articles on Eton, poured gallons of butter over me ('everyone tells me you are the one who' etc etc) and mentioned as great friends of his several O.E's whom I knew to be good chaps. So I had that disgraceful lunch with him and subsequently told him plenty about Eton—which he professed to admire immensely. He was excessively friendly, and really very pleasant. *BUT* in the next few days I wrote to him three or four times apropos of introducing him to Van Oss, and generally smoothing the way for him at Eton. He never sent one word of acknowledgement or thanks. Last Friday I lunched with Birley[1], who wanted to know all about the background of the articles, as the Governing Body might want to know. He was much amused at my not knowing that geniality is part of a journalist's stock-in-trade, and that they turn it off as soon as they have got from you all they want. (Incidentally, I had gently reminded XYZ that he had said I should see the articles before they appeared. I didn't—or afterwards either.) I have now got hold of the articles, and very poor stuff they seem. Several facts are wrong, and very many of the inferences etc drawn from those that are right. I lent XYZ a small book on Eton, and have sent a *not* very effusive postcard asking for its return. He hasn't yet sent it, and I am rather hoping he won't, as in the small hours a letter has been taking shape in my mind, of which the gist or nub is that its loss is a small price to pay for the revelation of what a Beaverbrook journalist regards as civilised behaviour, and ending by saying this is so far from the normal view that he may be surprised at my being able only in irony to call myself his sincerely. One or two more ponderings at 5.30 a.m. will do to polish it up. How I do loathe the Press!

There is a good deal of abusive stuff in the life of Middleton Murry which I am in the middle of.[2] Did you know him at all? If not I expect you have heard plenty about him from T.S.E.—one of the many who at any given moment one is not quite sure are or are not on speakers

---

[1] Robert Birley (1903–1982), then Headmaster of Eton. Knighted 1967.
[2] By F.A. Lea (1959).

with M.M. A very odd chap. I can't make much headway with all that introspection and metabiology, whatever that may ultimately be, but I rather like him. I don't much like K. Mansfield, and still less D.H. Lawrence (an old *bête noire*).

Last week I sat under your old hero the Archbishop of C. He was full of fun. He is resigning the Chairmanship of the Y.B.A. and there is a movement on foot for the committee to give him a dinner (£3 a head). The cream of the joke is that I think it will fall just beyond the date on which my term on the committee comes to an end. But I must tread warily; they may suggest a retrospective levy. A portentous man called Sir Griffith Williams is the moving spirit, and, like Habakkuk, is *capable de tout*. He is one of those men who *look* far more important than anyone can possibly *be*—as Desmond MacCarthy said very young elephants do.

I go to London on *Tuesday* and then stay for two nights at 7 The Grove, Highgate Village, N.6.

6 February 1960   *Bromsden Farm*

Adam reports that his English Extra Studies are divided equally between Keats (please send me an edition, he adds) and some novel published last month. No such nonsense would have been permitted in G.W.L.'s day.

I imagine the Beerbohms may have had Jewish blood: 'Brennbaum' was simply a slender disguise for 'Beerbohm'. All the literary blokes mentioned in those particular poems of E.P.'s are given fictional names.

My FitzGerald volume is not yet finally kiboshed, so don't let the Woodbridge library lose interest. I did just know Middleton Murry (I was at Cape's when they published his autobiography and other books) but only slightly. An interesting but intolerable man, I should say, though I haven't yet read this new biography.

I am gradually collecting objects for the London Library sale. Leonard Woolf has sent copies of the first six Hogarth Press books, which he and Virginia set up and printed by hand: they should fetch a lot. And the splendid old G.M. Trevelyan says that he can never repay the London Library, without which his early books could not have been written. He is giving us drawings by Domenichino, Romney and Edward Lear, as well as the manuscript of his own autobiographical essay!! He apologised for not bringing them to London, as he is too blind, so I am to collect them at Cambridge on Monday afternoon. I shall go down after lunch, attend a dinner at Trinity Hall as Graham Storey's guest, spend the night (chastely, *bien entendu*) with Humphry House's widow, catch the 8.45 a.m. train to London, and prepare for the London Library meeting, the Lit. Soc. *and* your visit to Soho Square. I do hope you won't have too much difficulty getting there from Highgate. Thank goodness the Railway Strike isn't till the following week. Last Monday was a foretaste of things to come. When I got to Paddington at 9.45 a.m. there were three hundred people queueing for taxis, and more for buses, so there was nothing to do but walk. Unfortunately I had two heavy bags, and when I reached Soho Square an hour later I was, as the Americans say, 'fit to be tied.' Every street was solid with stationary vehicles, loud with curses, and heavy with the fumes of petrol.

I have just been sent the proofs of the first volume of an American (two-volume) biography of Mrs Besant. She's certainly ripe for a volume, but will she stand *two*? And is this chap (a university professor in Chicago) the man for the job? I must start on it tonight. This morning my eye fell on *The Egoist* (I have a battered first edition—three vols—which belonged to Augustine Birrell) and I took down the first vol, found the first chapter enchanting, and quickly put the book back on the shelf in case I should be so beguiled that my work would go by the board. If I ever have a free day I'll go a bit further: when did you last try it?

Today the *sun* came briefly out, and I did my first spell of garden-work for many months: rain is prophesied for tomorrow, so Mrs Besant may get a look in.

I have sent for that new life of Conrad, which sounds excellent. The author is a nice intelligent fellow, very industrious and thorough.[1] No proofs of Oscar yet: Ruth and I are both longing to get at them—and we're both looking eagerly forward to 6 p.m. on Tuesday.

---

[1] Jocelyn Baines (1924–1972).

Again some of us lingered on after the rest of you had gone—Ivor, Roger, Tim, and Martin Charteris, because the divine good fortune emerged that Ivor Brown was on M.C.'s way home and that that home is only a few hundred yards from where I am, so a long and tedious journey was avoided. I was very well placed between Ivor B. and Tim. I didn't notice who your neighbours were: I hope they were good value. Did those empty chairs mean defaults at the last moment? Where was Peter F? Where, so to speak was Bohun?[1]

My sister took me off to a film yesterday—*Anatomy of a Murder*. Nice and long and mainly consisting of an American trial for murder. I enjoyed it, though my ears missed a good deal, and it was never really clear whether the young wife *had* been raped or not. All hinged on a pair of panties, a psychiatrist, and the fact that Mary was not the mistress of the murdered raper but his daughter. Perhaps the book will make all clear. There were several passages of which Queen Victoria would not have approved.

Life is full of mystery. This evening a photographer and young woman turned up out of the blue to take snaps of me talking about the family to the young woman. This is all for the *Queen* newspaper—unfamiliar to me—run by Francis Wyndham, a cousin of Pamela's and once in my house. A good lad with brains (something of a writer).

The railwaymen are obviously insane. We *may* escape something very like a general strike, but hadn't the boil better burst? How obvious it is that we can't go on in this atmosphere of perpetual strikes threatened or actual. But how is it to be tackled? The trouble is that democratic government demands (1) more brains (2) more unselfishness (3) more patience, and (4) more imagination than there is the smallest reason to suppose human nature will be able to produce for several hundred years. Aphorism by GWL.

Just finished another Trollope in the train, *Sir Harry Hotspur*—not very good, though of course readable as always. The characters are all black and white, and the young lady really does die of a broken heart, which they tell me does *not* happen—especially as the young man who broke it was a blackguard of vintage strength and cheated at cards.

[1] 'Where's Bohun?' (Bernard Shaw, *You Never Can Tell*, act iv).

Did you ever read the Tranby Croft baccarat case[1]—and if so tell me *why* Sir William cheated. His income was about £7–8000 a year. But my uncle who was in his regiment said he was suspected long before of cheating at cards by his brother-officers. Very rum. Who was the duchess who frankly cheated and they used to say 'Now, duchess, keep your hand up—no sly work below the table'? I like those old aristocrats, e.g. the one with kleptomania, whose valet's chief duty was to return in the morning the silver cruets and spoons which his master had brought from last night's dinner.

*14 February 1960**Bromsden Farm*

My Saturday writing plan broke down yesterday, for we were out all day, driving over to lunch with Patrick Devlin, the judge, and his wife at Pewsey, near Marlborough, where they have a beautiful centrally-heated Georgian house. My friend Christopher D., Patrick's brother, is there recovering from his ghastly operation, and I went up and saw him after lunch. Our new car has now had a radio installed— the first time we've ever had such—and on the way back we listened to the rugger international from Twickenham.

Duff reports that he is on the short list for a Commonwealth Fellowship (interview in March) and that three skeletons have been dug up in the excavation for a new building at Worcester College: victims of the Black Death, says Duff.

Did you realise that I was feeling exhausted and stupid on Tuesday? I hope it didn't show too much. My dinner neighbours were Tony Powell and Jo Grimond, whom I like very much. Peter had simply shirked, thinking the dinner was next week. I'm so glad you got a lift back to Highgate—what a stroke of luck! We must make sure that all future candidates are strategically placed round London to convey you home. Have you got your deaf-aid yet? It's no use going to the movies if you can't hear who has raped whom.

I might have known that Francis Wyndham was a cousin of Pamela's—everyone interesting is. His mother Violet, as I'm sure you

[1] For a full account of this famous case, see *Cheating at Cards* by John Welcome (1963).

know, was the only child of Oscar's friend Ada Leverson (née Bedding-ton) whom Oscar called The Sphinx. I have got a lot of O's letters to her, and I need Violet's permission to print a letter from her father, Ernest Leverson, who was a rich diamond-merchant, as well as a number of Ada's contributions to *Punch* (some very amusing) which I unearthed.

The day after I saw you, old Jonathan Cape died suddenly, and his *Times* obituary, which I had promised to do eighteen months ago, had to be dashed off in a couple of hours. Did you see it on Thursday? It was exactly as I wrote it, except that the editor had inserted the sentence about *Earlham*, which in my haste I had forgotten. All the same, 'best-seller' is an exaggeration in reference to *E*. The first edition consisted of 750 copies, and I suspect that the rushed reprints were of 500 each.

I'm delighted the strike is off, even though I shall now have to attend Cape's funeral at Petersham, near Richmond, at noon on Mon-day. I am also supposed to be writing Diana Cooper's obituary for *The Times*, but I find the task unsympathetic to the point of impossibility when the subject is alive and flourishing.

I think Sir William cheated because he liked winning, so that his wealth had nothing to do with it. Mind you fire that last shot at the unspeakable XYZ—don't weaken!

Next Wednesday I have to take the chair at a Foyle's Literary Lunch (I've never been to one before) in honour of Priestley's massive new tome *Literature and Western Man*, of which I've read a good chunk: it's a remarkable achievement, though I can't quite understand why he took the trouble to write it, or who exactly is expected to read it.

The American publishers of Oscar's letters have proved most co-operative, and I shall now be able to price the book (850 large, closely-printed pages) at 63/- maximum, and possibly 45/-. Anyhow the printers have at last been given the go-ahead, and proofs should start coming in before the end of March. Then the fun begins!

E.M. Forster has offered to give the manuscript of *A Passage to India* for the London Library sale! He says it's messy and incomplete, but it should fetch a tidy sum. I fear I shan't get it without another journey to Cambridge, and I'm always so short of time. You've no idea how often I envy you your comparative leisure to do and read what you want.

I didn't think you were in the least stupid last Tuesday, but that you were rather tired. And added the mental rider, 'and who wouldn't be?' Has any friend of yours *not* said at one time or another that you work at too many things? I trow not (though never quite certain what 'trow' means). How good you are at 'keeping your friendships in repair'; hardly a letter does not mention a visit to some ailing friend.

Old Cape must have been a good man. Your excellent obituary didn't mention, what some other did—that he had always had a particularly intelligent succession of readers, one of which was R.H-D. Does *Earlham* still sell? Very doubtful I imagine. To take trouble over *how* one says what one has to say on paper is still out of fashion. The man Naipaul who called *E.* 'estimable but rather dreary' still flourishes.

The first batch of your old letters will be shortly on their way home. I must see that they are in order. The fly in the amber of leisure to read all one wants to is that it belongs to a period of life when one gradually becomes more conscious of 'Time's hurrying footsteps' and Winston's 'surly advance of decrepitude'. The grim Scottish aurist says a permanently flat drum in my left ear is not temporary but eternal, i.e. old age. But some kind of hearing-aid will probably materialise in a week or two. They tell me the defect of it is that what one hears most clearly is one's breathing and the beating of one's heart. We shall see.

Alas, the man XYZ has returned the book I lent him with a tremendously smarmy letter, in which he pours far too many coals of fire on his own head and far too much oil and melted butter on mine. So the beautiful letter I was preparing for him is wasted. Housman would no doubt have kept it for the next harmless German who said something about the enclitic δή which H. disapproved of. These great scholars are very absurd with their pedantry and thin skins. They *sit* too much and get dyspepsia. Who was the scholar of Milton's day who was for some reason cut open after death, and his tummy was found to be half full of sand?

The Witch is delightful. I love the demure way she records the really incredible deeds and words of those irresistibly comic fairies—and the doctor, too old to know the sex of his patient, and the countess, buried, or rather not buried, in her hat. And I have enjoyed Nicolas Bentley's *A Choice of Ornaments*, though perhaps he does quote too often and too lengthily. Do you know him? I always liked whatever his father wrote—except of course his 10,000 leaders for whatever his paper was. He had an excellent style and any amount of humour and sense. Wouldn't you put *Trent's Last Case* very near the top of all 'whodunits'? I like the final scene at Simpson's, when Trent begs Mr Cupples to speak lower when asking for a glass of milk, on the grounds that the head waiter has a weak heart.

I am sure you are right about Sir William's motive—the same really as Iago's and T.J. Wise's. And perhaps the murderer(?) Wallace who in the end got away with what J. Agate called the perfect murder.[1] Bernard Darwin tells me there is no doubt that W. did it, but I don't know that there is any fresh evidence.

Tell me all about the Foyle lunch. I am always rather pro-Priestley, but I know nothing much about him. He may have jawed us a bit too much in the war, but he does, *me judice*, talk a great deal of sense.

20 February 1960   *Bromsden Farm*

I rather enjoy the false glow of non-stop activity which your letters cast on me: without them I might be overwhelmed by my own idleness, procrastination and lack of method, but I have only to remind myself 'George thinks I never stop working' to feel reassured once more.

Jonathan Cape's funeral on Monday was icy, and the clergyman so thin-voiced, old and doddery that I feared he might have to be shovelled into the same grave. The church at Petersham is a lovely old building with high pews, and a gallery round three sides of it. I travelled down by tube and taxi, but got a speedy lift back from a chartered accountant (Cape's and mine). He said that for years he had tried to persuade Jonathan to give some of his fortune to his five children, and so avoid at least part of the crippling death-duties, but the old boy always refused. Power to such as he is simply money, and if

[1] See volume iv of these letters, p. 150.

you part with any of your money you must lose some of your power. I understand this attitude without sympathising with it. I have never had any money (nor shall ever have) and my love of power is minimal: the Treasury will be lucky if they ever get anything out of me. Jonathan was in fact, despite my obituary notice, one of the tightest-fisted old bastards I've ever encountered, though his partner Wren Howard is even tighter. Still, one doesn't engrave a man's faults on his tombstone, does one?

The thought of my first batch of letters winging their way home is a sobering one, but perhaps one day I shall bless them and you— but the latter I do continually.

I'm longing to bawl into your hearing-aid, and only wish it was an ear-trumpet. My paternal great-grandmother used one, and she lived to be ninety-five.

I like your attribution of pedants' dyspepsia to their sitting too much, and hasten to quote (not, I fear, for the first time):

'Don't come flying out of your chair like that, Mr Venus!'
'I ask your pardon, Mr Wegg. I am so soured.'
'Yes, but hang it,' says Wegg argumentatively, 'a well-governed mind can be soured sitting!'

I only wish I had Dickens at my finger-tips, as Bernard Darwin has. Perhaps one day . . . ?

So glad you liked *The Witch*: the author was beginning to be rather a nuisance, sending her chauffeur round to every bookshop in London (including antiquarian ones) to ask if they had copies of the book, but mercifully she has now set off round the world by air, and by the time she gets back her detective ardour may have cooled. Nick Bentley is indeed a friend, and a most delightful fellow. Last year he too had a nasty go of jaundice, and his first drink (after, I think, the prescribed period of abstinence) produced such a severe relapse that he was in bed again for weeks. His father I saw but never knew: *Trent's Last Case* and the Clerihew should put his immortality beyond question.

The Foyle lunch was hard work. I took an old friend as my guest, a most amusing widow called Josephine Bott (see my *Hugh Walpole*, *passim*), and when we arrived Miss Foyle (dolled up to the tens and immensely refined) asked if I would receive the guests. I said I was her servant, so Jo and I stood solemnly inside the door and warmly shook hands with dozens of people as an enormous man in red called out their names with a roar. Tiny little old women with purple dresses and white fur hats and a surprising number of men. Jo almost got the giggles and tried to abandon me, but I made her stay, pointing out that we were in a strong position, since none of the guests had the faintest idea who *we* were, whereas we knew at least all their names. Several hundred people sat down to what proved a surprisingly palatable lunch (sole, chicken, ice-cream and peaches, white wine). I was between the two Priestleys, which was fun. After lunch I made a brief introductory speech, then Richard Church spoke well but dully about Priestley, and J.B.P. replied in his happiest and least combative vein. He said: 'When I arrived, the Chairman asked me why I always arrive at a function in my honour with a face of thunder (as I indeed had), and I'll tell you. Most of the time I'm glum because I'm not being praised, and on the rare occasions when I *am* praised I'm ashamed because I haven't done better.' Which I thought rather charming. The whole thing took more than two hours.

25 February 1960   *Grundisburgh*

Back of my hand to you six times! Your picture of yourself as a *dolce far niente* devotee, muddling through a slackish day, is on the same level of truth as Himmler's obituary reference to the unspeakable Heydrich as 'this good and radiant man'. Ask Ruth if it is an accurate self-portrait—or indeed anyone who knows you.

I see there was a side to old Cape which you touched on very lightly in *The Times*, but, as in epitaphs, a man is not on oath in an obituary. There are/is a number of people mentioned in your letters to me who will cut a very different figure after your letters—selected! —have been published. If the Lit. Soc. is on March's second Tuesday, that happily cuts out the Johnson Club dinner on the same day. How nice it is to make a choice between A. and B. when there is no rivalry. I hope Harold Nicolson will be at the Lit. Soc. dinner, as I want to tackle him about a remark he is reported to have made on Thomas

27

Carlyle—in today's *Times*, *viz* that he was 'a horrid old thing' whom he was delighted to think that nobody now read. If not misreported, it is below the level we expect from H.N. even as an *obiter dictum*— and as to the last statement, has not R.H-D just been reading the horrid old thing? So you must join in tackling him.

My hearing-aid is not yet to hand, in fact I still await a summons to the clinic. It is a rather sinister fact that several people who have the thing quite rarely use it. Like another friend whose first action when taking his seat at table, is to remove his dentures, which he says are just tolerable except when eating!

I notice in today's literary page in *The Times* that there is a sudden revival of interest in Southey, of all dreary dogs. Are you aware of this? It seems to be his political writings rather than his poetry. Or are people murmuring the tale of old Kaspar as they trudge to their work? I have always thought his couplet the most pathetic thing in the *Oxford Book* (except of course, for a different reason 'Meet we no angels, Pansie?')

> Yet leaving here a name I trust
> That will not perish in the dust.

—and hitherto, surely no hope has seemed less likely of fulfilment? Or am I addressing one whose heart always misses a beat when he thinks of how the water comes down at Lodore—easily the least impressive waterfall I have ever seen?

The ear-trumpet, yes. An aunt of mine had one, and one bawled into it placed in front of one at meals, not looking at her—rather like talking into the mike I imagine. Now and then it went out of order and screamed piercingly on one high note like a railway engine. She couldn't hear that and when it happened during a play or concert, she was not popular—in fact more than once had to leave the building.

At last, after really a very kind winter, we have one of those days which has, more than once in the past, been the prelude to thirty-six hours' rain. They say it is the same all over England. The sort of day which makes some take to drink. Do you know, by the way, the three reasons given by an American for declining an invitation to 'liquor up' —(1) that it was the anniversary of his brother's death, who had died of D.T. (2) that he was a teetotaller (3) that he had liquored up only ten minutes earlier? Not bad, I think, considering it dates from Victorian times.

Odd you should mention Dickens, because I have been recently re-reading all the *Martin Chuzzlewit* bits in which Mr Pecksniff and Mrs Gamp come (and *of course* the whole story of M.C. and Mark Tapley in America). Gosh! the man's mind was simply a *ceaseless* bubbling-up of fun and fantasy and the right words for embodying every notion, big and little. And how magnificently bad his character-drawing is! All his folk are black or white, e.g. Jonas Chuzzlewit and Tom Pinch— no iota of good in one or bad in tother—and both therefore very tedious. And Macaulay called *Martin Chuzzlewit* frivolous and dull, and refused to review it because he had dined with Dickens—a lovely Victorian blend of stupidity and gentlemanliness!

Your vignette of the Foyle lunch is lovely, and what a good remark of Priestley's. I haven't seen his new book yet, but the Ipswich librarian knows that there is such a book.

I am rather sorry that the new record for the high jump has been made by a man called John Thomas. We don't want any D.H. Lawrence in the athletic world.

27 February 1960   *Bromsden Farm*

I'm sorry to start this week by quoting your least favourite author, but Comfort has been reading *Pride and Prejudice*, and she says I am exactly like Mr Bennet: 'In his library he had been always sure of leisure and tranquillity; and though prepared, as he told Elizabeth, to meet with folly and conceit in every other room in the house, he was used to be free from them there.' I see what she means, and try hard to be charitable, but this room, which I made out of an old dairy so as to get away from the children, is now so much the warmest and cosiest room in the house that they tend to congregate here. Duff came over from Oxford for lunch, and Bridget is here for the week-end.

This morning I drove over to visit the Poet Laureate[1] at Burcote Brook, between Dorchester and Abingdon. One bumps up a dismal

[1] John Masefield (1878–1967).

drive to a low-slung desolate-looking house standing in the midst of much unkempt grass, with the swollen Thames flowing sullenly past. The old poet couldn't have been more charming: says he's getting shortsighted, but otherwise quite all there. We didn't mention his wife's death (I had sent him a letter of sympathy) and for all I know it may have been a great relief to him. He had ready for me three cartons, all packed and labelled by him, containing no fewer than *128* of his own books and pamphlets, in each of which he had written something—a quotation or other remark, sometimes about the London Library—and signed his name. It was all most touching. As I was leaving he said 'Is there anything else I can do to help?' I said: 'Certainly not: you've done quite enough—unless you can find us a tame millionaire'. 'Alas,' he said simply, 'my millionaire's dead.'

Talking of millionaires, did I tell you that I have managed to extract £500 from Mr Roy Thomson, the owner of the *Sunday Times* and many other papers? We have now passed the £10,000 mark—half way there!

On Wednesday I travelled again to Cambridge and visited E.M. Forster at King's. I found the dear old man surrounded with sheets of the manuscript of *A Passage to India*, which he was vainly trying to put in order for me. I told him I'd do all that for him, swept it up and took it back to London. After two evenings of sorting (when I should have been doing a hundred other things) I've got it into pretty good order, despite his appalling handwriting, and it should fetch a pretty penny. After all this sweat and toil we've received only some fifty lots, and we need 120. Somehow I must try to assemble the other seventy by the end of March, so that the cataloguer can get to work. T.S.E. has been laboriously copying out *The Waste Land* in Morocco, and yesterday I got a postcard from him, beginning:

> Oh Chairman, my Chairman,
> The fearful task is done!

I expect you saw the leader in today's *Times* rebuking Harold N. for his remarks about Carlyle: I'm sure it was written by Sir William Haley himself.

I long for further news of your hearing-aid. Perhaps you'll hear, not only your own heart beating and clothes rustling, but the bats squeaking in your belfry, the chip creaking on your shoulder, and the bees buzzing in your bonnet. Every man his own concert-party!

I can't help having a soft spot for old Southey, though I was quite unaware of any general feeling in that direction. Landor thought the world of him: a much greater poet than Wordsworth, said the old silly. But isn't the *Life of Nelson* rather good? I have the feeling that if one had the time and patience one might succeed in compiling a readable *short* anthology from S's works. A good biography of him was published in 1945 by Jack Simmons (or perhaps Simmonds: the title-page says one, the binding the other): it's worth reading.

I've always loved *Martin Chuzzlewit* (what a splendid name), but I remember thinking that Dickens's view of some of the characters had undergone considerable change as the book slowly appeared in its monthly parts. I can't remember now, but don't the Pecksniff daughters (particularly the one who marries Jonas) turn from monsters into almost sympathetic figures of tragedy? Or am I quite mistaken? One of the first things I shall do when I retire to N.W. Yorkshire is to re-read the whole of Dickens: there's something to look forward to!

2 March 1960   *Grundisburgh*

Pride and Prejudice is the Jane Austen I like best. As to the others my resentment (as of course you know) is composed partly of annoyance at myself for not seeing what so many great and good men are apparently unanimous in praising, and partly impatience with the amount of *Schwärmerei* there is about her by Walkley and David Cecil and all those voluble women. I believe to like *P. and P.* best is to join the groundlings who put *Pickwick* top of Dickens (where did I read lately of a piece of research which revealed the striking frequency of the occasions on which Mr Pickwick drank too much?).

What marvellous work you are doing for the London Library—Masefield, Forster, T.S.E. etc. I (knowing nothing at all about it) still feel that eventually an American tycoon will cough up a really fat sum. Or do they remember too well what Carlyle said about them? There was much to forgive in what Dickens wrote. I was amused and pleased by the *Times* leader putting H.N. firmly and justly in his place about T.C.—one of what I suppose to be the rare occasions on which H.N. spoke foolishly. But of course the thrawn old dyspeptic, like Milton, does arouse a really fierce antipathy in some. You, thank Heaven, are not one of them. And please read the very last paragraph in his *Reminiscences*, just after he had finished with Wordsworth, and tell me how can one *not* love the man who wrote that?[1]

Now, your letters. How you will laugh at me (and possibly, perhaps, be faintly pleased). I started arranging the bundle, re-read the first one or two, and without a pause settled down to re-reading *every single one*. I have nearly finished (each one took about five minutes); they range from October '55 to March '58. They are superb! What fun posterity will have, and how easily I foresee an able editor observing kindly that (if you reprint any), though G.W.L.'s are not in the same class, they at least did quite a good job in the midwife line. You will see some odd cabalistic signs in places—in one the name 'Gubby' makes a mysterious entry. Many questions and problems arise, and I must be sparing of them. In one place tears seem to have fallen, springing perhaps from acute sympathy with your railway accident in December '55. What is the story of 'Two Zoologists and a Flea' which you proposed to tell me and then didn't? Have you beaten Adam at chess since January '56? Wellington at the ceremony apropos of Borodino? Duff Cooper's 27 hats, Oscar's protest about his cress sandwich, Winston on his gaping flybuttons—the fun and fertility are inexhaustible, and if you please, in strong contrast with mine, you repeat yourself exactly once. If you think I am exaggerating, hand any three or four to Ruth and ask her candid opinion. She may find, as they did in Dr Jekyll's bible (was it?), some 'annotations of startling indecency (blasphemy)' made of course by Mr Hyde: some extremely funny flashes from the smoking-room, but she will take the same view

[1] In a few years, I forget in how many and when, these Wordsworth appearances in London ceased; we heard, not of ill-health perhaps, but of increasing love of rest; at length of the long sleep's coming; and never saw Wordsworth more. One felt his death as the extinction of a public light, but not otherwise. The public itself found not much to say of him, and staggered on to meaner but more pressing objects. Why should I continue these melancholy jottings in which I have no interest; in which the one figure that could interest me is almost wanting! I will cease.

of them as Landor did of the naughtinesses in Catullus's poems, and if she doesn't laugh at e.g. Mencken's story of his revenge on his traducer—but the hypothesis is absurd.

I *shall* bring this batch to you on Tuesday at 6, taking all the precautions that James Bond, when on the trail, took whenever he entered his room or got into a train. How absurdly readable Ian Fleming is. I couldn't resist *Dr No* in a Penguin. By page 40 (as far as I have got in bed) J.B. has already foiled four attempts to kill him. Dr No is as incompetent as Professor Moriarty.

My hearing-aid is still delayed. I don't think they trouble to be very quick with N.H. patients. My dour Scotch specialist clearly looks upon them as Himmler did on the Jews.

You put old Southey higher than I do (so far, by your letters, about the only thing we strongly disagree about is custard, which I love). I haven't read his *Nelson* for years. I remember admiring the end of it. I suppose Landor could be just as dogmatic and wrong in his judgments as Ruskin.

I see Oliver Van Oss has written what seems to me an excellent review of old Priestley's book in the *National Review*. It has the breadth and humanity of Priestley himself, and how nice to find a modern reviewer uttering full-throated praise. Do tell me what you think of it. And also, why J.B.P. gives a short parenthesis and no more to Milton; how can *he* be deaf to the organ-voice? Another question. The excellent N. Bentley has a lovely remark about M. Arnold's 'chilblained mittened musing', which is shrewd and telling about a good many of his poems, but what about Sohrab, Thyrsis, and Scholar Gypsy? Do tax him with this little catechism. We all have blind spots, and he *may* share this anti-Arnold spirit with Edith Sitwell and Lytton Strachey. M.A. *was* too pontifical of course and invited a sharp deflating punch in the stomach.

5 *March 1960* *Bromsden Farm*

Truly you're better than any tonic. I got home last night utterly exhausted after a trying week and not a trifle despondent. There waiting for me was your splendidly long letter in which you tell of

33

re-reading and *enjoying* all my old letters. Isn't that enough to raise anyone's spirits? As Yeats wrote:

> We have no gift to set a statesman right;
> He has had enough of meddling who can please
> A young girl in the indolence of her youth,
> Or an old man upon a winter's night.[1]

A momentary pleasure, when they arrive next day, is all one can hope for one's letters—and here are you, a man of the utmost taste, discernment, and, I'd have sworn, honesty, affirming that my old ones have amused you years after they were written. Can you wonder that today I wear my rue with a difference? One day I will pay you back by re-reading all *your* letters and overwhelming you with praise. Alas, I have forgotten every remnant of the story of the two zoologists and the flea (why on earth didn't I pass it on?). Now it must join Ould Grouse in the gunroom.[2]

I forgot to tell you that I asked J.B.P. about his unhappy trip to Australia, where he clearly put the natives' backs up, as he inevitably does wherever he goes. 'What did you say to upset them?' I asked. 'Nothing at all,' says he—and then, after a pause, 'I did say that their big cities reminded me of Wolverhampton after a long dry spell—but nothing else.'

On Thursday Christie's sent out a 'press release' about the London Library sale, and I was rung up by every newspaper in London. After lunch the B.B.C. telephoned to ask if I would be interviewed on television. I felt I must agree, but stipulated that I must be conveyed to Alexandra Palace and back in a B.B.C. car. This they arranged. I was on view for two minutes, twenty-one seconds, and the whole thing took exactly *three hours*! Have you ever been to A.P.? It was North London's answer to the Crystal Palace, and it stands like a monstrous folly on quite a high hill. One drives up a long circular drive, like the rings round a sand-castle on the beach. After dark the endless vista of coloured lights all round is very beautiful. Inside, the building is

---

[1] 'On Being Asked for a War Poem.'

[2] The anecdote mentioned, but never told, in Goldsmith's *She Stoops to Conquer*.

34

purely functional—studios and control-rooms and so on. I rehearsed my interview four times, trying desperately without watch or clock to keep within the allotted fragment of time. They were all very charming and helpful.

Next morning a widow sent the library a cheque for £2000, but no amount of flattering unction can persuade me that this had any connexion with my TV appearance. Be that as it may, we have now indubitably received £12,500 of the £20,000 we need, and the balance looks more possible daily. Also I have persuaded one of the independent TV companies to subscribe £250 *a year*!

I have, as you ordered, read the last passage of Carlyle's *Reminiscences*—with delight. I started my TV interview: 'The London Library was founded in 1841 by the *great writer* Thomas Carlyle . . . .' I knew you would approve.

Many of Landor's pronouncements were not literary judgments at all, but rather expressions of personal loyalty. He loved Southey as a man and didn't care for W.W. Therefore S. was the better poet. Incidentally, Southey's last recorded words were: 'Landor, ay, Landor.'

Your memory is not the only one that's going: I can't remember whether I told you about Ruth's son, Timothy. He is thirty and got married a few months ago, just bought his first house. Now he has to undergo the most serious heart-operation imaginable—they have done it only for a year or less, and it involves stopping the heart while they do the job. Apparently many recover completely, but others don't. To make bad intolerable they can't find room for him at Guy's for another fortnight, and in the interim the young couple are staying with Ruth, and you can imagine the underground tension. The boy is wonderfully cheerful and brave, and so, outwardly, is Ruth, but when she gets away to Soho Square she naturally relaxes and I do my best to comfort her. I don't know if she'll manage to be there at 6 on Tuesday, but if she does I thought you'd better be in the picture.

Did you know that the German for ice-hockey is Eishockey? I just found out, and it amused me, partly perhaps because Ei is the German for egg. Little things please little minds. A letter from America the other day referred to me accidentally as a 'publusher'—a lovely word. I am on the last chapter of Diana Cooper's last volume: it has been a fearful job, but there are some charming things in the book. I shall expect you on Tuesday, bringing *my* sheaves.

10 *March* 1960   *Gruudisburgh*
                                                            (*Summer-house*)

Once again a perfect London visit with the highlight 6–7 p.m. on the Lit. Soc. evening, which is itself, in my experience, of excellent quality. Am I curmudgeonly in saying that Gerry Wellington is *almost* first-class company? But anyway we had a good crack. Poor old Cuthbert shrinks visibly; he must weigh under eight stone and will just twinkle away one of these days. As my surgeon (a great man) once bluntly put it 'Yer know, Lyttelton, excluding accidents, there are, when yer come to it, only two ways of dying; you either dry up or swell up, and the first is more comfortable. You'll do the second.' A nice brutal man. But to go back to 6–7. How brave of the lovely Ruth to turn up and show no sign of strain. Honestly I cannot remember so striking a blend of charm and sympathy and sharp intelligence (how I should hate to say something really stupid to her—and I suspect I have). Which brings me to the blunt question (awfully non-U I expect) how is it possible *not* to be in love with her? So there—and I shan't be surprised if the answer to this is in the third person closing the correspondence. Still it has been a good one.

There are other problems an editor will some day have to tackle besides the two zoologists, *viz* was 15 January 1956 the last time you beat Adam at chess? What were you to tell me about the dentist at Didsbury (a ridiculous name)? And won't more light be wanted about the man who had a dipsomaniac daughter who was electrocuted by an electric iron at Beersheba, whose husband was manager of the Sodom waterworks?

In one letter you said your *Hugh Walpole* might be coming out in a Penguin. What has happened about that? I feel it should have precedence over *Lady Chatterley*.

That was a good party of Roger's—ultimately a benefaction of Lord Beaverbrook's. Rose Baring is a charmer, and Pamela's sisters are—well, Pamela's sisters. I nearly missed the 4.30 at Liverpool Street.

What business have all the No 9 buses to be full up at 3.30? Grotesque. What fun—if it is on, which it won't be—one would have in the next world contemplating London traffic in 1980. It was some ass of a saint who said that one of the chief pleasures of the saved *through all eternity* would be watching the torments of the damned. But *all* the time?

How they do go on about the *St Joan* Epilogue. My opinion (not that anyone ever asked it) is that it is quite in order but that the *expression* of it should be more dignified. They shouldn't all appear equally *little* men. What do you think?

I had nothing to read in bed last night, so picked up (why?) *Vile Bodies*[1] oh dear! I should have preferred the Koran, though it would have kept me awake longer.

I do hope there will soon be good news about Ruth's boy. My love to her.

12 March 1960   *Bromsden Farm*

Two little things I forgot to tell you last week: (1) when I looked out of my bedroom window here at 7.30 on Monday morning, just as it was getting light, I was enchanted to see five wild deer, grey and ghostly, in the field. By the time I had had my bath they had vanished into the wood, and now I only *just* believe in their existence. (2) Coming down exhausted in the train on Friday evening I was irritated from Paddington to Henley by two schoolgirls, who talked and giggled loudly without a break. I could have slapped them both with pleasure, and then one of them said, quite seriously, 'I've given up being beastly to Daddy for Lent,' and my wrath subsided.

What, if anything, makes you cry? I asked Harold Nicolson this question at the Lit. Soc. dinner, and he said: 'Three things only— patriotism, injustice righted, and misunderstanding explained. Tragedy never.' I agree whole-heartedly about patriotism: I can't see the Queen on a newsreel without a lump in my throat; but am less sure about the other two.

Poor old Cuthbert made an effort to sit next to me, but I had already buttressed myself with Roger and Martin Charteris—and then, when

[1] Evelyn Waugh's second novel (1930).

37

I saw Cuthbert silent, and his neighbour Tony Powell wilting with boredom, I felt a few tiny pangs of compunction.

I shall have to show Ruth some sentences in your letter, if only to sustain her during the last week of waiting for the boy's operation, now fixed for Monday 21st.

I think that 15 January '56 was almost certainly the last time I beat Adam at chess—and jolly nearly the last time I played with him, for he quickly got much too good for me. The dentist at Didsbury rings a bell almost as faint as that rung by the zoologists. My *Walpole* never appeared as a Penguin because the Penguin people ratted, after suggesting the idea to me. I was most disappointed, and so were Hugh's brother and sister, to whom I had told the good news.

I thoroughly enjoyed the luncheon-party and was charmed by both Pamela's sisters, please tell her. What is the other one's name?

I agree exactly with what you say about the Epilogue to *St Joan*, but it's many years since I saw it acted.

This morning I drove over to Oxford and fetched Duff home for his last vac. The traffic in the city was *épouvantable*. The new paper, the *Farming Express*, on which Bridget is working, will burst on an astonished world next Thursday, and she claims to be rushed silly in her office. The demise of *Time and Tide* is not unexpected, and it had sunk to a miserable rag since Lady Rhondda's death, when the subsidy was cut off. Still, I reviewed thrillers for it for fifteen years, and now there will be no more. I hadn't time for them anyhow.

The reason I've sent you no books lately is that I haven't published any: my absence last summer (when no new books were taken) is now making itself felt. However, we start again at the end of April, so look out!

Sunday morning.

Refreshed, and also slightly stupefied, by nine and a half hours of sleep, I return to the charge. The sky is grey, the bird-table thronged, the library fire most comforting. Surely you can't be in your summer-house today?

I have a few proofs to look over, but no manuscripts to read. In a fortnight the Oscar proofs will begin to arrive, and directly Fleming has finished his book about Younghusband, I shall have to go over it with a blue pencil. In fact I foresee a ceaseless stream of publishing work until June takes me back to Kisdon. And then, who knows?, *How Green etc* may tempt me! Now I am about to embark on that new life of Conrad by Jocelyn Baines: I can't remember whether you've read it. So far there hasn't been a good life of C.—oh yes, I have had a letter from Professor Theophilus Boll of the University of Pennsylvania. Clearly a fictional name—don't you think? but which novelist? Not quite outrageous enough for Wodehouse perhaps. You will know at once.

A nuthatch has just driven off the tits and is wrestling with some bacon-rind. It is raining steadily.

Next week looks like being a little less busy than last, and I am planning to try and take Thursday off, so as to take Ruth to Brighton for the day. We always love such excursions, and I think diversion is what she needs just now. You shall hear all about it.

17 March 1960   *Grundisburgh*

We are not at home at present as a new Aga and a new boiler are being installed, so we are with Pamela's sister at Wickham Market, hoping to be back by Sunday. But you know how it always is: 'Some of the pipes cannot be used again, being so silted up that it is a mystery how you got *any* hot water etc'. It is no crisis except in so far as old age can be called a crisis. P. goes over (seven miles) every day, having discovered how much better and quicker work is done if the owner is present and doesn't mind fussing, nagging, girding, protesting. I never can dismiss that horrid conviction that practically all work— not only of this sort—is done more speedily and competently by Germans. Don't *you* rage over the new pound notes where the important number is on the side under the counter's thumb? It is not inconvenient, it is imbecile. Incidentally isn't it a pity that the effigy of our pretty little Queen on it should bear no resemblance to her at all? No wonder old Carlyle more than once expressed exasperation at men's 'cursed ways of going on'.

Your deer! That sight was what Geoffrey Madan in his enchanting *Livres sans nom* called 'Sights of the Kingfisher', i.e. bits of dazzling luck. And I like your schoolgirl's Lenten resolve. I told two noisy schoolgirls on the top of a bus recently that they shouldn't make so much din in a public place, and to my astonishment they never uttered another sound. I suppose they thought I really *was* the great Panjandrum with the little round button at top.[1]

I cry repeatedly (like Winston) certainly at some aspects of patriotism, some ridiculously obvious sob-stuff in e.g. a cinema, but mainly at *words*, used as they are in e.g. 2 *Samuel* ch. 18, *Matthew* 26, the end of *Earlham*, of 'Sohrab and Rustum', of *Lear* (which old Samuel couldn't bear to re-read, though he was editing it!) and of course the 'Thus with the year' at the beginning of *Paradise Lost*, Book Three. As Cocteau (I think) said 'It isn't the pathetic that moves us, but the miracle of a word in the right place', which has a lot of truth in it. I agree with you that there is something very moving about the sight of our little Queen.

Oh yes, and I think I must tell *you*. My Aunt Lucy (Lady Frederick Cavendish)'s husband was murdered in Phoenix Park, Dublin, in 1881 and it broke her heart. She was very religious and quite enchanting, so full of humour and understanding; we children all loved her. Well, the murderers were rounded up and several put to death. The ringleader, Casey, nicknamed 'Skin-the-goat,' was to be hanged on a certain day, and the evening before Aunt Lucy sent his wife the little gold crucifix she always wore, as a sign of forgiveness—and other things. Of course *she* never told anyone, but Mrs. C. probably did. Anyway *old* George Trevelyan tells it in his Life of Macaulay, and says it is the most beautiful human action he ever heard of. That makes me cry whenever (very rarely) I have told it. It *could* be misunderstood, but Aunt L. was the most entirely genuine person that ever lived.

How right you are about Pamela's sisters—Sibell and Lettice both, like P. (and Madeline with whom we now are) magnificent people, *special* targets of fate. S. has lost two husbands and an only son, Lettice a husband and two sons—one in the war, the other, two years ago, run over by an underground train, of all fantastic ends; he thought he could nip across the line.

[1] From a rigmarole composed by Samuel Foote (1720–1777).

Time and Tide is the Chessman[1] of the periodical world. I see it has again been reprieved. Revivals *do* happen; I once again peruse *John o' London* in the Ipswich library, though how long I can stand the underbred swaggering cocksureness of Colin Wilson is doubtful. I read that he avers that Casanova was not immoral. Words are turning their coats. 'Dirty' will soon be a word of praise—just as 'brutal' was in 1937 Germany.

Theophilus Boll is straight from Peacock—like Dr Virgil Wigwam who writes about Scriptistics, whatever they may be. I always love the names which on the screen precede an American film. Even in the G.C.E. we get increasingly odd ones, e.g. two years ago Bee, Bones, Baffin, Bulger, and Blim. None such from Eton. There are still the ancient hierarchies of Campbell, Foljambe, Serocold, Howard and Hart-Davis.

I haven't read Conrad yet, but have just got the new book on Kipling and—in bed—an unread Raymond Chandler. As usual practically whenever Marlowe calls on a man the man is there all right—but dead. Why do I read him? God knows.

By the way will you send me my paper on reading without the schoolmaster, which I once wrote for Van Thal. The series it was meant to figure in perished a few months before it was due. What the devil was the paper called? I want to read it to the Leys School in a few weeks. Perhaps you have put it, as my father would have said, behind the fire.

I do hope all will go well with poor dear Ruth's lad on the 21st. I think of it constantly. Please give her my love. I don't pray much but aren't hundred-horse-power hopes prayers?

19 March 1960   *Bromsden Farm*

Your letter was faithfully waiting for me on Friday evening (yesterday). I do hope you're safely home by now, with all pipes flowing. I very much like and approve Cocteau's phrase (if it is his) about the

---

[1] Caryl Chessman, having at Los Angeles in 1948 been sentenced to death for multiple crimes, spent twelve years in the death-cell at St Quentin and was finally executed on 2 May 1960.

miracle of a word in the right place. My friend Humphry House couldn't read aloud 'whose dwelling is the light of setting suns' and the lines around it, without tears. On the other hand my Uncle Duff habitually cried when he was reading, and in the theatre, at almost any emotional passage, and in a way I rather envy that extra enjoyment of his. Your Aunt Lucy's action is certainly most moving—a beautiful and lovely story. Thank you for telling me. And now I shall go to bed and write more in the morning.

Sunday morning

The sun is shining, and Comfort is planting vegetables all over the place. A brick path demands my attention, the wild daffodils are out, and a few tame ones. Duff shot a deer last week (on Peter's orders) and I can't help being sorry, remembering that 'kingfisher sight' in the early morning. I'm against killing anything.

What is Lettice's surname?—her charming manner gave no hint of her tragic history. The agony of Ruth and her family has been protracted by the postponement of the operation to next Thursday, so concentrate your thoughts then. The boy is now in Guy's, being prepared for the ordeal. They keep telling him, or at any rate his young wife, the most grisly details, and mercifully they don't seem to upset her. For instance, while the heart is stopped and the operation in progress, the blood is pumped through the body by a machine, which, they cheerfully announced, has to be primed (like a pump) with three pints of someone else's blood. The whole thing makes me feel sick, but all I can do is to distract and comfort Ruth as much as possible.

What can I tell you of last week? It began in an underground 'dive' and finished in Henry's holy shade. Leonard Russell, the literary editor of the *Sunday Times*, asked me to lunch on Monday at a place called The Paint Box in a back-street near the B.B.C., which he had seen advertised. I arrived first and found it to be a pitch-dark basement with faint lights round the edges and a hidden gramophone playing incessantly. Two solitary men and a couple were sitting at widely spaced tables, groping for their food in the gloom. A strong smell of bad cooking pervaded everything. I sat down at a tiny bar to wait. Presently some curtains on one side were pulled back to reveal a tiny stage, on which a stark-naked Eurasian girl was reclining on the floor, with her back against a chair. She had a fine figure, but was clearly not allowed to move an inch for fear of breaking the law. None of the half-dozen people in the room paid the faintest attention to her, but I thought it only civil to face in her direction until my host arrived. He was extremely embarrassed and kept his back firmly towards the girl, who must, I fear, have been frozen. We played for safety with cold ham and an omelette. After about half an hour the curtains were drawn again, and soon the girl appeared in the restaurant, rather scruffily dressed and far less prepossessing. Later she carried on a piercingly loud telephone conversation in what I took to be Malayan, a few yards from our table. Apparently London and our other cities are full of such places, where tired business men can eat nasty food with a frozen nude in front of them. Perhaps even in Ipswich . . . ?

The best London Library news is that James Strachey (to whom I wrote soliciting) is going to give us the manuscript of Lytton's *Queen Victoria* for the sale! Willie Maugham is sending the manuscript of a long short-story, and Nancy Mitford a whole novel.

Our day in Brighton was the greatest fun and change. We walked by the sea, had an excellent lunch, briefly inspected *four* secondhand bookshops, and went to the movie *Anatomy of a Murder*, which we both enjoyed. I can't remember if you liked it?

Yesterday Adam was confirmed along with a hundred others, including Oscar's grandson. We had to sit on the knifeboard, under which run extremely hot pipes. The Bishop of Oxford spoke for much too long, and the boys grew restive. I suppose no-one can stop a bishop when the bit's between his teeth, but he ought to sense the right moment to stop. Afterwards we had a poorish lunch at London Airport and went to an amusing movie in Slough, called *Two-Way Stretch*. This is Adam's first half in the top Science division and he has come out second in the half's order, which seems pretty good. Bridget has started to mow the lawn and is calling for assistance.

Yes, it *was* Cocteau, though I don't know which work it comes from, being, let me tell you, wholly unacquainted with his writings. I am in fact a contemptible French scholar. I imagine your Uncle Duff was a very good one. I particularly like to hear of his crying over a book and in the theatre. When he had once got over my being a beak, I feel we should have got on very well—and frequently we should have mingled our tears.

Yes, deer must be shot I suppose, but not in my presence, thank you. One can think of a cow, pig, or sheep lying down but who ever pictured a deer other than moving with incomparable grace at whatever speed you like? (interval for instruction: a cheetah is the fastest of all—about 70 m.p.h.: in two seconds from stationary its speed is 45 m.p.h. A botfly goes 400 yards in one second, i.e. 818 m.p.h. End of interval for instruction).

Lettice was married to Geoffrey Colman (Oxford XI about 1913–14). A grand chap; head eventually of the great mustard firm, and one of those who really would have helped industrial relations. He was badly wounded in 1916, and died in about 1930, endocarditis I think they called it, the result of the wound. Never was there a sisterhood of greater courage than the Adeanes.

I shall certainly think of Ruth to-morrow. The tactlessness of doctors is very odd—and almost universal. I suppose if you are trained to regard the heart as a pump or a muscle, you just can't think of it as the 'fountain of sweet tears', or dancing with daffodils. *Do* our thoughts and hopes have the faintest effect on the Ancient of Days? Who knows? I find it hard to feel the confidence that many say they do, that all will be perfectly clear to us the moment we arrive in the next world. And I rather like old Allan Monkhouse's remark that he was not going to be easily convinced by what he called The First Cause's explanation of his main puzzles in his lifetime. Ruth will know that, with all the host of friends, every wish and hope I have is hers on Thursday.

Your story, by the way, of the man who had lost his memory has had a good press in Suffolk.[1] My doctor I thought would pass out, he

[1] See volume iv of these letters, p. 163.

laughed so much. I may tell you I am quite shameless in retailing them to fit audiences. You know the lovely Audrey Van Oss? She recently had a spell in hospital—often depressed, not getting well very quick. I told her in a letter of Winston's reply apropos of his fly-buttons,[1] and three days later she was back home. Of course the cure is an old one, and I need not remind you of Dr Battie whose impersonation of Punch made an ill boy laugh so much that his quinsy burst and the boy recovered—and Henry VII hired a man for six shillings and eightpence 'to eat coals before him.' It was, as far as I remember, about the only thing he ever did laugh at.

Your 'dive' adventure is grand. Every facet of it is a-gleam with character and fun. Fancy you *not* having time to write. Monstrous unfairness. I love your climax, viz the hypothesis that even in Ipswich there may be a place or places where tired business men eat nasty food with a frozen nude. I must do some research; there should be something bizarre in the alluringly-named Silent Street.

I much enjoyed *Anatomy of a Murder*, also *Battle of the Sexes* which was quite funny. But all the last week we have been at Madeline Wigan's (P's sister) while our stoves were being put in, and had our bellyful of TV non-stop from 5.00 to 10.30. Altogether about four things worth seeing, chiefly of course the Calcutta Cup match and a boxing match. Otherwise one is almost killed by the amount of *jaw*, as there is apparently hardly any music. By Tuesday I felt I never again wanted to hear what anybody thought about anything. No, I shall never have one. I shall go to a neighbour's to watch the Boat Race. Oxford is to win, they say, probably because they put the oars in the water with their feet, as the rowing-manual at Spottiswoode's said was essential. Tuppy always maintained 'with' meant in company with and not by means of. It *always* annoyed wetbobs when he mentioned it.

On Tuesday C.M. Wells's[2] dinner, his ninetieth birthday. He hasn't changed in the last twenty years. His forty-to-fifty-year-old pupils have—bald, fat, dewlapped, limping etc. G.O. Allen was there. He had just seen Statham who told him that Hall, 6 ft 5, was *much* the fastest bowler he or anyone else had ever seen; not even Cowdrey really enjoyed facing him. C.M.W. of course repeated W.G.'s saying

[1] See volume ii of these letters, p. 35.
[2] Former Eton master.

about fast bowling, *viz* that the faster it was the better he liked it. I gathered that G.O.A. regarded himself as of much the same pace as Larwood etc. But D.R. Jardine told me L. was a good deal quicker. John Christie[1] is the spit of Mr Pickwick, in good form. Only one eye and subject to angina pectoris, but quite contemptuous about both.

Our old stove would have lasted another ten weeks at most, our Aga another three or four, so we haven't acted too soon. Pamela purrs audibly whenever she enters the kitchen.

Adam's scholastic career is most impressive. I imagine you chatting with him on a summer evening about specific gravity. Who teaches him? In the Nineties all the science-beaks were absurd, though Porter had a touch of genius, and was a fine showman. He told K. Fisher who was brought in to re-organise Eton science (which P. thought was unnecessary) that all the science-teaching at Eton except his own was mere wind, and got the Johnsonian retort: 'But even so, my dear Porter, is it not better that we should have organised wind instead of casual flatulence?' K. Fisher was a good man.

P.S. I don't think you reached the sentence in my letter in which I expressed a mild wish to get from you the typescript of my paper called I think 'Letter to a Schoolboy'. It was all about how to read without having any truck with a beak.

26 March 1960   *Bromsden Farm*

I love finding your letter waiting for me, and any Friday evening at seven you can imagine me, newly changed into my comfortable old clothes, relaxed in my armchair by the library fire with a glass of hot whisky and the latest budget from Finndale House.

Last week was a nightmare of anxiety and strain. Ruth's daughter flew home from Italy to stand by, and that meant another person to cope with. Poor Ruth could settle to nothing, so I took her and the daughter to the cinema two nights running to distract them. (One of the films, *I'm All Right Jack*, was excellent, and I suddenly realised that I, a confirmed non-cinemagoer, had been to four within a week— one at Brighton, one at Slough, two in London.) On Thursday the

---

[1] Eccentric millionaire (1882–1962). For some years an Eton master. Founded the Glyndebourne Music Festival on his own estate 1934.

operation began at 9 a.m., and we were told to expect news about noon. In fact it wasn't till almost *two* that we heard all so far was well, and you can imagine the stress of the morning. They found his heart even worse than they had expected and say they can't guarantee how fit he will ever be. On the other hand, they say he couldn't have lasted more than a few months without the operation. I have just (11 p.m.) spoken to Ruth. She saw the boy today for the first time, and they say all is going splendidly, though his condition must be considered critical for another forty-eight hours.

In between all this I attended Jonathan Cape's memorial service at St Martin's, and took the chair for my old friend William Plomer when he read some of his poems to a collection of old dames in Foyle's bookshop. On Thursday I attended a dinner-party twenty strong, given at the Ivy by the head of the U.S. publishing firm Harper's. I had the ill-luck to sit next to Mrs Woodham (*Florence Nightingale*) Smith, who is voiceless and inaudible at nine inches' distance. Altogether the week was endlessly wearing—and next Tuesday the Oscar proofs start rolling in. Oh for Kisdon Lodge! I backed Eagle Lodge in the National, but it's still running.

Sunday morning

A cold grey day with a bitter north-east wind. I lit the library fire and it went straight out. Duff is kindly coping with it. Did I tell you that he failed to get a Commonwealth Fellowship? He was very disappointed, but on the whole I'm not sorry. By the time he came back from America he would have been twenty-six, without prospects and thoroughly used to being subsidised. Now he will have to get a job after he comes down from Oxford in June.

Yesterday I drove over and had tea with Lytton Strachey's brother James, a charming old boy with a white beard, blind in one eye, who lives with his psychoanalyst wife in a fine centrally-heated, book-infested house in a wood above Marlow. He has now translated eighteen of Freud's twenty-three books into English and still seems quite cheerful. He gave me the complete manuscript of *Queen Victoria*, beautifully legible, together with corrected typescript, corrected page-proofs, and a number of notebooks in which L.S. planned the book and took notes for it—what a haul! I found it difficult to thank him adequately. What will it fetch? I posted your 'Letter to a Schoolboy' to you on Friday. So sorry I forgot to mention it last week. Altogether I feel rather bad about your batch of essays, having seized them enthusiastically and then gone dead on them. The trouble is that there isn't quite enough, it seems to me, to make a book, and I don't suppose you feel like writing any more. Please let me have this one back when you've delivered it, so that they are all kept together.

I have started to re-read Dover Wilson's *What Happens in 'Hamlet'* and can't put it down. I expect you know the book?

30 March 1960   *Grundisburgh*

What a dreadful time poor Ruth has been having. I hope the acute anxiety is now past. It is a tremendous burden for a young man to shoulder just at the dawning of all his hopes and prospects. Can we agree with John Keats who in a letter wrote that when a great misfortune came to a man he felt inclined to congratulate him on being so challenged to show the resources of his spirit? I can't find the passage in what must be much the worst edited book in the world, *viz* K.'s letters edited by Colvin. In the first three pages there are six unexplained allusions and names. It is as bad as Aldis Wright's two vols of FitzGerald's letters. What did those old men *think* their job was? K. is of course fundamentally right in regarding man as capable of *any* degree of heroism and fortitude. Most of us, happily, are spared the uttermost tests.

You omitted to say what the menu at the Ivy dinner was. I lunched there four times and dined once, and the provender was superb. Is it still? I have some notion that the famous chef has gone.

Are you writing a detailed account of your money-raising activities for the L.L.? Because it really is a grand story. Strachey's *Q.V.*! Just imagine if you have two opulent Yankee fans in opposition! The price could rival those fantastic sums paid for pictures, many of which *can't* be worth all that. I suppose Agnew's will make a packet on that Gainsborough, was it?[1] My old pupil[2] must have done some fine reconstruct-

---

[1] *Mr and Mrs Robert Andrews*, bought by Agnew's for 130,000 guineas at Sotheby's on 23 March 1960. Now in the National Gallery.

[2] Geoffrey Agnew. Knighted 1973.

ing of the firm's fortunes; it was in very hot water fifteen years ago.

Many thanks for the 'Letter to a Schoolboy' which you shall have back in due season. I shall use quite a lot of it for the Leys School in May. The line I have in mind is not anti-science (though I shall have a little swipe or two at Hogben and co) but rather to show how *clarity* of style is essential to both literature *and* science—and how they can and must almost entirely acquire that on their own, with very little help from the beak. Do you think that is at all a promising line? Of course I am not anti-science (it is important that Adam should not think that) but only arrogant ignorant scientists—e.g. Hogben.

There is a good deal of fun in the papers just now. Are you well up in Francis Bacon's painting? His 'Sleeping Figure' in to-day's *Daily Telegraph* has strong emetic value (hailed of course as of immense power and originality). And I like the brothers Cheeryble on p. 19 who are suing the Attorney-General and a brace of policemen for £10,000, for charging them (successfully) with swindling. America of course does well with a 'special tariff' for black men at an eating-house which charges them 17/9 for a cup of coffee and then summons them for making a disturbance. But I feel no great liking for the boy of ten who can't quite remember whether he did or did not stab to death a girl of nine.

Pamela is now rejoicing over a new sink, which looks to me very like a quite competent old one, but in which she sees a score of superiorities. Women!

2 *April 1960*   *Bromsden Farm*

The Oscar proofs have begun to pour in, and I am already overwhelmed with sheets and sheets of paper, all requiring checking and titivation. I shall not badger you at this tiresome stage, but perhaps when the proofs are paged and manageable (in some months' time) you might be amused to read them and look for howlers?

I'm happy to say that Ruth's son appears to be mending most satisfactorily: her acute anxiety is over, but she is suffering a little from reaction after strain. I shall try to advance our Yorkshire holiday—to May if possible.

Colvin was not only the idlest of editors, but also the most unscrupulous. We shan't know exactly how much he cut, expurgated and bowdlerised Stevenson's letters until they're edited afresh from the originals, but I know of one letter which R.L.S. (in the midst of a haemorrhage) signed 'Yours in buckets of blood, R.L.S.' Colvin printed 'Yours, R.L.S.', with no sign of omission.

I'm sorry to say that the Ivy dinner wasn't up to much gastronomically—smoked salmon, *huge* segments of tough duck liberally soused in orange, and a goodish pudding. I fancy the chef must have fled, as you suggest.

The London Library sale is now fixed for the *evening* of June 22—which should give Christie's plenty of time to circulate the catalogue in the States. No astonishing acquisitions last week, except the manuscript of Rosamond Lehmann's last novel *The Echoing Grove*. Also Macmillan's coughed up 100 guineas, to bring our cash receipts above £15,600.

I think your suggested address to the Leys School is admirable, and am only sorry I shan't be there to hear it. Francis Bacon's pictures are too revolting for words—stockbrokers with two heads and no trousers, elemental horrors crawling up walls—give me *Dracula* any day!

Last week I dined out three nights running—nothing worth recording, but all very exhausting. Adam came home covered with glory, *viz* (1) Trials Prize, which seems to me to make him the top Science specialist in the school at sixteen, though he modestly says that several of his rivals were away on scholarships; (2) a prize for his *sixth* Distinction in Trials; (3) a prize for his third sent-up-for-good. Withal he remains his old self, very affectionate and simple and undemanding.

Duff has now cut all the grass, and in its ring of daffodils the garden looks very trim and springlike. P. Fleming has dumped on me twenty-three out of the twenty-four chapters of his Younghusband book, which we are now thinking of calling *Bayonets to Lhasa*—a better title, I think, than his original one, *Tibet 1904*. I shall have to read these chapters comma by comma, correcting and making notes or suggestions, and naturally I long only to pore over the Oscar proofs.

I'm delighted to see that Donald Somervell has expressed his intention of attending the Lit. Soc. on the 12th: he must indeed be much better. Will you be there? I do hope so.

You didn't answer my question about Dover Wilson, whose book I am still enjoying, alongside Bloggs Baldwin's new book, *The Mac-*

donald Sisters,[1] which has a lot of amusing new material in it.

I have refused an offer of £25 to drive to Teddington next Sunday and appear on Commercial Television with Ian Fleming, discussing his new book of short stories (which I haven't read). The money is tempting, but Sunday is precious for work and rest.

Today I drove over to Pewsey and lunched with the Devlins. My friend Christopher (the judge's brother) seems to be making a good if slow recovery after his frightful operation, and I am encouraging him to occupy his mind with a monograph on Christopher Smart[2], for which I have sent him cargoes of books from the London Library. He is a charming person, of the utmost naturalness and courage, and he's the only priest I've ever known (he's a Jesuit) who is *completely* unparsonic.

My publishing activities, having lain dormant since January, will start up again on April 28: nothing very exciting, I fear, or very saleable—except for a frightful book about the Wolverhampton Wanderers football club. The ghost-author is always unobtainable and the book is almost a year late—luckily perhaps, since W.W. are now in the Cup Final, and may win the League as well. Our first edition of 5000 copies looks like being exhausted before publication, which is more than can be said of most of my precious literary books. It only goes to show! Now Younghusband calls.

6 *April 1960*   *Grundisburgh*

What a relief about Ruth's boy! You and Kisdon will remove her strain, which must have been like a dead weight on every minute of her day. Give her, please, a message of deep affection from me. You needn't perhaps add the egotistical note that I rejoice delightedly to find that, at seventy-seven, the heart's blood is not dried up.

I shall love to be associated with your Oscar in any office. The most menial if you like. The best judges are agreed that few tie up parcels better than I do. I will help in any way I can.

Those old editors were curiously shameless. Macaulay who hated

[1] By A.W. Baldwin, younger son of the Prime Minister, whose mother was one of the sisters.
[2] Poet (1722–1771).

Croker (as apparently most people did) more than cold boiled veal, had no difficulty in showing up the monstrous liberties C. took with his edition of Boswell, and Froude—though I have forgotten the details—was pretty loose with the Carlyle material. I have been browsing once again in the Life, with the same feelings as of old. C's conviction (the same as Dean Inge's) was that democracy was a more than dubious form of government. Those who say that C's prophecies of disaster have been disproved, don't know or have forgotten that the *ultimate* crash that he foresaw might not happen for a century or two. *All* his lamentations a hundred years ago—love of money, lowering of standards, political humbug, impotence of religion etc—would surely be intensified to-day, if indeed the English language could carry any more than he put into it. If Gladstone on Ireland, and Dizzy on the Franchise, nearly killed him with exasperation, what would Barbara Castle have done? His imperviousness to feminine charm always amuses me—the obviously personable young lady from U.S.A. who called on him and was tersely designated as 'a diseased rosebud', Margaret Fuller 'a strange, lilting, lean old maid, not nearly such a bore as I expected'. And his horror at the portraits of himself is also rewarding: 'the portrait of an idiot who has taken glauber salts and lost his eyesight;' 'a delirious-looking mountebank, full of violence, awkwardness, atrocity and stupidity,' and of course the early one which he said was 'like a flayed horse'.

With Bradman as captain that black team would have won the rubber—or M.A. Noble. Both of them, they tell me, immensely superior to any English captain. Jardine just as intelligent, but cordially disliked by *both* sides—as I keep in reserve for any more than usually smug Wykehamist. (It is simple historical fact that the only tour in Australia led by a Wykehamist nearly disrupted the Empire.)

How proud you must be, and ought to be, of Adam. If it would give him the smallest pleasure, convey to him my congratulations. I forget whether he knows my grandson Lawrence. He too is an interesting boy, but lacks A's cutting edge. At the moment he is on the way to Greece with a party. I hope he will see the Acropolis by moonlight, *and* with the southern sun on the rich marble of the Parthenon—quite unique and unforgettable. The light seems to be coming out of the marble. It is worth remembering (or is it?) that Bernard Shaw wrote to Ellen Terry that he was glad to get away from Athens 'with its stupid classic Acropolis and smashed pillars'. One of his pronouncements that make one's toes itch.

I have just got into Priestley's book. Very enjoyable. I skip a certain amount when he is among foreign playwrights, but reluctantly, because he has a wonderful gift of phrase. He must be grand company. I wish he would write more regularly in the weekly press; his comments on the prevailing asininities are always refreshing.

I note that in the publisher's advertisements of *Breakdown* by Bratby, it is clear that we have now reached the point at which 'vulgar, tasteless, a beast of a book, repellent, garbage-can' are regarded if not as actually laudatory, at least likely to attract readers. And there are still those who approve of the general taste of readers in 1960!

I have been reading in bed about the absurd life of Selfridge. Nothing in the book has given me as much pleasure as the figure of Arnold Bennett in one of the illustrations. Every single item of his dress is wrong and the total effect is an overwhelming picture of the provincial snob. He never quite shed his upbringing did he? In one of his reminiscent volumes there is a snap of him and Dorothy in deck-chairs on the sands somewhere. A.B. is still wearing ordinary black *boots*. None the less he always strikes me as a good chap.

What *excellent* news about D. Somervell. He must have recovered marvellously. I wish I could be at the Lit. Soc. on Tuesday, but my sister is to be here for two days, and I must shirk. *What Happens in 'Hamlet'* I remember thinking *superb*, but I must read it again *at once*. Thank you for reminding me.

9 April 1960   *Bromsden Farm*

It's angelic of you to say you'll help with the Oscar proofs. I think I'll keep you for the page-proofs later in the year: they'll be much more convenient to read—just like an unbound book—and I hope less scrappy than these galley-proofs which are now pouring in daily. Eight expert well-wishers in various parts of the world are reading sets, and it looks as though their comments and queries may be longer than all Oscar's works put together. Endless minor points need attention, but there is no time. Mercifully the London Library sale is now complete except for a few stragglers, and the cataloguers are at work. Elisabeth Beerbohm's sister has given us two Max drawings for it.

Having finished *Sterling*, which I much enjoyed, I have embarked on T.C.'s *Reminiscences*. I found I hadn't got the first two volumes of Froude's biography, so that is postponed.

Adam's reports were the best I've ever seen, but he is in no way changed or spoiled by his success.

I thought you'd enjoy the Priestley book: I skipped too, here and there, but found much to admire.

I have just finished the manuscript of Peter's book about the Younghusband expedition—at present called *Bayonets to Lhasa*. It's a fascinating story very well told, but I can't see it selling as well as *The Siege at Peking*: it lacks comedy, and the Dowager Empress, and a proper climax, but you'll like it, I'm sure. It should be out in October or November.

I was sorry to read of Crace's death:[1] I was never up to him, but he was a friend of yours. Now I shall put the clocks on and resume this turgid scrapbook in the morning.

Sunday morning
A gale is blowing, and once again it looks like the library fire for me. I'm happy to say that Ruth's son is getting on splendidly: from tomorrow he is to be allowed non-family visitors, so Ruth won't have to battle her way to Guy's every day.

Last week I saw Diana Cooper, fresh from the De Gaulle banquet at Buckingham Palace. She reported Winston as totally *non compos*, and scarcely able to walk. I fear the old hero has lived too long.

Once again I dined out three nights running—too much food and drink, too much time wasted: 'So much to do, so little done.'[2]

I expect you saw that Peter Davies threw himself under a train. The poor fellow had for years been dying of some incurable disease, but this does seem to me a particularly inconsiderate form of suicide: just think of the driver of the train, and the people who have to pick up the remains! Sleeping-pills are surely the most civilised means, and

[1] J.F. Crace, Eton master.
[2] Tennyson, *In Memoriam*. Said to have been the last words of Cecil Rhodes.

going to sleep is itself pleasurable, but I suppose they don't work instantaneously and might leave time for a change of heart. Hemlock itself wasn't all that quick, was it?

We still haven't decided exactly when to go to Kisdon, but it may well be in May, which would mean my missing that Lit. Soc.—we'll see. The Oscar proofs are going to take so long anyhow that we can almost disregard them in our plans: they'll go with us for sure. Last week I got copies of the last nine letters which had hitherto evaded me, and now I know of none that I haven't got, though many more probably lurk here and there—especially in America. You must forgive my harping on Oscar: he is much on my mind just now.

Did I tell you that I have stupidly agreed to open the Antiquarian Book Fair on April 27? What on earth am I to say? This is only the third year they've held it, and the two previous openers were Lord Birkett and Miss Phyllis Calvert. Clearly they've tried Brains and Beauty, and are now reduced to the Beast. Somehow I must try and learn to say NO politely—a thing I've always found it hard to do.

13 April 1960   *Grundisburgh*

How good that Ruth's boy really is getting on well. I suppose it is still too early to say whether he will in due course be able to do a full day's work with head or hand. What a rum thing the whole of man's existence is—how, why, whence, whither—not one of the four questions ever answered. You will find many reflections of that sort in Carlyle's reminiscences. The *fundamental* difference between him and Macaulay is that C. never lost his sense of mystery, and M. never had one. I expect you may find C's lamentations for Jane a bit too much. In any recollections connected with her he writes as if she had died the moment before, and as if she simply was unique—body, soul, and mind. The old man had extraordinary tenderness, and yet you can see, from what she quotes in her letters of what he said, that this usually had a grumpy sound. I suppose the Scots are like that—his family especially. 'Pithy, bitter-speakin' bodies' some neighbour said about the whole clan.

I shall be greatly honoured by having the very smallest bit to do with the Oscar letters. Will the chorus of indolent reviewers see the immense trouble you have taken with it? Some will, no doubt, and the rest don't matter. You will have every right to be wholly indifferent to what they say—like T.C., content with the knowledge that you have done every blessed thing that you could.

Jan Crace was a great friend of mine, and I spent many hours last week writing a thing about him for *The Times*. They must have got it on Monday, but so far nothing has appeared. I have heard more than once that the present obituary editor is rather a cross-grained chap, and he has probably reacted rather violently from the too ample notices of Eton beaks in the past, but they ought not to ignore men of marked distinction in some line the public know nothing about (as I shall tell the bloke on Sunday, when demanding my manuscript back for the *Eton College Chronicle*). If you are director of a company, you are sure of at least six–eight inches, and giving intelligent boys a love and knowledge of the classics is better work in the world than passing a dividend. They will of course plead lack of space. Luckily Pamela insisted on copying it out and sending it to Jan's widow, who seems thoroughly happy about it and not to care twopence if *The Times* prints it or not. Very like J.F.C. himself!

I got recently a tiny volume of poems by Susan Glyn who is apparently about sixteen years old. They seemed to me very distinguished and wholly unintelligible (the bucket with a hole in it blaming the inefficiency of the pumps filling it!). She says she knows you (and of course gets a thrill out of it) but so far, she says, hasn't dared to tell you that she has written poetry. I have reassured her about your ability to survive such a shock, and I rather think left her with the impression that you are a prince among patrons. I wonder how you met her. Do you know her father, who for some obscure reason has changed his name from Geoffrey Davson to Anthony Glyn. I don't think his mother at all approves and I don't wonder.

I am *much* enjoying Priestley. Surely his pages on Wordsworth, Coleridge, Scott, Byron, Shelley, Keats could not be better—and what a lot he says in really very little space.

Where did I read recently a complaint about T.S. Eliot's dulness in conversation? Not that he is alone among great men. Housman could be deadly—partly from disdain, partly because, just like Kipling, he didn't *want* to give his opinions about this and that, except on rare occasions in congenial company, and with just the right amount of the right food and drink inside him. Too often, as Max Beerbohm said, he should have had a poached egg in his room. But he was very greedy, so paid much attention to the fare and none to his fellow-guests.

A poor day—dark, windy, wettish, and the cherry-trees and almond are looking somehow snubbed; all they ask is a little sun. But the brevity of the life of spring blossom saddens me every April and May—less than a week for many things. We should be having the nightingale here in a day or two, but somehow he is not the bird he was, or perhaps my ears are at fault. I have had my aid fitted, but I doubt if I shall wear it much. There is too much fiddling with adjustment and parking of batteries etc. They tell me I shall get used to hearing my own voice (my daughters rudely say that surely I must be *that* by now). I think I may find it useful when sitting on a committee, and so avoid (which old Monty Rendall[1] *didn't*) announcing as the next item on the agenda the matter they had just finished discussing. On Tuesday I go to a Christie play just to test the thing. If I could resume playgoing that *would* be a great gain. *Nous verrons*.

I didn't know Peter Davies, though I did all the others—a lively and attractive lot. I agree with you. Sleeping-tablets or a jump out of a window, but not in front of a train at Sloane Square. But suicides are incalculable—wasn't it Brutus's wife who died by swallowing red-hot charcoal? 'Many the ways, the little home is one'.[2] I suppose a doctor can do it without pain or delay.

Good luck to Duff and his Greats. Remind him at the right moment if necessary that all the greatest men got seconds. There is a lot of luck about it. You *can't* bore me about Oscar, so there.

Easter Saturday, 16 April 1960   *Bromsden Farm*

Undeterred by celebrations of the Crucifixion, our postman de-

[1] 1862–1950. Headmaster of Winchester 1911–1926. In retirement he restored and transformed Butley Priory, near Woodbridge in Suffolk, and was chairman of many committees.
[2] T.L. Beddoes, *Death's Jest Book*, act 1, scene 1.

livered your letter faithfully yesterday morning, so my holiday began most agreeably. I haven't got to Jane Carlyle yet, but was much touched by the tribute to T.C.'s father, and am now deep in the account of Edward Irving—it's all splendid stuff.

So far less than a quarter of the Oscar galley-proofs have arrived, but already my inner ring of helpers are flooding me with pertinent comments and queries. On Monday I am to dine at All Souls and receive Sparrow's animadversions to date. Most of the chorus of indolent reviewers will fail to appreciate the notes, but to hell with them. If *you* are pleased and satisfied I shall not have laboured in vain.

So glad you're enjoying Priestley. Why don't you write him a fan-letter?

By the way, I have just re-read *The Bridge of San Luis Rey* by Thornton Wilder, which 1 hadn't looked at since I bought and much enjoyed it when it first appeared—in 1927, when I was twenty. To my astonishment I now think it *first-rate*—a shaped and finished work of art—contrived, admittedly, but none the worse for that. Do read it again and see whether you agree. It seems to me to have improved and mellowed in thirty-three years, and I don't see why it shouldn't be read and enjoyed as long as books are read. I shall nervously await your reaction to this *ex cathedra* pronouncement.

You must give the deaf-aid a proper hearing, to coin a phrase, before you miss any of Cuthbert's witticisms.

The other day I was trying to find words to explain my dislike of Henry James's old-age revisions of his early work—and today I find that Max (I might have guessed) put it perfectly:

> One . . . wasn't glad that for the definitive edition of his works he did a lot of re-writing—a process akin to patching pale gray silk with snippets of very dark thick brown velvet. It was a strange sad aberration: and a wanton offence against the laws of art.

That was written in 1949, when Max was seventy-seven. Age couldn't wither him, any more than it can an old East Anglian friend of mine. Now to bed with T. Carlyle and Edward Irving.

Sunday noon.

On the Resurrection morning I slept till 10.30, and over my breakfast (one slice of bread and marmalade, one mug of tea) I read the second volume of a book called *La Jeunesse d'André Gide*, from which I was happy to learn that the French translation of *Wuthering Heights* is called *Les Hauts de Hurlevent*. Gide hasn't met Oscar yet, so I must push on.

Ian Fleming's new book, *For Your Eyes Only*, consists of five superbly readable long short stories, one of which might have been written by W.S. Maugham.

Bridget has gone riding, Adam (after attending Holy Communion in the village church) is pursuing pigeons with his gun, Comfort is scrubbing the kitchen floor, Duff is with his sweetheart in Wales. There is much rough work to do in the garden—clipping and path-laying and stone-carting: the sun is shining through the window, and I must away. I like to think of you sunning in your summer-house, perhaps thinking up a joke or a quotation for next week's letter. How many words, I wonder, have we now exchanged? A quarter of a million each? My *Hugh Walpole* is 180,000, but most of them are other people's words. Sorry about this ink—fountain is the right name for my pen. A lovely nib but an incontinent belly.

20 April 1960 *Grundisburgh*

Would Priestley care one twopenny.damn for a letter of appreciation, however genuine, from an elderly nonentity in Suffolk? I wish his book had been out when I was lecturing on Eng. Lit. I should have used it lavishly. Is it too 'advanced' for the School Library? Adam in due course would get a lot out of it, unless, as old Warre[1] said of M.D. Hill, he is 'delivered, body and soul, to science.'

I have just been reading R.W. Livingstone's *Rainbow Bridge*, all about education—very wise and urbane about science and 'vocational' studies etc. It was all the more surprising to find him describing Carlyle as 'that illustrious master of cant and self-deception'. 'Self-deception' of course you can saddle anyone with, whose opinions you don't share, but '*cant*'? If L. is thinking of its dictionary meaning of 'false or affected assumption of lofty morality' he is surely about as wrong as one can be about a man who, in his large output, mainly

[1] The Rev. Edmond Warre (1837–1920). Headmaster of Eton 1884–1905.

attacked various forms of cant. It strikes a crude and violent note which is quite uncharacteristic. (Like the tale I found recently of T.S.E. showing a fierce thing he had written to Ezra P. who said: 'No, that's not your style at all. You let *me* throw the bricks through the front window. You go in at the back door and take the swag'.)

My hearing-aid. Well, yes I do hear better with it, but it is, somehow, not all that gain. One hears so much else, plus a sort of old gramophone background noise. But I missed very little at the theatre last night, where we all went to see *The Unexpected Guest* by Agatha Christie. Very good fun. She is really devilish clever in making one suspect *everyone* in the affair, except the right one in the last minute. I think I shall keep the aid for such occasions—and especially committee-meetings, where everyone mumbles, and one sits at a long table. I shall *not* bring it to the Lit. Soc. and Sir Cuthbert's acidities shall waste their sweetness on the desert air. I am delighted to hear that Donald Somervell was there—because you don't attend the Lit. Soc. unless mind and body are functioning pretty well.

I am browsing in Johnson's Lives, *not* of the poets but of others, and constantly turning up nuggets, e.g. the reason for Blake (Admiral) not getting a fellowship at Merton, because of 'his want of stature, it being the custom of Sir Henry Savile, then warden of that college, to pay much regard to the outward appearance of those who solicited preferment in that society'. In fact Sir H.S. was a —? I will send you more as I find them. Meanwhile let me remind you that when he and Boswell supped with a farmer at Armadale, the fare put on the table was minced collops, fricassee of fowl, ham and tongue, haddocks, herrings, frothed milk, bread pudding, and syllabubs made with port wine. Those were the days.

I shall certainly read *San Luis Rey* again. I remember greatly liking it, and it is high time for a *re*-reading—on the whole life's greatest pleasure. I do like to think of you in the T.C. reminiscences— savouring (as so few seem to) the old man's tenderness and perception and never-ceasing consciousness of the eternities on which man's life so obscurely rests. His 'eternities' are now *jokes*—like Milton's God the Father. Priestley, the wise man, points out very pertinently that we haven't *emerged* from C's pessimistic forecasts; we are in the middle of them. The mills of God!

Les Hauts de Hurlevent is delicious. Do even the cleverest Frenchmen understand English fully? It may not of course have been a very clever Frenchman who translated 'The English always love the under-dog' into 'Les Anglais aiment toujours le ventre du chien'.

P.S. Love to Ruth (treble the normal because of not seeing her. But how is 'treble' possible?).

P.S.2. There is nothing in life I enjoy more than this correspondence.

P.S.3. So there!

---

23 April 1960   *Bromsden Farm*

I think you should write to Livingstone and take him up on Carlyle's 'cant'. Almost the only thing I have learned in thirty years of literary life is that *all* authors, whatever they pretend, *love* getting appreciative letters from readers. Authorship is a lonely business, and after the nine days' wonder of reviews etc, the ripples are apt to subside, and as far as the author knows no one is reading or enjoying his book. The most acceptable letters, therefore, are the ones that come after the initial splash has subsided. *Verb. sap.*

Where did you come across that splendid tale of T.S.E. and Ezra Pound?

So glad the hearing-aid is some use. We shall definitely be back before the Lit. Soc. dinner in June. Ruth's son is leaving hospital next week. I visited him in Guy's last week, and was amazed at how well he looked: modern surgery is astonishing.

I'm loving T.C.'s *Reminiscences*—still on Edward Irving.

Last Monday (Bank Holiday) I heard my first cuckoo (and another one today). The wild cherries just failed to wear their white for Eastertide, but are full out now. On Monday evening, after a lot of gardening, I drove over to Oxford; the road was filled with vehicles bumper-to-bumper in both directions; I hit the main road behind two 'coaches' and was unable to pass them for sixteen miles. Dinner at All Souls was uphill work. Besides the Warden there were only three other Fellows there—a rather dried-up Professor of Comparative Religions, a young philosopher with long hair, and the black Fellow (from Ghana perhaps) who never spoke. When the daylight died and the only light came from the seven-branched candlesticks on the table, you couldn't see him at all against the dark panelling of the Common Room until he opened his mouth and his very white teeth flashed out. Sparrow told me afterwards that the servants had complained of this fact. I gathered that they all regret having elected the poor fellow—falling over backwards to avoid any hint of segregation —and I daresay he feels pretty miserable too.

On Tuesday I lunched (chez Herbert Agar) with Sir Fordham Flower, brewer and chairman of the Stratford Theatre, and Alfred Francis, chairman of the Old Vic. As a result I think both these great concerns will contribute mildly to the Phoenix Trust. Flower was interesting about the results of advertising his beer on commercial TV, describing how the demand rose hugely *next morning*! whereas they reckon that ordinary advertising (press, posters and what they call 'point of sale') takes at least *three years* to produce any visible result. No wonder the TV companies are so rich.

On Wednesday I lunched in state with the Governors of the B.B.C., which was more fun than I had expected, since I sat between Hugh Greene, Graham's brother, an old friend, now Director General, and Thelma Cazalet, another old friend. Afterwards a meeting of the General Advisory Council, at which I spoke not a word. There was much discussion of B.B.C. interviews on sound and television, and it was generally agreed that, whereas private people being interviewed should be treated with care and consideration, public men were, as it were, fair game and could be more roughly handled.

On Wednesday evening I gave dinner again at the Garrick to my north-country poetess Phoebe Hesketh. Altogether it was a short but exhausting week. Two hundred Oscar galleys have now come in—just over a third of the whole—and the amount of detailed finicky work they need is appalling. I see no hope of their going back to the printer to be made up into pages before July or August.

This morning Comfort got a letter to say someone had left her £100 and I got a very grand one from Windsor Castle signed by Michael Adeane and saying that the Queen, God bless her, will present a book to the London Library sale. This was Harold Nicolson's doing, and the publicity value should be considerable.

Adam is ending his holidays with a dance every night, and will go back to Eton on Wednesday a wreck. On the same day I have to open the Antiquarian Book Fair at 11 a.m.—what next? I can't wait for the sheep and the curlews. I shall try and get the sitting-room in the flat redecorated while we're away—which will entail moving all those books. Many of them haven't been dusted for ten years—heigh ho!

27 April 1960   *Grundisburgh*

I think I shall see Livingstone when I go to Oxford in May or June. His Carlyle remark is such an oddly crude and shallow one for a good man to make. But you know practically all the modern remarks one comes across on T.C. (Harold N.'s for instance) are based, if not on sheer ignorance of him and his best work, on a view of him which is limited to his *Latter-Day Pamphlets* pro-Germanism, Might is Right, and the greatly overdrawn picture by Froude of his inconsiderateness to Jane. It must not, too, be forgotten that the old man never meant his *Reminiscences* to be published at all, with their morbid self-accusations, exaltation of Jane, and consequent denigration of almost everybody else. There is a sort of conspiracy to ignore his rectitude, courage, independence, insight and depth of feeling. Stimulated by your interest (which I find nowhere else) I have just re-read his magnificent essays on Johnson and Burns and am deep in 'The Diamond Necklace'. He will come back some day when the present silly queasiness about writing of any richness has gone. I think that T.S.E. and Ezra tale came in a review of some Yank who has just been explaining T.S.E.—the man whose book is reviewed in last week's *Spectator*—a review of which I understand hardly a single sentence.

Your daily doings once again fascinate and appal me. How do you get *any* work done? My letters must be very small beer after the talk you must come in for almost daily. But All Souls, like Trinity, was clearly disappointing (but for Sparrow). So many dons are dried-up or contemptuous or—like Housman—both. The exceptions—e.g. Jim Butler[1]—are good value, or old George Trevelyan, still foaming with rage over some injustice several centuries old.

[1] James Ramsay Montague Butler (1889–1975). Regius Professor of Modern History at Cambridge 1947–1954. Chief historian of the official war-history of 1939–1945. Knighted 1958.

You must be nearing the £20,000 mark for the L.L. Are you wearing black about your person for old Chapman?[2] I thought him a stiff old thing on first meeting him, but he thawed considerably in a few minutes. He gave us—I forget if you were there—a very slatternly talk at the Johnson Club, quite obviously implying that if any of his audience thought he was going to take any more trouble about it than a few random thoughts between snoozes, on the way from Oxford to London, could throw up, they were much mistaken. But I suppose he did plenty of good work in his prime.

Adam will find the half very restful after the holidays. It always amused me that Long Leave—meant as a mid-term *rest*—always sent the boys back exhausted with late hours and divers skylarking. And the clever beaks always arranged their football match v. the School on the Tuesday—and always won it, though often beaten in the first match. How does A. face a game of *cricket* to-morrow? Here to-day is simply a goodish day in mid-February. The cuckoo showed up (as always) on Shakespeare's birthday, but since then has got no further than 'cuck'. These hard dry Aprils are very tedious—and frequent. I should like to go and fell a tree, but my anile leech forbids it with the same tactless insistence with which he cuts off ham and bacon—my two favourite comestibles. I steadily gravitate to the condition of Sir Cuthbert.

30 April 1960   *Bromsden Farm*

I have spent most of this lovely sunny day kneeling in the garden, picking stones out of the new November-sown lawn. Excellent therapy, no doubt, but I am now suffering from some sort of double house-maid's knee and move with groans. Whether or not Carlyle intended his *Reminiscences* to be published, I am enjoying them almost more than anything of his—certainly more as a whole, for in most of his works one has to wade a good deal to get to the plums, if you will forgive a peculiar metaphor. This book is *all* enjoyable, the writing much more unbuttoned and less strained than elsewhere. I particularly like the description of a Warwickshire serving woman: 'correct as an eight-

[2] R.W. Chapman, editor of Jane Austen and Dr Johnson (1881–1960).

day clock, and making hardly as much noise', and when T.C. rode over to Hagley and thereafter 'Lord Lyttelton's mansion I have ever since in my eye as a noble-looking place', I raised a special cheer. I trust you to put Livingstone severely in his place.

The London Library fund has now reached £16,300, so we need only £4000 from the sale, which in fact I hope will produce more and so provide us with a much-desired surplus.

The Oscar proofs are now approaching the half-way mark, and the galleys themselves are becoming a burden. The trouble with a book of this length and complexity is that one needs an index at the typescript stage, and another for the galley-proofs, for unless one can remember exactly where each letter and each note come (which one can't) one wastes hours in searching. When we get to page-proofs (which you shall see) I shall have to compile *the* index, which will take many weeks.[1]

I was sorry to read of old Chapman's death: rude and curmudgeonly though he often was, he was a 'character' and he did the state of letters some service.

I have sent for Roger's new book,[2] and shall bear it happily off to Kisdon on Tuesday week—blessed day! We've been looking forward to it actively since last August, and now are like prep-school boys counting the days.

Last Wednesday I opened the third Antiquarian Book Fair at the brutal hour of 11.30 a.m. A few stray thoughts and an hour's feverish cramming produced a short speech which went down well, but I knew my audience (mostly antiquarian booksellers) and one day I shall leave it too late and dry up. Yehudi Menuhin was surprisingly in the audience, and I was introduced to him afterwards—very young and small and intelligent he looked.

On Thursday evening Ruth and I went with an American friend to *A Passage to India*, which we thoroughly enjoyed. The Indian lady-dramatist has made an excellent job of it, and the leading part is brilliantly played by a Pakistani actor. Afterwards we had a first-class supper with John Gielgud at Prunier's (*oeufs en gelée*, steak, an excellent claret, and a melting-in-the-mouth piece of cake).

[1] It took six months.
[2] *Hanover to Windsor* by Roger Fulford (1960).

John G. regaled us with a variety of good stage anecdotes, told with punch and finish. Vague and dreamy about most things, he is exact and always amusing about the theatre, having been, as he says, stage-struck all his life.

On Tuesday I dined with the James Lavers in the Boltons. Vyvyan Holland (Oscar's son) and his wife were there, and I was able to enlist Mrs V.H.'s support in my campaign to prevent V.H. from expurgating anything in the Letters. He owns the copyright and must be appeased.

Did I tell you that Bertie Van Thal is making a one-volume anthology from Agate's works (all of which are now out of print)? I shall probably publish it early next year, but I daresay it won't sell. Jock Dent has written an introduction. Bertie is miserable in his present job with Weidenfeld, and I've told him I'll take him on as an editor-cum-reader on July 1. I'm fond of him, and he's full of ideas for books.

I've still got those Max Beerbohm letters to edit, and I shall take them to Kisdon, just in case I have time there or feel inclined—though generally we find that looking after the cottage, fetching water from the spring etc, takes up most of our time, and when it's fine we just lie or sit in the sun. Write here this week: I'll be here next week-end. Now for more Oscar.

4 May 1960   *Grundisburgh*

How right you are about 'unbuttoned' Carlyle. That is why his letters are in the main so good (so much better than the overpraised Jane's, in which there is a spate of stuff about tweenies etc and her ailments). Some day you must browse in *Frederick* which has some of the fine 'grisly humour' praised by Meredith. What about his comparison of the activities of various dryasdusts who nose out a good deal of scandal with 'those dogs that after closely scrutinising the parts of shame of another dog, eventually depart with satisfied air, as though from a problem solved'. Not quoted alas, only remembered, and life even in Suffolk is not long enough to search all 7 volumes. I remember the allusion to 'Lord Lyttelton's mansion'—which, alas, after a life of exactly two hundred years is almost sure to be sold—if anyone will buy it. I don't quite remember how much my grandfather did about starting the London Library, but no doubt you will. He was a fine old chap—a good deal of an oddity. Have you come across Carlyle's perfect snapshot of Sir William Harcourt, 'a lawyering, parliamenteering, loud man', which my uncle Alfred particularly loved?

You were the big noise in the literary pages of the *Sunday Times* this week. I hope your chatty Leonard Russell may have been helpful with his allusions to the work you are doing. It will be grand when the sale is over, and the world knows how you have saved the L.L. 'Sir Rupert' is, *me judice*, an absolute certainty. Just as it should be.

I read in *Punch* an excellent review of *A Passage to India* by Eric Keown—known to you of course. He always seems to me pretty good. But how devastatingly unfunny—and often quite unintelligible—are the pictures nowadays, and I was much disheartened by the face of Cyril Connolly, all chin and conceit, and virosity. Dreadful! The two leaders in last week's *T.L.S.* were on an architect I had never so much as heard of, and *Pilgrim's Progress* which I have on the whole read enough about. The Pryce-Jones tradition continues; and he goes on with that insipid chatter on Thursdays.

The admirable Richard Martineau has written a first-rate obit of poor Audrey Van Oss, who was ill, off and on, for twelve years and fought throughout with unfailing courage. She won a county golf-championship *after* the doctors had told her she could never play again. She was forty-seven. Lovely to look at and (she was a great friend of ours) we can get some comfort from 'Adonais'—that is all there is for a death in the prime of life. I forget whether you knew her.

I hope there will be no expurgating by Vyvyan Holland. I trust you to make rings round him. That is interesting about Bertie Van Thal. I had thought he was with Barker. He was very friendly at one time— he and wife actually stayed a week-end here, but then he dropped me for, no doubt, excellent reasons. Was there no more sale for any Agates? The poor old thing was convinced of the immortality of the *Egos*. And they are surely much better than Arnold Bennett's *Journals*. Though A.B. met on the whole bigger people, he mostly made very little of them. But perhaps A.B. too is out of print? I will eat my hat if J.A.'s criticisms of Shakespeare plays are not jolly good.

You say nothing about taking *How Green* to Kisdon! You will never read it. I have some books like that, e.g. I know I should like Creevey, but I simply cannot start on him. Something Freudian I suppose.

I listened to and judged on Monday the Ipswich declamation prize. Not very good. Boys rarely seem to realise that you must get not only the meaning but the whole mood and tone and colour of a passage— feel it, in fact, before you can repeat it remotely well. They declaim 'Kubla Khan' as if it was Kennedy's gender-rules. But anyhow *not one* in the Cassius passage pronounced 'controversy' like the damned B.B.C.—with the stress on the second syllable. Don't you hate that?

7 *May 1960*   *Bromsden Farm*

Eves of departure are usually hurried and confusing. At *4 a.m.* on Tuesday we shall leave Soho Square in Ruth's tiny car, breakfast at 8 at Bawtry, near Doncaster, lunch on the moors high above Wensley-dale, and reach our cottage in the benevolent farmer's tractor at about 2.30 p.m. Before then a thousand loose ends must be tied or hidden away, countless details seen to. My pockets are stuffed with *aide-mémoires*, and all the time the Oscar galleys are piling up.

The weather today was perfection—lilac and apple-blossom out, wallflowers giving out their lovely smell. I drove over to Pewsey and lunched with the Devlins. The judge is charming, and I think might be a good Lit. Soc. member. Adam reports clean-bowling an opponent with his first ball of the season: perhaps the umpire hadn't called 'Play'.

I have finished the first volume of T.C.'s *Reminiscences* and am keeping the second for Swaledale. (By the way, T.C. refers to the Yorkshire moors as 'those mute wildernesses and their rough habitudes and populations'.) I particularly enjoyed, and sympathised with, the plight of poor John Murray (Byron's one)—do you remember?

> Stupider man than the great Murray, in look, in speech, in conduct, in regard to this poor *Sartor* question, I imagined I had seldom or never seen! Afterwards it became apparent to me that partly he was sinking into the heaviness of old age, and partly, still more important, that in regard to this particular *Sartor* question his position was an impossible one; position of a poor old man endeavour-ing to answer yes *and* no!

My ageing publisher's heart goes out to the poor old fellow: I know that feeling so well.

After watching the royal wedding[1] yesterday (I hired a television set for the day, so that all the staff could see it—and we all loved it) I think £25,000 was a very modest outlay for such general enjoyment and beneficial outlet for emotions. Reflect also that a great deal of the money goes in wages to the people who put up the decorations, and so benefits them. The royal yacht is permanently manned and maintained, so that fuel and food are the only extras for the honeymoon. As you see, I grow more militantly Royalist daily.

Leonard Russell's piece in the *Sunday Times* has so far called forth *eleven* new Oscar letters—none of prime interest, but several quite good—and more may still be reported.

I never knew Audrey Van Oss, but like to think that you brightened her last days with the story of Winston's fly-buttons.

So far Vyvyan is playing up splendidly, but the bits he most dislikes are still to come. I have suggested dedicating the book to him, his wife and their son—not wholly as a sop, but because it seems to me fitting. Mrs V. told me the other day that they look on me as almost one of the family, so there is hope.

There is no need to take *How Green* to the cottage: that great work awaits me there, if the mice have spared it.

Oh yes—I hate contrōversy worse than cold boiled veal—make no mistake about it. Last Thursday I went to one of the world's longest operas, Berlioz's *The Trojans*. One is in the theatre from 6 till 11—too long for me—but since my host Garrett Drogheda (our new Lit. Soc. member) is Chairman of Covent Garden, we were most comfortably accommodated in the Royal Box. Behind it is a private dining-room, where we ate and drank copiously during the three intervals. Two of my companions were Sir Solly Zuckerman, head of the Zoo and Government scientific adviser on defence (whatever that means) and his very agreeable wife, a grand-daughter of Rufus Isaacs. I was glad that I hadn't yet published the forthcoming book about the Marconi scandal. The opera itself has some excellent moments, but to a non-musical person the convention and idiom are hard to take, and it transpired that the name Aeneas is a difficult word to sing.

[1] Of Princess Margaret and Anthony Armstrong-Jones.

One evening Ruth and I had drinks with Alistair Cooke and his wife, there meeting the film-star James Mason, who seemed modest and agreeable. He had just finished playing the part of Carson in one of these frightful Oscar films. Incidentally, a musical version of *The Importance of B.E.* has just been successfully produced on Broadway. The old boy's definitely in the news.

Peter has at last handed in his Younghusband manuscript, and I can see that we're going to have a helluva job to get it out this year.

11 May 1960   *Grundisburgh*

You are now there—browning, probably already, happy as a sand-boy, whatever a sandboy may be, and Ruth somewhere in the immediate offing, looking quite lovely against the background of heather and hill—that endless sky which the children evacuated from London to the country in 1939 found so horrible and terrifying. Not that she depends on background. She would give grace to the goodsyard-wall of St Pancras Station. Fancy your imagining that I might have forgotten your holiday address! You remind me of an imbecile aunt who told my sister all about her (the aunt's) brother, who, in cold fact, was my sister's father. Otiose (or supererogatory) is the adjective isn't it, or hasn't anyone used either for years (except Max, of course)?

Adam has started well. As the foolish golf-reporter said of a player who was one up, he has only to stick to his lead to be sure of victory.

My excellent nephew from N.Z. was here on Sunday and confessed how little interest *he* takes in 1960 cricket—nothing like the same game as he remembers played by Hammond and co (and he never even saw Trumper!). Am I to be interested in an art practised by such men as Halfyard and Titmus? You may say what about Gaukrodger, but there is a certain magnificence about the ugliness of that, as in a Notre Dame gargoyle. And if you object to my saying there is so much sheer *bogus* in county cricket, look at the Sussex v Yorkshire match today, when in reply to Sussex's 280 Yorkshire made 281 for *none*, but lost the match. In match after match declarations are *de rigeur*, because three days without them produce nothing but draws.

In old days Yorkshire would have won easily with that start—and deserved to.

Poor old Murray. To deal at one time with Byron and later with Carlyle would have taxed any man's wits and patience. Publishing must be a very difficult vocation. For one thing the difference between silliness and genius must often be very hard to discriminate. One post brings Della Crusca or Dada and the next *Tristram Shandy* or Ezra Pound (a good seller, I imagine, though to me unreadable). And would any sane man spot *Lucky Jim* as the book which everyone *must* read?

I saw nothing of the royal wedding, though everyone says it was lovely. I don't feel strongly about the £25,000, and in any case always hate to find myself approving of anything done by Gaitskell and co. Everyone hereabouts has commented on the black depression on the Queen's face, and the rustic mind likes to invent the causes of it as jealousy, snobbery etc. But how can you rely on a photograph? Probably she was wondering whether she had left the bath-tap running; and anyhow, like her grandma, when she isn't smiling, she *does* look over-serious. You don't say anything of what they tell me are the countless rumours about and against the poor young photographer. Probably you will say, as Johnson did when surprise was expressed at his ignorance of some town scandal, 'By those who look close to the ground dirt will be seen'.

Two most intriguing books (isn't 'intriguing' a necessary word somehow, though an upstart? It seems to me to express something which 'interesting' doesn't) have just arrived from you with great appreciation. The one about a house[1] Pamela has bagged and is enjoying, and I have read *The Answer to Life is No*[2] with the greatest interest, though he is often too subtle for me. He is right down among the roots of human nature. I wonder what the reviewers will make of it. The blurb hints that the author could be spotted—but not by G.W.L. Anyway—though you hate being thanked as much as Jan Crace did—gratitude is, as ever, your portion.

I shall miss his memorial service, and my lecture at the Leys School, for a rather humiliating reason. I had a heavy fall on the top of a bus yesterday and have cracked a back rib. The leech prescribes rest for at

[1] *The Living House* by George Ordish (1960).
[2] By Wrey Gardiner, published anonymously (1960).

least a week and says at my age etc a cracked rib is not to be sneezed at. Not that I would dream of trying. Every movement is infernally painful. Dressing is purgatory; changing position in bed is hell; merely to clear the throat *very* gingerly would start Himmler or even Heydrich chuckling. And I always thought a cracked rib about equalled a mildly sprained ankle. The only *soulagement* to my feelings is that it was not my fault but that of the damned bus, which stopped with a hideous jerk as I was making my way to the steps, and hurled me to the ground, where I must have caught the edge of a step. Apparently a lorry suddenly got in the way. Pamela wants to sue the bus, the lorry and whoever made rather a blind corner on the road. Bless her.

I have a letter from Wilfrid Blunt with whom you have recently corresponded. A good man. He says he can't imagine how you get through what you do. Nor can I or anyone else. I suspect Ruth must sometimes have urged you to leave me out *this* week when you are clearly overdone. 'After all the old stuffy has had any amount of good stuff from you, not to mention forty or so excellent books.' She has every possible reason for saying that, and, to use that slightly stupid expression, I couldn't agree with her more. But not one of your letters shows any sign of strain (I have read and re-read each one pretty carefully) so I want nothing at all to change.

The opera! It is an immensely ridiculous art-form surely; 'an exotic and irrational entertainment' the old man called it,[1] but it survives with apparent ease for all its absurdity. When King Mark found Tristan making love with Isolde, instead of laying T. out with one swashing blow, he merely lamented the situation for twenty-two minutes in notes of indescribable fatness (he was a superb basso-profondo). What is the Oscar film in which J. Mason appears as Carson? It hasn't come Ipswich way, but then lots of things don't. I have just read Roger's book. A very pleasant bit of bookmaking indeed. The royal family circle must always have been fascinating—in one way. Not one single solitary remark ever made indicating the slightest understanding or appreciation of anything at all three inches below life's surface or two inches off the beaten track. What did George V and VI *read* in their spare time? Our little Queen I believe is fond of

[1] Dr Johnson, *Life of John Hughes.*

Jane Austen. John Raymond in his new book of criticisms has one of those articles on J.A. which always irk me—practically putting her above all other novelists that ever wrote.

Well, the thought of you two at Kisdon is a very happy one. Tell me *all* about it and send any spare snapshots you can. I shall forget when I get them that picking a letter up and opening it is a definitely painful movement—but not mentally.

15 May 1960   *Kisdon Lodge, Keld*

Even as you unerringly remembered this address, so you will doubtless recollect that the postal arrangements, especially the outward ones, are erratic. Our good farmer, Mr Hutchinson, duly brought up your excellent letter, and will always post things for us, but we never know exactly when he's coming, and sometimes miss him. In fact I hope this will reach you by Tuesday, but while I am here you must be patient with delays.

I don't know what a sandboy is either, but we are certainly as happy as any two of them. Our journey went smoothly according to plan, and we arrived to find the cottage swept, scrubbed and polished, with a good fire burning (all done by the Hutchinsons). Within a few hours it seemed we had never been away. The first night we slept exactly twelve hours (10.30 to 10.30), since when we have averaged ten hours a night. The first morning, when we were fetching water from the spring in the next field (six gallons, carried in two buckets and two plastic water-carriers given us by Elisabeth Beerbohm) in hot sunshine, Ruth spotted a ring-ousel's nest in the stone wall. On Friday we almost stumbled on a meadow-pipit's, and now the only regular birds of Kisdon whose nests we haven't found are the snipe and the golden plover. (We have found curlew, grouse, plover, lark, redstart and yellow wagtail. Also sandpiper.) The fields are thick with wildflowers, which Ruth arranges in the most enchanting way all over the cottage. Just now there are kingcups, primroses, cowslips, oxlips, forget-me-nots, anemones, heartsease and masses of deep purple orchids. We have been to one village sale, where in an afternoon of pure enjoyment we spent 21/6 on a looking-glass for the bedroom,

73

two pillow-cases, three curtains and a quantity of plates and dishes. The weather has been Aprilish—hot sunshine between hailstorms—but we are just as happy inside as out. Oscar proofs arrive most days and we are busy checking the letters against photostats of the originals. *How Green* is still on the shelf, and so are Roger's book and the second volume of T.C.'s *Reminiscences*, which I brought with me. So far I have read a good Buchan (*The Dancing Floor*), part of an idiotic woman's memoirs (in search of Oscariana) and a chunk of the first volume of the big new edition of Swinburne's letters. Unfortunately the two vols so far published (out of six) go only to 1875, which is exactly where Oscar's letters begin, but I find them most interesting all the same.

I'm glad you got some enjoyment out of *The Answer to Life is No*. The author's name would certainly *not* be known to you. He has published a number of books, but, as you can imagine, they were all failures, and I told him I would publish this one only if it were anonymous. He reluctantly agreed. I still hope the very fact of anonymity may arouse some interest. Since he wrote the book I gather that his financial position has improved as a result of his letting his basement to a call-girl who pays a substantial rent.

We are both most distressed by the account of your accident. Must you travel on the *top* of buses? I've often almost come to grief myself in the same way. Your doctor is surely right to prescribe rest: do please obey him: we don't want to lose you.

Ruth is outraged at the suggestion that she might ever, in any circumstances, try to prevent my writing to you. So you had better make your peace in your next letter.

Up here—and nowhere else—I always keep a brief daily diary, and Ruth is even now reading the entries for 1955–58, reminding me of many incidents we had both forgotten. The grandfather clock is ticking placidly; the Aladdin lamp sheds its splendid light; the fire burns brightly, and another is already lit in the bedroom. There is no sound outside, save now and then the mournful cry of a curlew. If one stands outside the cottage door one can see four lights strung out along the bottom of the valley: three are in farmhouses and the fourth in the telephone-box in Keld. It is on all night, and doubtless we all pay for it. The lady who keeps the only shop in Keld is stone-deaf and has been courting for thirty-five years. This year we hear she has acquired a deaf-aid (*verb. sap.*) and has so far regained touch with life that she insists on shutting the shop at the regular hour of 6 p.m. (and then removes the deaf-aid to avoid hearing the knocks and shouts of the outraged villagers) instead of obligingly staying open till all hours, as she has done for many years. The couple who run the Keld post-office are giving it up on July 31. They are sick of being tied all day and everyday for £4. 10. o a week, which is apparently all they get. No one else is keen to take the job on, so perhaps there will be no post-office next time we come. The old-age pensioners are already pitifully asking how they will get their money. Our village, you see, is full of its own problems, although the population is something like thirty-eight.

Much love from us both.

The plot thickens. The doctor—like all of his trade a simple psychologist—told me I had a cracked rib, by which he really meant not cracked but broken, confident that the milder word would soothe me. But after two days it seemed to me that the pain was altogether on too majestic a scale for a mere crack, so I had it X-rayed, and that revealed *three* ribs temporarily but effectively bust. They are now sullenly mending. I can now clear my throat without feeling sick, and can walk much as usual, though, to adapt Flurry Knox on Miss Bobbie Bennett,[1] you would still look a long time at Deerfoot or Jesse Owens before you thought of me. The body is very odd. I asked the doctor if anything I did in reason could have a bad effect, and he answered 'only staying in bed'—rather as if, say, an ingrowing toenail *could* result in gastritis. Apparently passivity when wounded invites pneumonia.

But how bored you will be with all this. Pain makes one a fearful egoist. Your letter arrived second post yesterday, which is only one post late (but what about your p.o. disappearing?). Your letter breathes happiness, which is wonderfully refreshing in 1960. All

[1] In *Some Experiences of an Irish R.M* by E.Œ. Somerville and Martin Ross (1899).

Lytteltons are hopeless ignoramuses about birds and flowers, but I like their names, and though the shape and size and colour of practically all remain mysteries, somehow the thought of you both surrounded by ring-ousels, meadow-pipits, redstarts, oxlips and heartsease gives me a lovely holiday feeling, vicarious though it is. We are not very rich in birds here, though I have a suspicion my ears may be partly to blame. But alas the nightingale has been banished from his old group of trees by building, and his note is distant and sounds discouraged. No longer 'singing with fear for none, true on the note, sharp at the edge, loud, fat with tone, with a trill and a tremolo to make you frozen with wonderment to hear' (from *How Green!*).

I am still puzzling over *The Answer to Life is No*. He seems to have such a lot to say which often does not emerge into intelligibility. Even short apparently simple statements; e.g. what the heck does 'I have brought my humming-bird to the glass of time' mean? I doubt if you will make a penny out of it, but what do I know? I have seen no review yet. Pamela is entranced with the other book; she hasn't finished yet. I raced through the new life of Charles Kingsley. A tedious old hearty in many ways, but a goodish chap I expect. Not up to Newman's class with the foils, but wasn't he mainly right? And wasn't there something faintly repellent about Newman, described by Scott Holland as looking 'as delicate as an old lady washed in milk'. Remembering many boring pictures of saints in the galleries and churches of Rome I like K's calling them 'prayer-mongering eunuchs'. And after all he did write the finest English hexameter, *n'est ce pas*? 'As when an osprey aloft, dark-eyebrowed, royally crested.'[1] Do you know about N. saying of Manning: 'Ah yes, Cardinal Manning, ambition, ambition, ambition.' Some kind friend told M. who flushed and riposted: 'And shall I tell you what was wrong with Cardinal Newman? Temper, temper, temper.' Both bullseyes, no doubt.

Ruth! The finest defence ever made of what at first sight looked harsh was of course Johnson's to a lady who said when they had met previously, he had called her a dunce. 'Madam if I had thought so, I certainly should not have said so'. That shall be mine adapted. And I will add that anyone who had been in her company for ten minutes, and thought she could ever do or say anything mean or ungracious or

[1] From 'Andromeda.'

76

jealous or stupid would be instantly certifiable. Any further reparation you think I should make shall be instantly made—and all with my very best love.

Boswell was a great standby last week, when each day was a long ache punctuated by stabs apparently of a dagger both sharp and serrated. I was pleased to be reminded of the mathematics lecturer, who, when he bored his audience, was made to yawn by their deliberately yawning, and invariably dislocated his jaw when he did, and could utter no word till his man was sent for to set it.

I say how *savage* reviewers are on a man who is out of fashion. Poor old Barrie kept on getting it in the neck last week, and a day or two ago one young man said *Margaret Ogilvy* was *nauseating*, an idiotic exaggeration. You can say that to modern taste it is sometimes sentimental, but no more. Much of it (e.g. the chapter 'RLS') is very charming, and I love the old mother's reply to J.M.B., after she had said how proud Jane was and she would have been to look through the door at Thomas Carlyle and think how famous he (her mon) was. J.M.B. said 'Yes but what when he roared at her (Jane) to shut the door?' 'Pooh! a man's roar is neither here nor there'. That surely is part of what every woman knows. Of course he *could* be tiresome. How cross old Agate was at his commenting on 'the courage of flowers' in wartime, going on and looking so bright and happy.

No, let us use words rightly. What *is* nauseating is the cant, very current just now, that one of the first essentials of civilisation and culture is that *Lady Chatterley* should be published unexpurgated, not in the least because pornography is popular, but because every teenager is passionately anxious not to miss a word D.H.L. wrote. One man ten days ago actually wrote that D.H.L.'s physiological details, interspersed with words commonly met with only on the walls of public lavatories, really made the book cleaner than when they were left out!

My nephew was here recently. He says there is not much hope for Hagley.[1] It is too near the Black Country and, there being only one park-keeper, toughs and teddies swarm at will in the park. When they want to come into it, they kick out three or four palings and come. There is a good deal of fern and bracken in the park, and the sardonic

[1] George Lyttelton's ancestral home in Worcestershire.

keeper told Charles that much of the recent rise in Birmingham's population was the result of what happens in the Hagley bracken every summer evening. Old George finished building the house *exactly* two hundred years ago. *Tout passe, tout casse, tout lasse.*

22 May 1960   *Kisdon Lodge, Keld*

To say the least, your doctor sounds to me an ass—but they are all the same, seldom knowing what is the matter, and failing to treat their patients as responsible grown-ups. Thank goodness you had the X-ray: *three* ribs *broken* is surely something to boast of. I do hope they're mending, however sullenly.

Your soft and affectionate answer has turned aside Ruth's wrath, and she sends you more loving messages than I think it good for you to read.

I visited our shopkeeper the other day for an ounce of tobacco. Certainly her deaf-aid has brought her to life. I also discovered that her only means of getting bread these twenty years has been an itinerant vendor who drives up the dale once a week with a travelling shop. But she has never been on speaking terms with him, so every week a neighbour, some way off, buys and pays for the bread and then carries it down to her.

This week we had three sunless days of bitter east wind, which kept us at the fireside and greatly benefitted the galley-proofs of O. Wilde. We have now checked 448 galleys against the photostats of the originals (finding just enough errors to make it worthwhile and amusing) and await more by tomorrow's post. The dear fellow has still two and a half years and a hundred or two letters to go. I should be doing lots of other work on the proofs, but our days seem all too short and full, and we still sleep our solid ten hours each night. I have almost finished the first volume of the Swinburne letters, and mostly find the matter more interesting than the manner. To his Etonian friends A.C.S. went on using Eton slang ('in the bill', 'after twelve' etc) for many years. Naturally enough the American editor has failed to notice or remark on this, but otherwise he has done quite well.

Although I have never seen Hagley, I hate to think that it is finished: will it become a loony-bin or what? Ruth is now enjoying Roger's book, and I shall read it next. *How Green* still looks reproachfully from its shelf. No more birds' nests, but plenty of birds and flowers: I'm glad to think that their very names gave you some pleasure. The wheatears (the word, they say, is a mangled form of 'white arse') have just come back: they lay delicious little blue eggs in walls and under big stones: we have only once found a nest.

They sent me a proof of the London Library sale catalogue, which I think will look quite impressive: you shall have a copy when I get back. It all seems delightfully far away, and I spend *no* time anticipating the ghastly pile of letters which must be accumulating in Soho Square. I gave E. Blunden this address, and his letter got here in *three days* from Hong Kong! He writes cheerfully, but clearly longs to see some cricket and get among the secondhand bookstalls.

We are in the middle of prolonged and delicate negotiations which we hope will lead to our getting (at a cost of £30) water piped to a (so-far non-existent) tap in our kitchen from a spring in the next field. The owner of the field seems very friendly, but the blacksmith from the fairly neighbouring village of Gunnerside is dilatory: we opened negotiations almost a year ago. We're very happy climbing over the wall each day and spooning water out of the animals' (spring-fed) drinking-trough with an enamel mug, but we can foresee days when we might prefer an indoor tap.

We have been for one long walk—a circumambulation of Kisdon. It took six hours, including two hours for picnic lunch and reading on the river-bank. It was hot and sunny, and we saw *no one* except a very distant farmer on a horse. Tomorrow, if it's fine, we plan another such walk, to visit a ruined farmhouse called Crackpot Hall, which is set in an astonishingly wild and beautiful place. There are spectacular waterfalls (here called 'forces') at Keld, which is where the Swale proper begins.

You must forgive the disjointedness of this letter: we are so relaxed that concentration is difficult, and I just scribble down whatever comes into my head. Write here again this week. We shall sadly return at or soon after the end of the month. I must be home for the Fourth of June. Only one more, which will be my tenth as a parent. Nurse your broken ribs.

79

There is a delightful holiday air about your last letter, slightly reminiscent of Tennyson's lotus-eaters reclining by their nectar, far away from everyday affairs. Just as it should be. And I fear you must find my half-baked observations on literary topics sounding very like the bloodless twittering of ghosts that Aeneas heard in Hades. Never mind; I have your assurance of loving messages from Ruth (though how right you are in realising how easily septuagenarian heads are turned).

You are pretty right too about my doctor—a good man, but like his tribe a childish psychologist. My ribs have abandoned their attempts to emulate the rack and the thumb-screw, and now merely ache, and that apparently they will do for another three or four weeks. However, at seventy-seven an ache is neither here nor there—or more accurately, if it isn't here it will be there—and I am back in circulation, if that is not too big a word for my mild activities. I am coming to the Lit. Soc. on June 14, though probably my doctor would purse his lips over the possibly dangerous effect of meeting Lockhart or Sir Cuthbert. I am told Lockhart's book has a reference to me—rather an inaccurate one it sounds—in connection with K.G. Macleod. But is anything ever *entirely* true?

Any news about your shopkeeper is welcome. I hope her non-speaks with the travelling baker is/are not only because of deafness. Those village animosities can be Olympian. Here Mr Dunnett has not spoken to Mr Willy Cook for seventeen years; Mrs Patemorrer, though living next door to her, will deny to her last breath any knowledge of the existence of Mrs Pizzey.

The Victorians had something we haven't. I have just got from the library Sir Charles Petrie's *The Victorians* and am a little disheartened to see in the index that Tennyson is mentioned twice, Carlyle and Ruskin not at all. Surely that is to describe a country's military activities and omit the artillery? The Ipswich library is in rare form nowadays; the last four new volumes it has acquired are *Pawn-power in Chess, British Monetary Experiments, Public Enterprise in Sweden,* and *Theoretical Elasticity.* I believe *you* would read the last long before *How Green.*

Hagley won't be got rid of till my nephew comes back from N.Z.— over two years, but I see no hope after that. The cussedness of things! My brother sold ten years ago a lot of land near Birmingham and got £110,000 for it. Very nice? Well, today it would easily fetch £1,000,000, and as my nephew says, you can do a lot with a million, and even get parlour-maids and gardeners.

What do our top-chaps care about old tradition, family seats etc., venerable and obviously valuable institutions like your L.L.? The Inland Revenue clearly contemplates bankrupting Shrewsbury, and takes the infantile point of view that as parents have so far faced the increase of fees, they will go on doing so. But in several schools I know the limit of parents' patience and indeed capacity is pretty near. Beaks' pay will continue to rise, and, let me tell you, few are worth more than they are getting now, though nobody dares say this in public. But enough of that. Fancy talking about education when you are listening to the white arse carolling away! I wish you could buy Crackpot Hall. What an address to have, and what fun counting—on the fingers of one hand—the people who did *not* make a joke about it.

We have a new neighbour here, one Patrick Barrington who used to write excellent light verse in *Punch* and elsewhere. (Do you remember his pet hippopotamus which he nursed through hippopota-measles and hippopotamumps?) Last week he came to tea at 4.30 and left at 7.45 without once drawing breath. Pamela says it was my fault and I encouraged him in capping quotations etc.

Meanwhile special thanks for *The Living House* which I greatly enjoyed, and Pamela adored. Fascinating and original. Is there *any*-thing the man doesn't know about lepidoptera and coleoptera etc? I have seen only one review of it so far.

Love to Ruth—it must have been someone very like her the poet had in mind when he wrote No 70 in the Oxford Book, original edition.[1]
P.S. I very seldom cob you in a mis-spelling, but shouldn't 'benefitted' be 'benefited?' Beak! Pedant! Prig!

[1] 'There is a lady sweet and kind' (Anon).

I am writing this out of doors, in a sheltered dip behind the cottage in hot sunshine. Ruth is beside me, repairing some gay curtains (destined for the bedroom) which we bought at that (one and only) sale. A cuckoo is calling across the valley. There is no other sound. I meant to write to you last night, but by ten o' clock I was too sleepy. The final batch of Oscar galley-proofs (ending up with No 542) reached us on Saturday, and we spent most of yesterday (a still and warm but largely sunless day) checking them against the originals, finishing after tea. We breakfasted this morning at 10.15, and after seeing to the fire, washing up, making the bed and fetching the water, *nous voici*. The post leaves the village below at 3.15, and when we post this we shall also fetch the milk and the day before yesterday's papers.

In the same bundle as the last Oscar proofs there arrived *all* the galley-proofs of Diana Cooper's third volume. (What, you may ask, is holiday, and what work?) But there are only 160 of them, and I should be able to read and correct them all during to-day and tomorrow. I may conceivably have to go to Chantilly next week, to go through them with Diana, but that depends on her movements. We shall leave here in great sorrow on Wednesday, stopping the grandfather clock and locking the door soon after 11 a.m., and reaching the noise, dirt and stuffiness of Soho Square about 9 p.m. Two days in the office, and then to Bromsden for Whitsun, the Fourth etc—looking forward to your letter greeting me. We're determined to get up here again for a week or two, possibly in August, by which time the spring should have been tapped for our water-supply. Did I tell you that both the farmer who owns the spring and the blacksmith who is going to do the job are called William Calvert? No relation, but luckily good friends. Ruth is also plotting to get a little calor-gas cooker to take the place of the Primus. Soon we shall be as sophisticated as the Savoy Hotel.

Ruth can't wait to look up No 70 in the *O.B. of E.V.*, which we haven't got here. So far our chief anthologies are *Nightingale Valley*, compiled by William Allingham (1862)—an excellent book: do you know it?—and a good Everyman volume called *A Galaxy of Shorter English Poems*, or words to that effect.

(The sun has momentarily gone behind a cloud, and a curlew is calling.)

Last week we made two longish walking expeditions—one to Crackpot Hall, where we would indeed like to live (jokes or no jokes), for its situation is superb, but the central part of the house collapsed some years ago—the result, they say, of centuries-old lead-workings under the hill. The other expedition was to various places, including Summer Lodge Tarn, a large and rather sinister mountain lake, miles from anywhere, in the midst of bog and heather, where thousands of black-headed gulls come every spring to nest—it must be a good sixty miles from the sea. They build their nests in reeds on the edge of the tarn, and rise in screaming multitudes at one's approach. Later they gradually settle, and apparently each bird unerringly flies straight back to its own nest. They are beastly birds, constantly dive-bombing the open nests of peewits, curlews etc and destroying their eggs. Often one sees a peewit driving the much bigger and more powerful gull away. If my last letter had a holiday air, what will you say to this one?

I don't think a great deal of Sir Charles Petrie—indeed, as Oscar would say, I never think of him at all—and so am not surprised at the deficiences of his index or his book. The Ipswich library seems to deal largely with what C. Lamb called *biblia abiblia*: you must let Patrick Barrington loose in it. He was at Eton with me, and I rather liked him. I thought 'benefitted' looked funny when I wrote it: I trust you to point out all such solecisms. I won't promise to write them all out ten times, but I shall probably remember them.

I have finished both large vols of Swinburne's letters One can't *like* him much, and his shrill tirades against 'the Galilean' and in favour of the Marquis de Sade are tedious and childish. But his devotion to poetry is fine, also his passionate championship of Shelley, Blake, Landor, Victor Hugo etc. There are four more vols to come.

Goodbye, dear George. I wish you could see the magical beauty which lies all around me.

At this moment you two must be approaching the sodden and un-kind midlands, every minute or two a mile further from paradise, 'so late their happy seat'. But I am afraid you will take rather a sardonic view of the subsequent lines 'The world was all before them where to choose Their place of rest'.[1] The last word will *not* seem to be *le mot juste* to you; I suppose Milton really meant 'abode'. If not Adam too might have indignantly asked how 'rest' was in key with all that menacing stuff about the sweat of his brow. I remember how un-attractive each year at Eton the resumption of the collar was every September—always glorious weather, and the realisation that there was some sour stuff to come before the feet could be again on the fender. And football in September was usually just as incongruous as cricket in May. I once inadvisedly caught a very hard hit in a trial match at Cambridge. Brilliant and all that yes, but not worth the split hand which the bitterly cold day brought about.

Comic about your Calverts (the chief factotum at Pamela's home Babraham was one William Calvert for years). It is much the same here; Pipes and Dunnetts swarm, all disclaiming any relationship with each other, though everyone knows they are connected, however different their social levels.

We went on Sunday to an exhibition of modern pictures at Fram-lingham (the home of P's sister, Lettice Colman). To my Victorian eye most of them looked like a painter's palette before scraping—a mess of bright confused colours. They literally said nothing to me what-ever. But the afternoon's entertainment was an address by Roger on George II, which was excellent value, and very characteristic, humor-ous, naughty, impish, very easy to listen to. But the room was rather hot, and one or two of the weaker brethren—and sisters—got rather repellently drowsy, mouth sagging, head drooping obliquely. A famous ex-international polo-player composed himself for sleep from the start, then woke up with a jerk and strode out of the room, watch in hand, giving the impression that he had to catch a train. But he did ample justice to an excellent tea half-an-hour later. Yesterday R. was lunching with the Lord Beaverbrook, not on business, just a friendly

[1] Part of the antepenultimate lines of Milton's *Paradise Lost*.

lunch, the Beaver apparently having forgotten that in a correspondence with R., not long ago, he said what R. had said in some speech referring to the *Daily Express* was 'most offensive'. Not that he really could have cared much. Only yesterday three judges stigmatised the *Daily Express* and *Daily Mail* in unmeasured terms. I shall be interested to hear R's account of his lunch. I fear he won't be at the Lit. Soc., as he and Sibell are taking a holiday in Spain.

Summer Lodge Tarn is a good name, in spite of its sinister aspect. Lakes can look really rather terrifying. There is a small one near here, closely surrounded by trees, black, absolutely silent; no bird comes near it. And Wastwater amid all those grim screes is pretty unfriendly. Do you know Loch Ness? The mother of a boy in my house was drowned there, and her body was never found, all of course put down to the monster.

I am glad to see *John o' London's Weekly* has revived, and there has been some interesting reported talk with Gilbert Murray; *inter alia*, that Henry James meant 'The Turn of the Screw' to be terrifying to every reader, but was convinced it was a failure as he dictated it to an unemotional Scot, who, after each hair-raising episode, merely asked 'What next, please'. And I like G.M.'s telling of the great (but absurd) Cambridge philosopher McTaggart that he always wore a string round one of his waistcoat buttons. 'Why?' 'I keep it handy in case I should meet a kitten'. The White Knight in person. But so were a good many Cambridge dons half a century ago.

How right you are about Sir Charles Petrie. *The Victorians* is poor stuff—superficial, chatty, quite inadequate. Reviews are misleading; only one that I saw observed that a survey of the Victorian age was an odd one which mentioned S.W. Gore as a tennis-champion but said nothing of his brother the great bishop. No, it won't do.

Love to Ruth. I don't *think* she will mind what poem No 70 *O.E.V.* says, but one never can be sure.

P.S. I have lost nine pounds avoirdupois.

Once again I write out of doors, but this time *in the shade*! The house is covered with huge red roses, and the laburnum-blossom is drifting down over me as I write. (I wish you didn't always have to come here at midwinter.) Outside the library window, in the morello cherry tree, a flycatcher has a nest with five eggs. Over the porch in the clematis a pied wagtail has built, and under the eaves the house-martins have returned in their dozens. A cuckoo with laryngitis is calling in the wood. Altogether a pastoral scene of high summer, but my heart is aching for the windy uplands, green green valleys and surrounding majesty of peaks. We drove south sadly in hot sunshine on Wednesday, and have both felt pretty miserable and *désorientés* ever since. What Henry James called 'the real right thing' takes a lot of snapping out of. At Soho Square the accumulation is appalling. Every-one I have ever heard of or dimly known seems to have written me a long complicated letter. Vyvyan Holland wants me to expurgate the later letters, and altogether my heart sinks. Kisdon is the place for me.

Ruth has gone to her son's cottage in Essex for the week-end. She was enchanted to discover the identity of No 70 in *O.B.E.V.* and is much looking forward to seeing you at 6 p.m. on the 14th. When do you leave for London? It mercifully looks as though I shan't have to go to Chantilly, since Diana is coming to London, but I may well spend next Saturday in Oxford, getting Sparrow's remarks on the Oscar letters and checking the ones in Magdalen. I'll hope to write to you on Saturday night and post it on Sunday.

I thoroughly enjoyed Roger's book: if this is book-making it's most agreeably done. Am now reading Cecil Day Lewis's autobio-graphy *The Buried Day*. I appear once with my name misspelled. I shall warn Cecil that when *my* autobiography appears it will contain many flattering references to C. Day *Leavis*. That should draw him!

Adam came over yesterday for the Fourth and spent a quiet day in the garden. Comfort took him and a girl-friend back for the fireworks. He seemed in good form, enjoying everything. He is supposed to be in Lower Club, but they haven't yet had one club game: instead they masquerade as the Third Eleven (XXXIII) and Fourth Eleven (XLIV), for which A. played against some school or other and took three for one.

Duff's Schools began at Oxford on Thursday. He telephoned yesterday to say the first three papers weren't quite as bad as he'd expected —which may or may not be a good sign. Adam's G.C.E. (Advanced and Science) begins on the 22nd (the day of the London Library sale). Yesterday Comfort looked at one of last year's Maths papers and couldn't begin to understand a single one of the *questions*!

Experts are predicting high prices for some of the manuscripts-at the L.L. sale: I only hope they're right. Christie's say that a little preliminary champagne always has a tonic effect on the bidding, so I'm trying to raise some more money for that. T.S.E. is all for it, and I'm sure will receive the guests most graciously. Did I tell you that I asked Birley to contribute to the sale, and he sent a copy of the Nonesuch Press Herodotus? It's a lovely book, which I wouldn't mind having myself. E. Blunden reports that a Hong Kong schoolboy wrote 'In Hong Kong there is a queer at every bus-stop'. I have told him that in London the answer would be 'So what?'

Ruth and I went to the Robert Morley Wilde film on Thursday and thought it rotten, except for the Trial dialogue, which is *verbatim* from life. We shall try to see the other film too. Next Friday is R's birthday and I am hoping to take her (on Thursday) to the new Rattigan play about T.E. Lawrence, which sounds pretty good. Sometime soon we are going to check that immensely long Oscar letter (*De Profundis*) in the British Museum. There is too much to do, and I don't much want to do any of it. Have your ribs quite recovered? It will be a sad day when you can no longer scramble up to the eyrie in Soho Square.

9 June 1960   *Grundisburgh*

As I hope you know, the widespread conviction that, without my counsel, the finances of the Abbey School Malvern would be entirely precarious compels my annual visit to Oxford, where the Finance Committee meets under Sir Douglas Veale. I am staying with Roger and Lavinia Mynors. Last night I was taken to dine in Corpus and had a pleasant talk with the Vice-President, and the printing pundit whose name, I suspect, has half-escaped me when I say it was Regler.

It was an oddish dinner for a guest-night, all cold, slabs of unidentified but not wholly untoothsome made-up meats. A good white wine, and of course I followed (was it?) Saintsbury's advice in preferring Madeira to port or sherry. I spoke with several others; more than one claimed to know R.H-D. (who doesn't?). One literally called him 'a great man' and clearly meant what he said, so you will see I was in the right atmosphere.

Pamela and I spent last week-end in a curious *omnium gatherum* at her brother's near Cambridge. A picturesque French lady was there, who, Robert Adeane told us, has had three children by Picasso, whose pictures R.A. does much to boost at the Tate. The house is full of ultra-modern paintings which to my ignorant and philistine eye look like the uncleaned palettes of painters—just a confused mass of colours. The one question one must *not* ask is 'What is the subject'? That puts one at a stroke back among the fans of Alma Tadema and Watts.

I hope the shades of the prison-house are gradually becoming less black? You suspected that Vyvyan Holland might be tiresome. There can surely be no point in expurgating O.W. I do hope you will be able to overrule him. Does he think that at this date O.W.'s moral opinions can be glossed over or whitewashed?

I leave for home to-morrow and go to London on Tuesday—the day your letter usually arrives. But, my dear R., you have far too much round your neck. We meet on Tuesday 6 p.m. Why not give yourself a brief rest from writing to G.W.L.? You really should. I shall be climbing your stairs at 6 and shall always do so, moving with the slow and rhythmical steps advocated by mountaineers.

I haven't yet read *The Buried Day*. Your suggested revenge for (I imagine) 'Davies' is excellent, though Roger Mynors tells me that Leavis's *pupils* are devoted to him, even after ceasing to accept all he says as gospel. I suspect he may be one of those apropos of whom G.K.C. (was it?) wrote 'If you want to keep your dislike of someone alive be careful not to meet him'. Macnaghten (H) at Eton constantly got letters from the Rev. H. Daman, spelling his name McNaghten. At last M. riposted 'If you go on leaving out the first 'A' in my name I shall address you leaving out the second 'A' in yours'. These witty old pedants!

Oxford is looking lovely—or would do if the traffic was not impossible, and the populace far too numerous. The streets are full of examinees fresh from a paper—though 'fresh' is not the word. Most are a bit pallid and strained. I hope Duff is not one of these—in fact I am sure he isn't. Adam, I think, has gone well beyond Eng. Lit. (O level) and will pass his tests with colours flying.

I like 'a queer at every bus-stop'. I think it may be true here, but what do I know?

I missed the Oscar Wilde film in Ipswich and am glad at your saying it is rotten. Anyway I know the trial almost by heart.

I was mildly interested by John Lehmann's second autobiographical volume[1] and quite a lot by *Waterloo*.[2] It seems that both Napoleon and Wellington made any number of what would appear to be almost fatuous blunders and misapprehensions. As for Ney, he never once did anything right. One constantly has the feeling of hideous carnage, but the sum total of English casualties is very small beer besides *one* day of the Somme or Passchendaele. Is there an expert in the Lit. Soc.? B. Fergusson? Tim? Probably Peter F. knows as much as anyone. My old brother, who never wrote a line, knew all there was to be known about Waterloo, and I was interested to find that this new book says just what he did about the undeserved load of blame which historians, following Napoleon, have put on Grouchy. Does one know the full truth about anyone or anything? And yet the air is thick with the dogmatisms of 'spokesmen' every day. The latest BBC change from facts at 9 to facts and comments at 10 will diminish my listening still further. It is grim evidence that people have got to the point of wanting their minds made up for them. 'Tell us what we *ought* to think'. And yet individuals I meet still seem to have some independent notions.

11 June 1960   *Bromsden Farm*

Your account of the conversation at Corpus is clearly apocryphal, but none the less welcome. Ridler is the name of the Printer to the University—a very nice and able man.

[1] *I am my Brother* (1960).
[2] By John Naylor (1960).

Duff has finished his Schools, for better for worse, and next Friday retires from Oxford, though he may conceivably be recalled for a viva in July. Yesterday he came over, and, in a fit of post-examination euphoria, cut *all* the grass in the garden between lunch and tea. This made the brick-path look so weedy and unkempt that I have spent most of today putting it in order, housemaid's knee or no.

Last week in London, though a short one, was well-nigh intolerable. Apart from the noise, heat and stink, my office was seldom free of callers and the telephone rang incessantly. Everything had stood still during my absence, so all books are behindhand. Vyvyan Holland is trying to make me bowdlerise Oscar's letters. Of course I won't (still less will I falsify some of them, as V.H. suggests) but the copyright belongs to him and I see a deadlock looming. I can't tell you how fed up I am with it all—and how I long to retire to Kisdon's happy hill.

Needless to say, Ruth has sustained, sympathised and comforted in her inimitable way, though she finds the London scene as unattractive as I do. Next week her daughter is arriving from Italy with a four-year-old child and an Italian girl, to await the birth of a second child somewhere about the end of July. This will clearly be a great nuisance. You mustn't mind my unburdening myself to you: it will be a joy to see you on Tuesday.

I met Leavis once and thought him quite revolting—dirty, messy, rude—but perhaps he grows on one. I shall certainly give him no opportunity of so doing.

The new *John o' London's* seems to me pretty poor: they refused to take Swinnerton back.

You must ask Gerry Wellington about Waterloo: I fancy he knows a good deal.

16 June 1960   *Grundisburgh*

An excellent evening, as always, only needing the presence of Ruth to make it perfect. I was glad to have a crack—for the first time—with James Laver, who was most pleasant and interesting. So too was Gerry Wellington. I asked him a good deal about Waterloo, and you may (or may not) be surprised to hear that the Duke did not make all that many mistakes. But, as the D. himself said, there are so many different versions of what happened that he really became quite doubtful whether he had been there himself. Jonah and Ivor and I sat for another hour afterwards. J. does seem much better, but is still breathless and the doctors are now really on their mettle and making test after test. Pamela's diagnosis is that it is some form of hysteria, as they all say his heart and lungs are as sound as bells. Maybe. We have a neighbour who now and then cannot walk across the room—in fact can do little else but tremble, and it is nothing at all but nervous imagination. It seems to me half-way to the firm belief that you are either God or a poached egg, which are apparently the commonest hallucinations, but somehow I don't think Jonah will end by thinking either. I like old Ivor very much, but doubt if he is a happy man. Yet as his old thrawn fellow-countryman said, nobody conscious of what is below the surface, i.e. the fundamental tragedy of man's life, can possibly be really happy—not even Leigh Hunt, 'idly melodious, as bird on bough'.

Your frank derision at my delicacy emboldens me to tell you that in your last list *The Laughing Fish*[1] sounds exactly the kind of book I love reading in bed. Sleep always comes to me late and goes early. On Tuesday night I had very little and put it down to your admirable vintages. But as I again had a hot head last night after a teetotal day, the cause must be elsewhere—hysteria perhaps. But how could an evening when Cuthbert and Lockhart were both absent induce hysteria? I suspect that after seventy-seven something goes a bit wonky every few days; all the bearings are getting a bit loose.

Lockhart's book[2] is mildly interesting in places, but doesn't amount to much—and why do I savour and rejoice in all *your* vignettes of heath and birdery at Kisdon, but never want to accompany him fishing in obviously lovely places? I am all for hearing about the playing of a salmon, but the description must be as skilful as the playing. Lockhart's writing is colourless, and after a time one gradually ceases to share his deep interest in Lockhart.

How good it was to see D. Somervell again—and looking so well—surely one of the very nicest of men.

[1] By Selwyn Jepson (1960).
[2] *Giants Cast Long Shadows* by R. Bruce Lockhart (1960).

Next week from Tuesday to Friday I shall be at North Foreland Lodge—Mr Chips to the life. Dreadful. Last year I brightened their young lives through my chair collapsing at girls' dinner. But I cannot expect such a stroke of luck again.

17 *June 1960*   *Grundisburgh*

I wrote and sent off my short-measure letter yesterday, and to-day arrives really the noblest non-birthday present that ever was—*five* books if you please, of magnificent variety and obvious readableness. I am equipped with occupation for my abundant leisure for weeks, not that next week isn't a bit depressing with *three* speech-days and a committee meeting. This goes to Soho Square, as I doubt if, posted to Bromsden F. to-day, it would reach you to-morrow. Well, what can I say but 'bless you' again. They say that prayers reiterated gain in force (how do they know?) so perhaps blessings do too. And how the devil can I ever hope to repay you in any way at all?

We dined yesterday in a small company, in which was a goddaughter of Malcolm Sargent's, and a lifelong friend of Vyvyan Holland's, so I walked warily. The lady told me that M.S. is fundamentally an unhappy man and very lonely—marriage broken, daughter dead. *Pauvre humanité*—another Eugene O'Neill in fact. Our eupeptic Victorians despised Euripides, especially in his view that the best thing of all was not to be born, the second to die as soon as possible. And Omar K. had no vogue of much account until Victorianism was on its way out.

18 *June 1960*   *Bromsden Farm*

I shall just scribble a page tonight, and continue in the morning. I spent most of to-day in Oxford, which was boiling hot and stuffed with mostly very unattractive people—bearded youths naked to the waist, negresses and other exotics, all sweating and jostling. I lunched at All Souls with Sparrow and John Bryson of Balliol. They have both read the Oscar galleys and are most enthusiastic. Bryson gave me material for three splendid new footnotes. Afterwards Sparrow and I walked down to Magdalen library, where we spent two hours checking their Oscar letters, Sparrow reading them aloud while I followed on the proofs. The road going and coming was packed with vehicles bumper-to-bumper—hideous! It is becoming increasingly clear that this part of the proof-correcting is going to take weeks, if not months, and I must just face the fact and get through it all as fast as I conveniently can. Now for bed and more of T.C.'s *Reminiscences*.

Sunday morning

The second volume of T.C. is excellent: I'm still on Jeffrey, with Jane to come.

Comfort is much disheartened because the squirrels have taken to lifting up the strawberry net, popping underneath and eating all the fruit. It has taken them twenty years to learn this trick, the little pets. A farm cat has destroyed the flycatchers' nest—tooth and claw everywhere.

Even as Cuthbert at the dinner-table sheds around him a baleful aura of *ennui* and *malaise*, so do you, my dear George, surround yourself with an infectious gaiety and pleasure. Whenever my eye falls on you, your noble brow, towering above its brachycephalic neighbours, is always the centre of laughter and anecdote, wit and repartee. Truly your presence always raises the Lit. Soc. level to what it's supposed to be. You mustn't mind my slipping away after dinner: I have almost always had enough by then, and Ivor is delighted to have you to himself. No, I don't think he is a happy man—a disappointed one perhaps.

As I left, James Laver said to me: 'What a delightful person G.L. is'. Needless to say I put him right.

Ruth was much pleased by the edited selection of your messages that I passed on to her. The advent of her daughter, grand-daughter etc has temporarily submerged her in a welter of cooking and tiresome domesticity, poor lamb. I sent you a parcel of books last week: *The Laughing Fish* shall follow.

Air travel is surely the most tedious and time-wasting invention ever—for meeters and see-ers-off, that is, and often for travellers too. Ruth and I went to meet her daughter at London Airport on Wednesday. Her plane from Milan was scheduled to arrive at 10.35 p.m. (a tiresome enough time in itself) but a telegram from Milan announced a postponement till 11.55 p.m. (This L.A. first denied and then corroborated.) We got there at 11.50, and, after some anxious minutes, the plane landed at 12.15. Customs etc took so long that it was almost 1 a.m. before we were able to drive away.

Next evening (Thursday) I dined with the Huntingdons at Roehampton: he a Labour peer, she a beautiful woman and good writer (Margaret Lane)—both charming. I was driven there by Lord Montagu of Beaulieu—and his wife. The other guests were Dorothy Dickson (marvellously preserved at sixty-four), Paul Dehn (Agate's godson) and a glamorous American woman. She drove D.D., P.D. and me back to London, and I set fire to a whole box of matches in the back of her car. Paul Dehn deftly put it out, but the car was full of fumes, and it transpired that none of the windows would open. The American lady explained this by saying that the car was borrowed.

22 June 1960   *Grundisburgh*

What a very nice letter to get! I remember my old tutor (or 'tootor' as my aunts always pronounced it; and it was a dear old Victorian snob great-aunt who, when a relative married a Headmaster of great distinction, said gloomily, and frequently: 'No, I must say I do think it is rather—as in 'gather'—dowdy to marry a tootor') Arthur Benson saying (not that no one else ever said it) '*Everybody* likes praise, deserved or undeserved, though many will pretend they don't'. But if you *will* produce such easy and charming people as James Laver to sit next to, how can I help bubbling away? And the excellent fare you provide does what it should to blunt their critical faculties. I am not so sure about your reference to my noble (*sic*) brow '*towering*' above those of my neighbours. The Creator has a frequently malicious sense of humour. He sent me into the world with an outsize head, and fifty years later gave me Paget's Disease, of which one of the results is a slow but steady increase in the size of the head. I don't yet—like Jeeves—take no. 9 in hats, but am not so very far off. So I adopt the feeble but very human device of practically never wearing a hat. Don't sympathise about Paget: it honestly doesn't bother me at all; there are many varieties, some hideously crippling, some quite harmless, and it was worth the exorbitant (I thought) £5. 5. 0 that I paid to the great Rowley Bristowe twelve years ago to be told a) it would trouble me very little and b) don't waste any money going to Droitwich. I was glad especially to hear b), as, with the possible exception of Stourbridge and Dudley, Droitwich is the most unattractive of places. Wigan—like Hell—has something majestic about it. Not Droitwich. Hester Alington was nearly drowned there, as the water is so salt that if you go upside down in it you can't right yourself. Didn't that happen to Kinglake in the Dead Sea?[1]

I have just finished the life of Eugene O'Neill you sent me. *Very* absorbing. As with so many geniuses the commonplaces of moral judgment are best left unexpressed. That picture of him in the frontispiece is really appalling in its tragic misery. Tell me about his plays. I have just got three or four of them from the library but not yet embarked on them. I remember somewhere in the book it says that they are—like so many of Shakespeare's—much better when acted than when read. I don't take much to Carlotta somehow. Am I wrong? Agnes sounds much nicer. And what is Shane doing now? And is Oona's marriage a success? Why did E.O'N. object to Charlie Chaplin —a greater genius than himself?

You told me the Bennett-Wells letters weren't up to much. After about p. 67 the editor had rather to scrape the barrel, and they don't talk enough about other people and things. But they say many shrewd and perceptive things. How right B. is about W. as an artist. But he was wrong surely in putting—who was it? *someone*, in one of W's lesser books—above Mr Polly as a comic character.

I shall tackle Druon when I get back. What a noble present you sent me. You always assert that gratitude is not your due, but again I remember Arthur Benson. 'Never take a kindness for granted, however regular or repeated it may be'. And if that isn't wise and just advice I'll eat my hat.

Your squirrels are, I hope, those grey criminals, not the little red fellows. Show them no mercy. Tree-rats they should be called.

Dorothy Dickson's looks thirty or forty years ago were entrancing.

[1] A.W. Kinglake (1809–1891) found it difficult to swim in the Dead Sea (*Eothen*, 1844, chapter xiii), but made no mention of capsizing.

I know of one young man who really did put an end to himself for love of her. Wasn't her daughter also a smasher? What has happened to her? Paul Dehn I surmise is making a name. What was that strikingly good play, revue, fantasy, pageant? of his somehow connected with Shrewsbury? James Agate thought a lot of him.

I am at the present moment at North Foreland Lodge surrounded by 'a knot of little misses', feeling, *à la* J.M. Barrie, how much nicer girls of fifteen are than boys of that age—so unshy and intelligent and friendly. Too strong perhaps. Boys can be very nice too.

What shocks one has. Harry Altham, President of M.C.C., *approves* of modern cricket—even of matches in which every innings till the last is declared and the result is awfully sporting and exciting—and bogus. A game which you lose after using only half your resources, in order to please the crowd, is to my mind rather a silly game. So I was always taught by C.M. Wells, who had the greatest contempt for cricket that wasn't serious. He didn't mean 'solemn'.

26 June 1960   *The Swan Hotel*
Newby Bridge, Lancs
(My bedroom is called Coleridge)

It's biro to-day, on a bench on the bank of the River Leven—in hot morning sunshine. It was charming of you to write an *extra* letter last week, and your regular one reached Soho Square just as I was setting off for Euston. Full of questions it was and lively comment. Droitwich, which you roundly condemn, has been the salvation of Comfort's stepmother, who goes there twice a year for her rheumatism or arthritis and always with benefit. I daresay she doesn't worry about the scenery or other horrors.

Eugene O'Neill's plays are mostly excellent to *see*, but I imagine less so to read. Shane is still a drug-addict, Oona's marriage is a tremendous success. She has six or so children and is reported placid and beautiful. All three of E.O'N.'s wives are still alive. Clearly Carlotta is intolerable, and E. could never forgive Agnes for having behaved so well. *What* a story!

Dorothy Dickson's daughter—Dot Hyson—is indeed a smasher.

She married the actor Anthony Quayle and renounced the boards, sensible girl.

The London Library sale exceeded all conceivable expectations—realising a grand total of £25,600!!!! Added to the £17,000 we have already collected in cash, this more than doubles the sum we originally appealed for, and should keep the Library solvent for some years. The high spot was the manuscript of Forster's *A Passage to India*, which, you remember, I travelled to Cambridge to fetch, and brought back higgledy-piggledy in my brief-case. Believe it or not, this fetched £6500—from America. Next highest was £3800 for two address-books belonging to T.E. Lawrence, and £2800 for the manuscript of *The Waste Land* which I persuaded T.S.E. to copy out last winter. The manuscript of Strachey's *Queen Victoria* fetched £1800, that of Maugham's *Up at the Villa* £1100, and so on. It was a very exciting, if hot, evening. Ruth and I dined first with the Eliots at their flat and went along with them. At dinner we spoke of Shaw, and T.S.E. said he thought S's best plays were *The Chocolate Soldier* and *My Fair Lady*—which I think better criticism than it sounds: there's nothing like a few good tunes for bolstering up a rather outmoded play.

When the T.S.E. manuscript was knocked down for £2800, the audience clapped and cheered and the old boy beamed modestly. We are devoted to him, but worried by his breathlessness and general frailty. His marriage is a tremendous happiness to him.

I arrived here on Friday evening in perfect weather, and yesterday (when the radio told of rain at Wimbledon and darkness at Lord's) the sun burned down all day from a clear blue sky (as it does to-day). There is mercifully no spare-room in the Ransomes' very uncomfortable cottage, so I am quartered in this excellent hotel, a few miles away, and they have hired a large Austin for the week-end. It has a wicked gear-change, but is otherwise okay. Ransome is pretty immobile—shuffling with a stick—so yesterday I drove him all day through the lakes—Esthwaite, Rydal, Grasmere, Thirlmere, Ambleside, Derwentwater, Keswick (where I visited Hugh Walpole's grave), Bassenthwaite (we picnicked on the road above the lake) and on to Cockermouth (birthplace of Wordsworth), where we sat in the sun by the Derwent, from which Ransome has pulled innumerable sea-trout and salmon. He is much grieved by the (scarcely acceptable) realisation that he will never be able to fish again. To-day I shall drive him about some more, and tomorrow morning take train for London, where another over-crowded week awaits me. I am reading Peter Quennell's new book *The Sign of the Fish*, which you must order from your library: it's autobiographical, and its theme is an enquiry into the ever-fascinating question of why writers write. P.Q. himself writes beautifully. I hope you can read this scrawl.

29 June 1960   *Grundisburgh*

I really should have sent you a wire about that magnificent auction for the L.L. which gave *me* immense pleasure, knowing something of your ceaseless efforts for it. Now who will paint your portrait to hang near that of Thomas Carlyle (and isn't my grandfather somewhere there too?). How does Comfort like the prospect of being Lady H-D. in the next honours list or two? It is inevitable—unless you refuse like John Christie and get a C.H. instead, even more distinguished they tell me. I do hope you are indulging in an orgy of self-satisfaction. I feel fairly confident that Ruth will see that you do. It is a very splendid achievement.

My letter. Yes I know. 'Questioning is not the mode of conversation among gentlemen'. And you may make the same retort as J. made to B. who feebly said he was encouraged to do it because J. was 'so good': 'Sir, my being so good is no reason for your being so ill'. But your knowledge of men and things in the world of drama, literature and indeed the world generally is so much greater than mine that I just have to pick your brains. And so you will continue to be good and I to be ill. It is one of your crosses.

Eugene O'Neill. I have read four of his plays, which seem to me fully to explain the appalling despair in his face. In *Desire under the Elms, Strange Interlude* and *Mourning Becomes Electra*, human nature is portrayed as of almost unrelieved blackness, 'no cakes or ale nor nothing pleasant'. I found them quite absorbing to read, and they must be terrific on the stage. *The Iceman* I am finding rather boring; all the conversations go on too long, in fact the whole play is too long. In bed I am enjoying the Jepson story you kindly sent. But how did your reader overlook 'corpus delic*tus*' on p. 70?

To revert to O'N. and your grim dictum 'He couldn't forgive Agnes for behaving so well'. Isn't that first cousin to D.H.L.'s insufferable trait of writing with the most venomous malice about those who had most helped him? Katherine Mansfield said there were three Lawrences—the black devil whom she hated, the prophet in whom she did not believe, and the man and artist whom she revered and loved. But I did not know him as a man, and am not clever enough to appreciate him as an artist, so all that is left is Nos 1 and 2, alas! But couldn't his executors have offered you something for the L.L. sale? Perhaps he thought it should be razed to the ground and the site sowed with salt, as that old ass G.B.S. suggested for Oxford.

The names of the places you passed through with Ransome— Rydal, Thirlmere, Bassenthwaite sound like vintages (though W.W.'s home *would* be called Cockermouth) but you ought to keep away from Westmorland. Nostalgia can be very debilitating. '*Tendebantque manus ripae ulterioris amore*'.[1] Virgil knew all about it. It would be worse if you weren't fairly soon getting another spell there.

Do coalmine disasters always hit you in the wind? They do me. Is there a grimmer death than being cut off by a fall of coal and being slowly suffocated or starved? I agree with the man who wrote that no man should be doomed to such a life. But then where would our fires and factories be? Other bad news in to-day's paper is that in a few years' time the larger apes will be no more throughout Africa. What will life be without gorillas? Apparently they are the mildest of animals, even if they have faces like enlarged H.K. Marsdens.[2] But you mustn't anger them; if it comes to a showdown you won't win. An irate gorilla once gripped a gun-butt so tightly that his fingers sank into the wood, and in a tug-of-war he can pull over seventeen men with one hand. He has a very sensitive spirit and can suffer acutely from disappointment—like (also improbably but truly) the pike. If Ruth is not chez No 36 on July 12, I shall show how strong my kinship is with both. I shall be there, though I oughtn't to be, as there will be a mort of exam-scripts here. The next three months are my busy ones. My real holiday-month is February, and a plucky lot

[1] 'Their hands outstretched in longing for the farther shore' (*Aeneid* vi, l. 314).
[2] Eton master.

of use that is. Love to R, and gently point out that to cast no eye upon her from April, no—March, till October is an infliction the Inquisition might have thought up.

P.S. And there are a lot of questions in this letter too; but practically all of them are rhetorical.

First—before I forget it—will you be an angel and propose Adam for the M.C.C.? He will be seventeen on Monday, and so eligible under the latest rules. I think—don't you?—that you know enough, at second hand, of his cricket interests and prowess to avoid perjury. Last week the *Chronicle* congratulated him on receiving his Middle Club, when he had not in fact done so, and the paper now has to retract and apologise. Many boys would be upset by this clumsy mistake, but Adam seems unmoved. Apparently the Lower Club side is now considered the Eton Third Eleven, and the Middle Club side the Fourth Eleven (and they play matches as such), while dear old Strawberry is left in the cold. As you will see, proposal entails both your signature on this form and a brief letter. If you can send me both in your next, I'll ask Fred Coleridge to second him. Adam is home for Long Leave, very cheerful despite his G.C.E. (A & S) which is in progress. To-day we all drove to Aldwick, near Bognor, and had our first swim of the year. There wasn't much sun, but no rain fell, and the sea was *warm*—very refreshing and enjoyable.

I have had three or four charming letters about the London Library sale, including one from Harold Nicolson, but have been too bedevilled with other things to spend much time in self-satisfaction. Your harping on an imaginary knighthood is a delightful fantasy. In the extremely unlikely event of one being offered, my instinct would be to accept. I have no worldly ambition (only peace at Kisdon) but while one is engaged in the merry-go-round, it seems churlish to refuse any rewards from the sideshows. There is surely a great deal of snobbery—straight and inverted—in these matters. My old friend Edward Garnett refused a C.H., saying that it was 'given only to dentists'. He was a lifelong 'agin-the-Government' radical, but I have heard many people sneer at honours of all kinds because they are mostly given to nonentities. True, but one might well refuse to do *anything* on the same grounds.

There my pen gave out and I went to bed. Now it is eleven o' clock on grey Sunday morning. So glad the O'Neill plays interested you: they are indeed terrific on the stage: even *The Iceman* held Ruth and me gripped for all its length.

I shudder at corpus delict*us*: I suppose I must have missed it in the typescript, but can't imagine how. Can I have been skipping?

My last day in the Lakes was hot and sunny: I drove A.R. all over the place. We lunched at Gosforth, in the shadow of the Atomic Pile, and then sat by the sea at Ravenglass, an enchanting little dead-end, consisting of one straggling street leading to nowhere, a huge natural (high-tide) harbour, said to have been used by the Vikings and not since, and beyond it a large island or isthmus which is a bird-sanctuary where several kinds of terns nest. I should have liked to join a boat-load of people who were being taken over to see it, but Ransome is too crippled to get into a boat. Altogether his situation is pitiable, for he needs a strong male nurse constantly in attendance, but has only his wife, who at the moment seems headed for a nervous breakdown, and is mildly irritated by the poor old boy. I left them feeling utterly exhausted, despite the wonderful weather and lovely scenery. Last week was black with engagements, none interesting enough to chronicle.

July 5 or 6, anyway Wednesday   *Grundisburgh*

Form filled in and enclosed for Adam—with great pleasure. I always resent 'block capitals', but as they might easily say the form was not properly filled in, I do so, not in block capitals, but in the script of Cardinal Bembo's secretary[1]—and I doubt if any candidate has been so sponsored before. I hope it won't stand in his way. Is there a possibility of his getting his eleven next year? That *would* be fun. I should

---

[1] In 1513 a papal brief of Pope Leo X was written in exquisite italic by an anonymous chancery scribe and signed by the Pope's secretary Pietro Bembo (1470–1547), who was later a Cardinal.

like to see you behaving exactly like a cat on hot bricks, and I can think of no other circumstance that would bring that about. A cricketer of such imperturbable nerves as A. has great potential value.

The Ladies Plate gave me immense pleasure. Bobby Bourne told me at Xmas the VIII would be nothing much; but on Saturday he said that quite suddenly, a week before Henley, they '*clicked*', like some machinery being adjusted and lubricated, and he went to Henley full of hope. Peter Haig Thomas five or six years ago told me he considered Bobby was in the 'Havvy' (de Havilland) class as a coach, and whatever rot he might (and did) talk about much else, he never did about rowing (like Flash Harry and music).

Of course you must accept the knighthood when (n.b. not 'if') it is offered you. You are right about the snobbery of those who sneer at it (or mere conceit, like Housman refusing the O.M. because Galsworthy had it). I have in my day done a little wire-pulling when Anthony Bevir[1] was in charge. But he is so no longer, and in fact is fairly deep in liquor nowadays. I regret the elevation of Hobbs and Gordon Richards but that was a sop to our *soi-disant* democrats. Surely old E. Garnett was quite wrong about the C.H. being given to dentists. Wasn't he mixing it up with the M.V.O., fifth class, which, the legend was, Edward VII gave to his bridge-partner who left the declaration to Tum, who had four aces.

Very interesting to hear that you and R. were thrilled by *The Iceman* on the stage. It just shows you can't judge by merely reading. I think the debased Yankee diction and slang rather got on my nerves (or 'noives'). The complaint that nothing happens except talk is of course as irrelevant as it was in Shaw's prime. Do any of the characters emerge as 'likeable' on the stage? Perhaps that is irrelevant too.

I was a little disappointed in the new Druon.[2] Didn't quite get the point of it, which of course may not be his fault; but his other books I recall as having plenty of subtlety as well as vivid colour, and in this one I get only some of the colour. What do *you* think of it?

You know, Rupert, the fundamental—and slightly depressing—

[1] Anthony Bevir (1895–1977). Private Secretary to Prime Ministers Chamberlain, Churchill, Attlee and Eden. Knighted 1952.

[2] *Alexander the God* by Maurice Druon (1960).

difference between my letters and yours is that yours are full of interesting things you have done, and ditto people you have seen. I, having done neither, am reduced, largely, to not very inspiring chatter about what I have been reading—with an occasional diversion onto, say, gorillas or other large animals for which you do not share my taste. What can be done about it? Nothing that I myself can see. Shall I tell you what Miss Smith (nicknamed 'the Drip') said about teaching Eng. Lit. to girls who confuse Ben Jonson with Dr Johnson and are not in the least abashed by her horror? Shall I tell you how I scored off the Inspector of Taxes last week, or that the reason why George Dunnett the local carpenter won't now go up a ladder, is not because, at seventy-five, his balance (like mine) is untrustworthy, but because, his weight being eighteen stone, he is sure that sooner or later a rung will wilt beneath his foot and bring him 'with hideous ruin and combustion down'?[1] No, the beer is very small and not comparable for a moment with your rich and varied vintages. I can't (honestly) think why you like my letters, but I believe you do. One, I suppose, of the anfractuosities of the human mind. Well there it is.

Now a small problem. Henry James wrote to R.L.S. that *Tess* was '*vile* . . . pretence of sexuality . . . abomination of the language' etc. But in *The Legend of the Master*[2] I read that in a later letter to R.L.S. he said that in spite of its faults it had 'a singular beauty and charm'. Well, where *is* that letter? It isn't in Percy Lubbock's two huge volumes; it isn't in your selection of his letters. But he oughtn't to be left with that slightly obtuse judgment. I am delighted to re-find that he regarded Carlyle as 'perhaps the very greatest of letter-writers'. But I suppose H.J. was not far wrong when he wrote 'your demolitions of the unspeakable Froude don't persuade me that C. was amiable . . . perhaps the most disagreeable in character of men of genius of equal magnificence'.

[1] Milton, *Paradise Lost*, book I.
[2] A compilation, by Simon Nowell-Smith, of anecdotes about Henry James (1947).

Considering that your last excellent letter began 'My dear Peter', and that you forgot to include in it the letter of recommendation for Adam to the M.C.C. (bring it with you on Tuesday if you can remember) you're jolly lucky that this letter doesn't begin 'My dear Cuthbert'. Anyhow you made up for it by your splendid substitute for 'block capitals'. Alas and alack, Ruth will not be with us on Tuesday, as she is being taken that evening to *Der Rosenkavalier* at Glyndebourne, which, as you know, means leaving London in full evening dress soon after lunch. She is most distressed at missing you once again. Her second grand-daughter was born safely on Monday morning, and will soon be back in Ruth's house, together with its mother, father, sister, nanny and Italian girl—a regular menagerie with which R. simply hasn't time to cope.

Last week, for most of three days, we escaped to the comparative peace of the Manuscript Room of the British Museum, where we checked the manuscript of Oscar's *De Profundis* (his longest, best and most important letter) against our proofs. The manuscript was given to the B.M. by Robbie Ross in 1909 (to ensure its not falling into the hands of Lord Alfred Douglas) with a fifty-year embargo on anyone's seeing it: R. and I are therefore almost certainly the first people who have scrutinised it properly, and to our surprise and great excitement we discovered that the so-called 'complete' version (first published in 1949) is a travesty of the original (it was printed from a wildly inaccurate typescript of Ross's). At least 1000 words were omitted, many hundreds misread, paragraphs transposed and goodness knows what. You can imagine what fun the checking was. I fear my proof-correction-bill will be appalling (I would never have set up from the printed version if I'd had the faintest inkling how corrupt it was) but the *Letters* will benefit enormously from containing the first complete and accurate version ever to appear.

You are quite right about Druon's *Alexander*. It was intended as the first volume in a series of *biographies* of Famous Bastards: Druon is one, and is therefore interested in the subject: he prefaced the book with a long introduction proving that all the greatest men in history were illegitimate (this seems to me idiotic: who knows who's legitimate for certain?). Anyhow the series never materialised, and we were left with this isolated volume. I decided I couldn't possibly publish it as a biography in English, so I changed its title, removed the introduction, and put it out as a novel—to all which Druon most helpfully agreed. *The Times* gave it a good review on Thursday, Raymond Mortimer is doing it in the *Sunday Times*, and the Critics are to discuss it tomorrow, so it should be well on its way. But it's nowhere near so good as his French history novels: I've just corrected the proofs of the new one, *The She-Wolf of France*, which will appear in the autumn. It includes an appallingly graphic description of the murder of Edward II in Berkeley Castle.

I think I have (at Soho Square) a typed copy of the James letter to Stevenson about which you ask: if I can find it I'll send it along. Remind me of it on Tuesday. Meanwhile here is a splendid piece of Oscar, rescued by us from the B.M. last week. It describes the recipient's father, Lord Queensberry:

> And I used to feel bitterly the irony and ignominy of my position when in the course of my three trials, beginning at the Police Court, I used to see your father bustling in and out in the hopes of attracting public attention, as if anyone could fail to note or remember the stableman's gait and dress, the bowed legs, the twitching hands, the hanging lower lip, the bestial and half-witted grin. Even when he was not there, or was out of sight, I used to feel conscious of his presence, and the blank dreary walls of the great Court-room, the very air itself, seemed to me at times to be hung with multitudinous masks of that apelike face.

Good strong stuff, eh?, and you are almost its first reader. I'm longing to get the book into page-proof, so that you can have a go at it. But when will that be? How long, oh Lord, how long? I have no time to work on it properly, and I keep on letting myself in for tedious, time-wasting and quite unnecessary chores. Tomorrow (Sunday), for example, at 3 p.m. I am opening an exhibition of Victorian first editions at Stratford-upon-Avon. Why, in God's name? you ask, and I can only say that I felt sorry for the organiser, who means well. I shall speak for ten minutes (goodness knows about what), and I shall waste *eight hours* doing it. This includes all the driving, and luncheon with the Priestleys at their new home, Kissing-Tree House, Alveston, just outside Stratford. Angus Wilson is staying with them for the week-end, I believe.

I have just read the new Michael Innes, which is great fun, and am now embarking on Tony Powell's latest. Mind you get the Peter Quennell book: it is reviewed in the current *Spectator* by Evelyn Waugh with a feline savagery which can only come from an old friend with a grudge.

We have a glut of raspberries, now rotting in the rain. The worst of growing fruit is that one either gets *none* or *much too much*. One hates to see it going to waste, but everyone else always has too much at the same moment. Anyhow thank God we're not in Cuba or the Belgian Congo! I can't wait to get back to Kisdon. London life has lost its spell for me. The noise in Soho Square seems to increase daily. Please come and add to it at six on Tuesday.

14 *July 1960*   *Grundisburgh*

Short measure this week, which should come as welcome relief. I arrived back yesterday to tackle a mountain of scripts on *Julius Caesar*. All the last twenty-four hours the morons of Liverpool College have made hideous with their half-baked ineptitudes. I am always mystified by the beaks of these third-rate schools. They go through the play repeatedly, and you would have thought that one time or another, on meeting the line 'Ate by his side come hot from Hell', someone might have asked and someone might have said who *Ate* was;[1] but so far of forty candidates *not one* has got nearer than saying Ate was Satan. And a good many spell Caesar Ceasar, and that I put to you is even worse than addressing someone called Rupert as Peter. The mystery of that still baffles me.

Tuesday again was an excellent evening—though Ivor, poor man, can't eat kidneys, and old Cuthbert practically can't eat anything. But I have never seen him (C.) in better form. Tim thought Peter F. was too heavy-handed in his ragging of the old chap, but from what

[1] In Greek mythology the goddess of vengeance and mischief.

I saw he thoroughly enjoyed it—and he certainly stayed longer than he normally does.

I say, did you see that dreadful grief that poor dear Pam Spanoghe has had—only daughter, aged eighteen, killed in a motor-accident? It simply doesn't bear thinking of. Elisabeth was the apple of her eye, and, I am pretty sure, her one real happiness in life. She is fond of the son, Benjie, but I think he was always second to E. What *can* one say on these hideous occasions that is of the smallest use? And yet one must say something. Fate is always quite indiscriminating in bestowing rough deals—no sign of ever thinking A. has had enough of them, let's send some to B. who has had few or none. I can't quote it, but Allan Monkhouse made a good remark once to the effect that he wasn't going to be satisfied with any but the best defence that the First Cause put up about the injustices etc of what Henry James called 'this horrible world'. I like the deliberate way in which the old agnostic avoided the name God.

I hope Ruth enjoyed Glyndebourne. I wonder if she met John Christie. He is a very Pickwickian figure now, physically as well as mentally, which he always was. He took enormous trouble over everything at Glyndebourne down to the smallest details. There is something engaging about what one could call the Prussian thoroughness, but for the sly fun in it, that in the cast's lavatories the ladies' seats are of different sizes, because, as J.C. simply explains, the rumps of prima donnas vary greatly in size. He once gravely admitted that the shapes as well as the sizes varied, but regretfully decided that it was too delicate a problem to tackle.

I very much want in October to sit next to D. Somervell, which I haven't done for a very long time. I had quite a lot of talk with Sir C. much of which, on his part, I didn't hear—to his obvious pleasure. I don't think we shall have him with us much longer; he looked incredibly thin and weightless on Tuesday, and I suspect, to use Carlyle's expression, is 'twinkling away' pretty quick.

I hope you are settling down to Oscar in every moment of spare time. No more Stratford jaunts. But you are hopeless.

I thought those kidneys were particularly good, didn't you? But Cuthbert and Ivor between them can eat practically nothing. Cuthbert's presiding kept him well away from me. When I rang up Tim to congratulate him on his barony, he reiterated his belief that Peter was too brutal with C., but I daresay he prefers rough attention to none. I had a good evening with Donald S., Leslie Hartley, Jonah and Tony Powell. In October we must certainly arrange for you to sit next to Donald. If you do, you must encourage him to let me see the anthology of wit which he has been compiling all his life. As I told him again on Tuesday, his retirement is just the time to polish it up and off, so that I can publish it, but he is shy about it.

Yes, I did read the Spanoghe tragedy, and wrote Pam a hopelessly inadequate little letter: it simply doesn't bear thinking of, as you say.

Ruth loved Glyndebourne and reported all the arrangements first-rate, working like clockwork and well thought out. She always sends messages of love and devotion, but I don't always pass them on, fearing to turn your head.

On Wednesday we went to *Ross*, an excellent play about T.E. Lawrence,[1] miraculously well acted by Alec Guinness, which held us both spellbound.

I only wish I could follow your instructions and concentrate on Oscar, but yesterday the proofs of *four* of my most important autumn books arrived simultaneously—bad planning you will say, but one simply has to push books through with different printers as quickly as possible. So goodness knows when I shall get back to Oscar.

Yesterday on my way to Paddington I looked in for half an hour at the nursing home where T.S.E. has taken refuge. What with asthma, breathlessness and determined admirers, peace is hard for him to find. He was in excellent spirits, reading a detective story, with a Penguin book of crossword-puzzles beside him. He is determined to preside at next Tuesday's Annual General Meeting of the London Library, returning immediately to the nursing home. He is unwilling to order a car for the afternoon, mistrusting the discretion of firm or driver (so far are our great men persecuted by the press!) and I have promised

[1] By Terence Rattigan.

to fetch and return him in a taxi. 'You're a great comfort to me', he said, and my heart melted. I truly love him, and so does Ruth—so you see you have a rival!

19 July 1960   *Grundisburgh*

I did nothing about Tim's barony, thinking he would prefer *not* to write a letter. I cannot quite make out—is he now Lord Nugent? Pamela says not but I am not sure. I shall certainly do what I can about Donald Somervell's anthology of wit. He mustn't be shy about it. The late Rev. P.A. Donaldson, Master of Magdalene, used to maintain shyness was a form of conceit. Once at dinner someone couldn't quite remember a certain song, so Donaldson sang it through. He had an unattractive voice.

I am sure old Cuthbert *enjoyed* Peter's badinage. I think he took Peter's list of his pessimistic views as in some obscure way a compliment. But I shall be surprised if he lasts until October; there is *nothing* of him inside those clothes.

I am sorry to hear T.S.E. is so frail. He has been only once to the Lit. Soc. since I have been a member. I had his company and greatly enjoyed it. He is clearly one of the best and nicest of men. I wonder why (or if) he likes Ezra Pound, whose utterances, many of them, reveal him as a really prize ass, but I suppose he isn't really, though I suspect Graham Hough thinks he is. Do you think G.H. is right in his view that whereas Wordsworth's and Coleridge's revolt inaugurated a century of new poetry, T.S.E.'s and Ezra P's 1920's revolt is so far sterile? Do you and can you read Auden? He says nothing to me, but that means nothing. Oh no, I see you share my view of him. What does T.S.E. think of Auden? I read a pleasantly sour review of A's recent volume,[1] though Connolly still seems to think he is very fine— and no doubt he too thinks so.

I wrote this yesterday at the club, and resume now having finished with the young women. They weren't so bad as I expected, their chief defect—as always—being to 'sow with the whole sack'. When asked to describe 'a day at the village school' most of them described

[1] *Homage To Clio* (1960).

the walk to school, the building and furniture, the schoolmistress's appearance and clothes, the two mistresses who succeeded her and the Inspector's visit, which took place once a year. They write like Herodotus in fact, though less entertainingly. Do you remember his tale of how some drug was discovered? It was like the house that Jack built. He began by describing the home of the explorer, then the boat in which he set out to sea, and how he rowed it, then his fishing-tackle, then the fish he caught, and how he extracted its liver from which he extracted the drug. In fact there is every reason for supposing it was nothing less than cod liver oil.

I thought Waugh on the Quennell book poor stuff. Mildly sour without any 'tang' to it. Meanwhile tell me about T.E. Hulme, who, they all say, is very important, and I recall nothing that he ever wrote. I looked at his life in the library and did not find him attractive. But it was fairly petty of the John's people not to admit him to their list of war-dead after 1918, because of some row they had had. I find some claim that T.S.E. owed him a great deal. Is that true?

It is very wrong of you not to hand on anything nice that Ruth says. You don't perhaps realise that my generation of the family is profoundly diffident—quite the opposite of my uncles ('all cheek and charm' as Inge said), who, as a result, all got jobs which they weren't quite up to—except my father who had no ambition at all. But you evidently think my head is easily turned, or perhaps, with the Doctor, that 'there are few things that we so unwillingly give up, even in advanced age, as the supposition that we still have the power of ingratiating ourselves with the fair sex'. Well, I don't care, and continue to send her my very best love, knowing full well though I do, what a peck of dry dust at seventy-seven she must think it (and quite rightly). What *would* life be without illusions?

24 *July 1960* *Bromsden Farm*

It is Sunday morning—grey and overcast—and I have more work to do before to-morrow than I can possibly accomplish, even without sleeping to-night. This is partly my fault for having spent most of Friday and Saturday on a jaunt to Stratford. I was driven down by

Diana Campbell-Gray (née Cavendish), a charming widow whom I have known for thirty years. We stayed with my ex-wife, Dame Peggy, in a very comfortable cottage in the country nearby and in the evening saw P. act in *The Taming of the Shrew*—a negligible play which in this production they have made enchanting. I last saw it in 1927, when it was the first play in which I appeared (playing a non-speaking servant) as a student at the Old Vic. This fact, combined with Peggy's astonishing youthfulness and beauty in the part, took me back forcefully, and with exquisite melancholy, to the time when we and the century were in our twenties. This in its turn made me long to write down some impression of those days. My love for Peggy, which will be with me always, was (I now see) chiefly an intellectual and spiritual passion, tied up with poetry and music, drama, youth and spring. Basically it wasn't a physical passion at all—which is why the marriage foundered—but all the rest is still there, although we seldom meet, and a brief visit like this can be an inspiration. Forgive me for pouring it all out to you: it is still very much in my mind, and you are my conscience.

You're quite right about Cuthbert's frailty: when I helped him up from the sofa before dinner it was like lifting a parcel of bones wrapped up in tweed.

T.S.E. wasn't well enough to preside at the Annual General Meeting of the London Library, so I had to ask Harold Nicolson, as Vice-President, to deputise. He agreed with his usual quick kindness, but made a fearful hash of the proceedings, getting things wrong and leaving out some of the agenda, which I managed to force in later. E.M. Forster turned up (as an ordinary member) and I particularly asked Harold to say something nice about him. But H. muttered that he (E.M.F.) was a grossly over-rated writer (which is to some extent true, I think) and scarcely mentioned him. I managed to remedy this, when it came to my turn to present the Report, by saying a few words about the sale, and pointing out that, except for the chap who gave us £10,000 anonymously some years ago, E.M.F. (by giving that manuscript which fetched £6500) was the greatest single benefactor in the Library's history. This got him a round of applause—which he certainly deserved—and made him beam with pleasure.

Next day I visited T.S.E. in the nursing home to report. He was in excellent spirits, but his breathing is very bad. He is hoping to go home to-morrow, and to his wife's family in Leeds on Thursday. Later they're going to Scarborough for a fortnight, but I fear they will have left before R. and I get to Kisdon, whence we could easily have driven over to see them.

As for Ezra Pound, he is (or rather was) one of those people whose *influence* is infinitely greater and more important than their writings. He undoubtedly had a great and beneficial influence on both Yeats and Eliot, and yet his own works seem to me largely wind and rubbish. T.E. Hulme wrote practically nothing, and I think you can safely pass him by.

Your description of Herodotus and your female examinees reminds me of the Warburg Institute, for they feel obliged to trace every irrelevance back to its origin, so that forward movement becomes almost impossible. I hope you will read Quennell: as a book it lacks shape and cohesion, but there are fine things in it, and it is beautifully written.

If you don't hear from me again you will know that I have been suffocated by the proofs of other people's books.

27 July 1960   *Grundisdurgh*

Plebeian paper I grant you, but I can no other. Next week I should have my head above water, and see about a visit to the Ipswich stationer. But even that is not certain, as in a rash moment I said I would look over and mark essays by juveniles at Oxford schools—the whole thing organised by the Oxford Preservation Trust. Well last year about seven schools sent altogether thirty–forty essays. This year one school kicks off by sending 101; their manuscripts are of all shapes and sizes, elaborately bound and illustrated by themselves— a really ghastly job, and I am plucking up courage to send them all back with a few well-chosen words of hatred and contempt. And I' rather think my eyes may be temporarily giving out. Little bouts of double vision—one eye at cross-purposes with the other. The doctor plays his comfortable trump card by saying it 'will probably pass off. It is not the thing to say then 'But supposing it doesn't'.

I love your 'pouring out' as you call it. What else are great friends there for? Your story is a wonderfully interesting one—and oddly enough has a strong resemblance to H.G. Wells's first marriage, which I was reading about yesterday.

They still refuse to cough up P. Quennell's book in the library, though I know it has been accepted. In *John o' London* last week there was an article about English words, and *inter alia* the wrongness of 'from whence'. I remember Cardus was on the mat for using it, and when he feebly said x. and y. well-known writers used it, the formidable C.P. Scott said: 'They wouldn't have in my paper'. C. ought to have taken leave of C.P.S. with the words 'Then I will lift up mine eyes unto the hills from whence cometh my help'. But I suppose he would have been instantly sacked.

Harold Nicolson ought to have remembered that, on an occasion like the L.L. general meeting, mentioning benefactors is in the same category as obituaries; 'In lapidary inscriptions a man is not upon oath.'[1] I rather agree with you both about E.M.F. It is odd that no one has ever set about debunking him—or have they? I was much bored not long ago by *The Longest Journey*, but then, as you know, I am poor at novels.

Shall we ever see T.S.E. at the Lit. Soc. again? He sounds in rather poor case, I fear. All the examinees in the G.C.E. (Alternative Ordinary) paper wrote of him with great respect—obviously dictated —though they based it on qualities which I rather doubt his claiming. What would he think of 'child-like', 'old-fashioned', 'bitter' and 'very reminiscent of Pope'? The cumulative effect of reading second-hand pretentious rubbish is in the end depressing. One lot of candidates referred with airy omniscience to Baudelaire, Dante, and Nietzsche; one young puppy was condescending about Nietzsche's 'phrose' (*sic*).

30 July 1960   *Bromsden Farm*

This last week has been a nightmare of proof-reading and index-making, from which I am still reeling. Oscar has now lain untouched for five weeks. Although there are two long manuscripts to be read

[1] Doctor Johnson.

and corrected, I brought down also the Oscar galleys, together with an armful of letters and notes which have collected, and this afternoon stole half an hour for the old labour. The delay doesn't matter much, except that for proper annotation and cross-reference one should have *everything* in one's head, and mine is now stuffed with irrelevant and boring details of the R.H-D. autumn publications.

Did you see that Duff got a second in Greats? I think it very creditable, since he was up for only three years (instead of the usual Greats four) and did a lot of other things as well. Now he is in search of a journalistic job, and the *Sunday Times* (Roy Thomson group) boys are proving most helpful.

I hate to hear of your eyes playing you tricks; couldn't you arrange to correct *fewer* rather than more exam-papers, which you seem to be doing just now?

I doubt whether we shall ever again see T.S.E. at the Lit. Soc. Apart from his physical weakness, he is so happy at home. They went off to Leeds last week to stay with her mother.

Comfort came up to London last week and went to a couple of theatres, which she enjoyed. She stayed at the flat, but I scarcely saw her, so engrossed was I in everybody's proofs. One night I dined with Veronica Wedgwood, where I met Sir Somebody Something, one of the joint heads of the Treasury, and so one of our chief rulers. He might have appeared, without make-up, as 'Self-Love' or 'Complacency' in a morality-play like *Everyman*, though his performance might have been thought a little exaggerated. As you will have gathered, I didn't take to him. When we left it was pouring with rain: he had a government car and chauffeur waiting but was too nervous to take us an inch out of his own way, so I and another chap were deposited in a streaming Oxford Street. God save us from such piddling bureaucrats!

Ruth is still overwhelmed by her grandchildren, but directly they all go back to Italy we shall hasten to our beloved Kisdon. About August 24 or so.

Have you got Lytton Strachey's *Portraits in Miniature*? I took it down this morning and read the little essay on Carlyle: some good things in it. Have a look.

Only eight grandchildren! I shall tell Ruth how lucky she is only having two. Please give my respectful greetings to the lovely Rose, and congratulate Bobby on winning the Cricket Cup after his Henley triumphs. Did I tell you that Adam *did* get his Middle Club in the end? So his scug-cap days are over. Mine never were.

3 *August 1960*   *Grundisburgh*

It really is heart-rending to hear that for five weeks you haven't been able to get at Oscar. You must be in a continuous state of irritation, and what is more wearing than that? Shall you get some chance at Kisdon? Winston or somebody defined the perfect holiday as 'a change of work', but there should be at least a period of *dolce far niente* at first.

I am delighted to hear of Duff's second in Greats. All the *best* men have got seconds from Newman downwards. Housman was ploughed, C.B. Fry got a fourth. People like Blue-tooth Baker[1] get firsts, do nothing very striking, and end up as Warden of Winchester. About the most brilliant scholar ever at Eton was Carr Bosanquet, of whom you have never heard—irretrievably lost as some kind of permanent official.[2] But one thing he did which should not be allowed to die. He described *The Yellow Book* as a book 'which binders would buy to bind and bounders would be bound to buy'. Which I am sure you will agree is pretty good. You have a good brainy pair of sons—but I am sorry to see Adam did not figure in the schools' chess championship. I expect he is more pleased with his cricket colours. Why *shouldn't* he get his XI next year?

My 'diplopia'[3] is nothing to do with excessive reading of exam-papers, and indeed is really very unimportant. Some years ago an oculist said I had 'splendid eyes'. As I have worn specs since 1900 I demurred, to which he said 'Oh yes, the focusing needs adjusting, but I was speaking of their sound lasting prospects; they will easily last your time'. And it is true they have never ached or given me the smallest trouble.

[1] Harold Trevor ('Bluey') Baker, Liberal politician (1877–1960).
[2] Robert Carr Bosanquet (1871–1935), archaeologist. Director of the British School of Archaeology in Athens 1900–1906.
[3] Double vision.

Quennell is still on his way, and I am first on the list. I shan't be disappointed. The *shape* of a book never enters my consciousness, but the *writing* does. Ivor gave me a month ago his *Dark Ladies* (i.e. Helen, Sappho, Cleopatra, and *the* Dark Lady) which I enjoyed, but entirely understood why, as he told me, it had no sale. There is too much historical information, and there isn't now the interest in (or knowledge of the background of) those old myth-histories that there used to be. It astonishes me all the more that Druon's book should be so popular (though delighted for the publisher's sake). I frankly found it rather hard going—so many bloodthirsty battles and necessarily all the same, and I couldn't somehow get very much interested in Alexander himself. But I *am* enjoying the Andrew Young poems[1]—so lovely and *short*, and every one with its flavour, and very soon shall be enjoying the Stanley book.[2] *Thank* you, as always. Stanley once came and lectured to the prep-school where I was. I can't imagine how they got him, as I suppose he was then (1893) at the top of his fame. For a long time he was looked on as a pushing little bounder, but I suspect he was a pretty good man, and that public opinion, led by the papers, was just as untrustworthy in the Nineties as in the subsequent Sixties.

Sir Somebody Something! Yes, you make me shudder. Those stuffed shirts are—what is the word? Shall I venture on 'rebarbative'? Rather a good mouthful, but I am not absolutely sure what it means. Couldn't you somehow have managed to hit him in the wind or even tread on his toe? Jacks-in-office are the devil.

I thought I had *Portraits in Miniature*, but it seems to have vanished. I seem to remember old Carlyle being described as 'that dry, neglected crater', as of an extinct volcano, which I suppose he is. So few appear to be conscious of (a) his enormous power of pen and (b) his glorious humour. But you and I know all right.

Next week I go to Cambridge for a week for tedious (but not badly paid) work on the G.C.E. borderline cases, and rectifying the blunders of examiners. I shall be here to get your letter, and shall answer it from the University Arms Hotel, which will be full of Yanks, affable but strident. Humphrey and family will be here just when I am not.

[1] His *Collected Poems* (1960).
[2] *Stanley's Way* by Thomas Sterling (1960).

Did you see about his loss of his trumpet and its return? It was actually in the 9 o'clock news, being apparently of equal importance with Lumumba and Castro and Cousins etc. No doubt some genial gossip-writer will hint that he had it stolen on purpose—like a film-star's jewels. I once asked who William Hickey was, and got the caustic answer that he was several people. 'No one man, or even woman, could be such a cad as W.H.'—a nice wide-flung denigration.

Luncheon is imminent and I must stop. It will be a good noisy meal, though luckily not all at one table. The children are in the kitchen, the grown-ups in the staff-hall next door. Two of my grand-sons are born teddy-boys, their motto being that anything like a book, hat, tool, or utensil of any kind is merely there to be destroyed, damaged or thrown away *quam celerrime*. One of the most boring traits in *all* the young is the irresistible urge to take away my stick. But there is a Mede and Persian law on *your* stick, which so far holds good. I shall bring it to the October Lit. Soc.; but am pleased to tell you that *at least* four people have already said it is the best they ever saw. But perhaps it will bore you stiff. You must pretend it doesn't. Apropos of boring I picked up the Shaw-Mrs Patrick Campbell correspondence after many years and found it *quite intolerable*. His voluble amorousness in letter after letter very quickly turned my stomach. What do *you* think? Give my love to Ruth. The idea of her as a grandmother is wholly incongruous. But then Nature *is* incon-gruous. My aunt Georgina married Lord Leicester and found *two* step-daughters several years older than herself.

6 *August 1960*   *Bromsden Farm*

This heavy sunless weather induces, I find, an immense lassitude, not to say sleepiness, which goes ill with work of any kind. Today I drove over to Wiltshire to lunch with the Devlins, and it was all I could do to keep awake, even on the way *there*!

On Monday Comfort and Adam are journeying to Scotland, to spend a fortnight with my sister, so write to Soho Square this week. On Friday Ruth and I are nipping over to Dieppe for the week-end. We plan to bathe and eat and laze, and visit Oscar's post-prison retreats. We both need freshening up—the grandchildren are over-powering Ruth—and we can't get away to Kisdon till the 24th. I shall try and scribble you a line from a café-table.

Duff looks like starting his journalistic career on the *Western Mail* at Cardiff in a week or two. Meanwhile he is toiling nobly in the garden.

Carr Bosanquet's quip about *The Yellow Book* is brilliantly good. I warned you (or meant to warn you) that *Alexander the God* wasn't up to Druon's usual standard. I knew you'd like Andrew Young, and you'll certainly enjoy the Stanley book. Incidentally, after I had passed Diana Cooper's proofs for press, what should I find but the hideous LYTTLETON (referring to Oliver)! An S.O.S. to the printer just caught it. Phew! What would you have said to me?

I'm much looking forward to meeting my stick in October: I daresay it will be a case of love at first sight.

To-day, when I might at last be spending an hour with Oscar, I am (for love of Max) correcting the proofs of Sam Behrman's forthcoming book on him (not published by me).[1] In it he records Max as saying that he was so disgusted by the Shaw-Campbell letters that he couldn't finish the book: so you are in good company. Now I am going to bed: more in the morning.

Sunday morning

After nine hours' sleep I feel a little brisker, and it's as well, for there is plenty to be done. Yesterday when I reached the Devlins, I found the judge in a secluded corner of the garden on a *chaise-longue*, reading a book on birth-control. 'Too late to be any use', he said, ruefully indicating his delightful family of four sons and two daughters. I think he might be an excellent member of the Lit. Soc.

On Tuesday I am making a lightning dash to Edinburgh to see the Estate Duty people about Dorothy Walpole's estate. Admirable though my co-executor is (he's a Writer to the Signet) his knowledge of copyright and publishing procedure is minimal. I am travelling each way by day—first class at the Estate's expense, 4 p.m.–10.40 p.m. This will give me more than twelve hours in which to read and correct a typescript about the Marconi Scandal. I am to spend the intervening

[1] *Conversation with Max* by S.N. Behrman (1960).

night with Robin Walpole, the surviving brother. I feel sure those two days will be the hottest and sunniest of the summer.

Adam is now learning to drive—on our car—and I tremble for the clutch and brakes. No news of his A levels yet: I think the end of August is the time. I shall think of you in Cambridge, discussing pass-marks with your fellow-examiners and going to strip-tease movies in the evenings.

10 August 1960   *Grundisburgh*

I have greatly enjoyed the Stanley book, and am glad to be corro-borated in my belief that, for all his bounding and pomposity, he was a fine and immensely tough chap. How he survived really passes one's comprehension. And I rejoice to have my opinion of Shaw's letters corroborated by M.B. What other support on a question of literary taste is needed?

I say, Rupert, your autumn list! If I wasn't quite sure I had quoted Mr Squeers before I would now. Druon back again on his own ground, Peter Fleming, and old Shaw on music—about which he is always first-rate reading. Also his dramatic criticism. I was delighted to find Max, when I met him at Butterwick's, put it at the top of his writings. Why does one never hear of Janet Achurch except from him? And he put her right among the Terrys and Bernhardts. *Trumpets from the Steep* is a fine challenging title[1]—if one precisely knew its relevance. I am taking Middleton Murry and Ivor's *Shakespeare in his Time* to Cam-bridge—and a new Carter Dickson for bedtime. Mind you tell me if and when you ever come across a first-rate detective story. The last Allingham I read was very poor.

I have got used to Lyttleton (though always annoyed by it). Half the pedagogues who send me exam-papers get it wrong. I feel inclined to fire Housman at them: 'Accuracy is not a virtue; it is a duty'. Yet another book about the chippy old Cassandra by a Yank lady called Hawkins. She claims to have talked repeatedly with Gow—who denies ever having heard of her. She says *inter alia* that the Oxford exam called 'Moderates' (*sic*) has as its Cambridge equivalent the 'Littlego',

[1] Of the third volume of Diana Cooper's autobiography.

in which Housman examined. It surely is not easy to be much wronger than that.

Odd that you should mention Behrman, because I have just returned to Wilfrid Blunt a lot of stuff by him on Max B. Talks, not yet gathered into a book—which surely must be the one you are proof-reading? Is M.B.'s remark about the Shaw letters in it? Because I didn't notice it. Anyway my memory nowadays is hopeless.

Why not Mr Justice Devlin in the Lit. Soc.? Judges are almost always the ripest company (I was omitting the 'almost' when I suddenly remembered old Avory, whose talk I believe was as dry as his skin, and one can't say more than that).

That was a sour leader in *The Times* about the Oxford by-pass. They *must*, as David Cecil says, take it at *any* cost well clear of Oxford. (But they won't.) We are all engaged in plans and policies which were profoundly stigmatised by Juvenal, *'propter vitam vivendi perdere causas'*,[1] or in our own less dignified idiom 'not putting first things first'. Did you see that remark by a woman in a traffic-block in Oxford 'They never ought to have put a university here'.

Love to Ruth. Why has the poor dear to take her grandchildren so seriously? Probably because she is a much more conscientious grandmother than I am a grandfather.

P.S. I have just discovered that there was a saint Bugga (*D.N.B.*). It almost reconciles me to the approaching collapse of civilisation.

P.S. *In Quest of a Mermaid*[2] is *good* reading. What a real fairy godmother you are!

13 August 1960   *Bromsden Farm*

As you see, I am not in a waterside café in Dieppe, awash with brandy and local wine, but at my old post in my library, with the rain falling steadily outside. We had to cancel our trip because Ruth felt she couldn't leave all her family, and maybe it was just as well, for the seamen's strike seems to have disorganised all yesterday's Channel services.

[1] 'For the sake of life to lose life's aim.' (Juvenal, *Satires* 8, 83).
[2] By J.H. ('Elephant Bill') Williams (1960).

Duff and I are here alone, but tomorrow if it's fine enough, Ruth is going to bring down a carful of her family for a picnic lunch.

Duff is expecting a call to begin his life's work at Cardiff, and meanwhile he is feverishly repainting the kitchen as a surprise birthday-present for Comfort. This evening he went to a cocktail-party nearby and on the way home shot three rabbits from the car with a .22 rifle. Nothing like being an all-rounder!

How are the giddy examiners at Cambridge? Plenty of night-life for them I hope. Tell them to read the strip-tease article in this week's *Spectator*, and they'll surely arrange the next examiners' meeting in Soho.

My trip to Edinburgh went according to plan. Very comfortable all-Pullman first-class carriage, in which, each way, I consumed a whacking tea and an immense dinner. The tea was especially good, and since it is a meal I usually miss, I particularly enjoyed it. I stayed comfortably with Hugh Walpole's brother, and woke on Wednesday morning to hot sunshine and a sky of unclouded blue. Edinburgh was looking its loveliest, and I rejoiced to see so many of its noble squares and crescents unharmed. The Estate Duty people proved very amenable, and the interview was over so quickly that I managed to fit in three-quarters of an hour in the best of secondhand bookshops. Altogether a most agreeable interlude. I have always liked Edinburgh, though I daresay one would tire of it eventually. Only ten days now— and then Kisdon, *laus Deo*!

Sunday morning

The sun is shining, but Ruth has just telephoned to say they can't come after all, as her daughter isn't well. So Duff will carry on with his painting, and I, inspired by his example, shall do some needed tidying and gardening. Peter and all his family are shooting grouse in Scotland. Oscar is with me, but untouched: at Kisdon I simply must read him straight through, but I should like to get rid of all the attendant letters and notes (a thick pile) before we leave.

Last Thursday I went to Sotheby's (now closed for the recess, after doing a year's business of almost *seven million pounds*) to see about the approaching sale of Max's books etc from Rapallo—a very touching but intensely amusing and interesting collection, for Max used to annotate and illustrate everything. Merton are to have enough to make a permanent exhibition in the Max Room, and the rest are to be sold. Mrs Reichmann, the owner, is threatening to give me one of the most valuable books, but I don't think she should be so generous. Across the room (at Sotheby's) was the splendid library of C.H. Wilkinson of Worcester College, waiting to be catalogued. It isn't so much the worms who get everything in the end, as the auctioneers. Except for insurance, auctioneering is surely the safest racket imaginable—no risk, a sure percentage, and endless material (including often the same objects sold again and again). And they're all immensely pleased with themselves, as though they were creating the masterpieces they sell. But I suppose an annual turnover of £7,000,000 is enough to turn the solidest head.

Now I must stop chattering to you and do some useful work. The trouble is I much prefer the chattering. How many million words have we by now exchanged? Enough anyhow till next Saturday. Write *here* this week.

18 August 1960   *Cambridge*

This will be rather a scrappy affair, I fear, as we are a good deal behindhand—owing to a posse of imbecile examiners who give three for a set of answers that deserve thirteen and vice versa, and then write reports which we spend half a day re-writing in English. Well you see what we are up against. Two of our examiners, moreover, have almost totally illegible hands, and one has the impudence to pick holes in the scripts of the candidates. There have been one or two good things, e.g. in the essay on 'Jazz' in which several candidates mention Humphrey and one writes 'Humphrey Littleton (always so spelt) is the leading English trumpeter, and—like many others—plays best when he is drunk'. What can one do about that? We have been once or twice to the pictures—nothing much until last night when we saw Edith Evans in *The Importance of Being Earnest*. Excellent fun, though some of the wisecracks date very emphatically. I was interested to see Dorothy Tutin, who is whole-heartedly adored, believe it or not, by Granny Gow. I don't blame him. Her Cicely was entirely charming. 1 haven't read the play for years, and please tell me if: Lady

B. 'My nephew tell lies?? Impossible! He was at Oxford' is a gag or not. I have a strong suspicion that it is—but it got the loudest laugh of the evening.[1] Margaret Rutherford was somehow wrongly cast for Miss Prism—too bulky and amiable, but the rest were all right. What a magnificent absurdity it is—and how O.W. must have enjoyed writing it.

You must tell me all about the sale of M.B.'s books—and of *course* you must keep whatever is given you. Sotheby's *would* make £7m p.a. now that Cyril Butterwick is one of them. He always falls on his feet and must put by a tidy annual packet. Whenever he bought a share it at once rocketed—and fell like a stone the day after he sold it. Mine always do the opposite.

I am reading Middleton Murry in bed. A good critic surely, but I find it very easy to get out of my depth with his aesthetics. I am delighted to see that *Lady Chatterley* is again postponed. One of my colleagues says that, unexpurgated, it is D.H.L.'s best novel. He is a northern professor of philosophy and ought to know better. But the inner circle of D.H.L. fans are deranged in their wits. Leavis is only about 450 yards away from this hotel. I shall not call upon him.

Apologies for this vapid (and rapid) scrap, but you won't mind with Kisdon so near. Keep Ruth's family away with broom and bayonet—and give her my love.

20 August 1960   *Bromsden Farm*

The blessed day approaches. If you should suffer from insomnia on Tuesday night, think of us at 4 a.m. on Wednesday, when we shall set out from Soho Square in Ruth's tiny car, lights on, streets empty. Out through St Albans and Dunstable to Northampton. At 6 a.m. we stop by the roadside for coffee (from a thermos) and biscuits. Mounting excitement as the morning lightens. On through Market Harborough and Leicester to a road which bypasses everything till at 8 a.m. we reach Bawtry, just south of Doncaster and *inside Yorkshire*. There we breakfast at the Crown Hotel. Sundry shopping at Bedale,

[1] 'Untruthful! My nephew Algernon? Impossible! He is an Oxonian'! (*The Importance of Being Earnest*, act iii).

123

Leyburn and Hawes; a picnic luncheon high on the pass between Wensleydale and Swaledale—first taste of that incomparable air and silence—then drop down into Swaledale and report at 2 p.m. to our farmer, who will be ready to drive us up Kisdon in his tractor, with all our luggage, books and provisions. Thereafter perfection.

Meanwhile the best news is that Adam has been awarded a State Scholarship, which seems to me excellent at seventeen. So far as I can gather from the mass of bumf they've sent, you get £50 a year even if you're a millionaire, and the rest (if any) depends on your income. He and Comfort come back from Scotland on Monday night, and I shall give them breakfast in London on Tuesday.

Duff starts his reporting at Cardiff on Monday. He has blued his savings (£200) on a 1955 Ford Popular, which looks sensible and roadworthy.

I am desperately trying to tidy everything up before Wednesday, so as to keep Kisdon for Oscar and idleness, but no sooner have I cleared everything off than some other horror crops up.

Your Cambridge outing didn't sound very gay. I certainly don't remember that line in *The Importance*, but will look it up. Fancy Granny Gow falling for Dorothy Tutin: he should journey to Stratford to see her Cressida, which is said to be excellent.

The question of my present from Max's sister-in-law is now happily resolved. She wanted to give me the plum of the whole collection (a biography of Bernard Shaw heavily annotated and extra-illustrated by Max), which Sotheby's have valued at £500+. I managed to persuade her to give me instead (1) a first edition of Oscar's *An Ideal Husband*, with a caricature of Oscar by Max on the flyleaf; (2) Max's copy of the first edition of *The Importance*, inscribed to him by Oscar, and with four most interesting notes by Max. These Sotheby's had valued at £150 and £200, so I have done pretty well, and am quite delighted. Both books have suffered forty years of Rapallo sun, but inside they're fine.

I have been asked if I am willing to be called as a witness for the defence of *Lady Chatterley*, and shall reluctantly agree. I'm all against the prosecution, though in fact I think it a sentimental, contrived and occasionally ridiculous work. Anyhow they must surely have plenty of more important witnesses.

Some of Ruth's family have gone back to Italy, but she won't escape from the others till we drive north. She is exhausted, poor lamb, and I daresay we shall break even our own high record for hours of sleep. We usually have a coal fire in the bedroom, and dropping off to sleep there in the flickering light, in the certain knowledge that one won't wake for ten hours, is so unspeakably agreeable that I sometimes try to keep awake a little longer to prolong the enjoyment. Very different from the incessant car-park noises in Soho. As you can see, my thoughts are there already, and I have to keep pulling myself back to the proofs and manuscripts which must be coped with before I leave.

I had a most touching letter from Geoffrey Faber, resigning from the Lit. Soc. because he now realises he will probably never see London again. This makes a vacancy, and the whole cumbersome business of an election (which I was hoping to avoid this year) will begin again in November.

Next week's letter will be pastoral-rhapsodical, and I may call in Ruth as collaborator.

24 August 1960   *Grundisburgh*

I get a vicarious glow from all you say about Kisdon—before, during, and after. My mind's eye reproduces it very convincingly as resembling that enchanting country along the Roman wall, or that surrounding the hamlet—it may be no more than a farm—which has the appealing name of Pity Me, which is somewhere up in the Walter Scott country, or at any rate Melrose. As to the mind's ear, I conceive the cough of a sheep or an occasional curlew as pretty well all you hear when the wind is low. What of the mind's *nose*? The sense of smell is the most vivid remembrancer of all five. Now and then I am recalled instantaneously to the prep-school I went to in 1892. What are the 'murmurs and scents of the infinite'—'weald' shall we say instead of 'sea'[1] or is it a little too literary and garden-of-Englandy? Four a.m. is a noble hour to start at. Please tell me exactly what you have for breakfast at Bawtry. It should surely be one of those great breakfasts

[1] Matthew Arnold, 'The Future'.

125

of fifty years ago. The North used to be good at them. I still remember the one I had at Scotch Corner thirty years ago. Wensleydale and Swaledale!—you must by then be feeling as full of music as Milton was when he wrote of 'Horonaim, Seon's realm, beyond The flowry dale of Sibma, clad with vines'.[1] Let me share your happiness in that lovely land you will reach at the otherwise prosaic hour of 2 p.m. Every and any daily detail will be a delight.

What a very distinguished pair of sons you have. That State Scholarship is a fine achievement. Will Adam go for a scholarship at Oxford in December? He sounds of the right calibre, and Etonians nowadays do sometimes get science scholarships, which they never did in my day, though one or two, like Alfred Egerton,[2] went to the top eventually, plus an ornithologist or two. Does Duff start by sending 'stories' about a man found dead at Bognor, which are ignored or cut down to four lines? Don't even the Montagues and Nevinsons start like that?[3]

Cambridge *wasn't* very gay—the whole day practically taken up with reading the work of the victims of very inept teaching. A name here and there pleased me. Among Browns and Joneses of some very English school there suddenly appeared *Parapolidikok* which I assure you is real, though it oughtn't to be. One good story I heard, which I hope you haven't. Old Maugham, talking to a girls' school about the art of writing short stories, told them that the essential ingredients were religion, sex, mystery, high rank, non-literary language and brevity. The schoolmistress next day told her young charges to try their hand at writing one according to this recipe. After a minute one raised her hand and said she had finished. The incredulous mistress told her to read it out, and she did: 'My God!', said the duchess, 'I'm pregnant. I wonder who done it'. That girl should surely go far.

Lady Chatterley. It is absolutely essential that you should not for a moment think that I am in *full* disagreement with you. I wholly agree that this police-court attempt at censorship is ridiculous. The fatuity

---

[1] *Paradise Lost*, book I.

[2] Alfred Egerton (1886–1959), Professor of Chemical Technology in the University of London. Knighted 1943.

[3] C.E. Montague (1867–1928) and H.W. Nevinson (1856–1941), leading journalists.

of a lot of men in the jurybox, every one of them straight out of a drawing by the late George Morrow[1], listening to E.M. Forster testifying to the deathless beauty of *Lady C.* cannot be described in words. But what nauseates me is the flood of *cant* which so very many of those who support the publication pour out. I read that there are 250,000 copies ready, and what the defenders say (or imply) is that this mass of readers wants to read it because it is a (or *the*) masterpiece of the great genius D.H.L. And everybody knows that the great sale will be to all the adolescents in the country who, like George Forsyte, have a liking for the 'nubbly bits'. I have actually heard a man maintain that the book, expurgated, may be dreary, but the addition of D.H.L.'s fourth-form physiological crudities makes it a work of genius. If my view is Victorian, well I can't help it—but I would maintain that the inhibitions, the dislike of seeing all these crude words for the sexual functions flung onto the page, are every bit as 'natural' as the impulse to fling them. It was wrong to write the book, and it is wrong to print it. Them's my views. 1883 was a great year for 'squares'.

Comic, your saying Gow should go to see D. Tutin at Stratford. He has already been, I think twice! He has seen every part she has played in, and is just as critical over the way she plays as over a colleger's elegiacs. What pleases him is her acceptance of and agreement with his strictures. Old Edith Evans, of course, was splendid as Lady Bracknell, but I was rather horrified by her striking ugliness. She is plainer now than Dame Edith Sitwell, and one can't say more than that. Have you heard any of these poetry recitals by the authors? Someone told me that the records of Dylan Thomas reading are magnificent. I remember thinking him the only one worth listening to when he was alive. The Dame, I gather, is inaudible.

Best love to Ruth. Don't go and say that I have sent *'regards'*. I like to think of her enjoying peace perfect peace, with loved ones far away. Mind you both come back completely rested, ready to face even the world of 1960 with equanimity.

[1] *Punch* artist (1870–1955).

I went outside just now to write to you, but the fickle sun withdrew, so I am back in our sitting-room at the big table. On the other side of it Ruth is working away at Oscar, checking the formidable lists of recipients and manuscript-locations. This letter won't go down the hill until our farmer comes up to milk in the late evening, so won't be collected till to-morrow, and should with luck reach you on Wednesday. Your letter was faithfully brought up by the farmer on Thursday. Our drive north went according to plan, except that it rained the whole way, and three different minor things went wrong with the car, so that we reached Bawtry three quarters of an hour late. We did indeed have a fine breakfast there—porridge and what they call 'a full house', i.e. egg, bacon, sausage and tomato, with masses of toast, butter, marmalade and tea. Since we got here we haven't left our hill-top except for a brief shopping expedition to Hawes on Saturday. Yesterday was my fifty-third birthday, and we celebrated it cosily in blissful isolation. Apart from its magical view, the first thing that strikes one with wonder here is the complete *silence*—a blessing almost unknown in most places today. At this moment for instance, with the door open, I can hear *nothing* except the tick of the grandfather clock and the faint bubbling of a milk pudding which R. is cooking on the range. The mildest cheep of a bird, let alone the mournful cry of the curlew, is a noticeable event, and when there is no wind (as now) we can occasionally hear the distant barking of a dog far down the valley. The weather has been mixed, with rain most days and intermittent sun, but we are equally contented indoors and out. We have never been to the Roman Wall, but I feel sure your comparison is pretty exact. We have often planned that and other such expeditions, but once we get here we never want to move, and our days seem so few and so fleeting. One day perhaps we shall have world enough and time. You ask about smells, and I don't quite know how to answer, for one's first impression is of the astonishing *absence* of smells, and of the purity and freshness of the moorland air. Just now, when the sun shines there is also the lovely smell of cut grass, for the wretched hill-farmers, who began their haymaking in June, are still not through with it. The field in front of us is cut but not gathered, and field behind not even cut. Three fine sunny days and we shall be helping with large wooden rakes, as we did last year.

So far we have slept ten or eleven hours each night, with an occasional after-lunch nap as well. Our promised tap and pipe are not yet fixed, so we still climb a stone wall each morning and fetch six gallons of lovely spring-water from the next field. Our two Aladdin lamps still warm our evenings, and for my birthday Ruth gave me a little lamp for my side of the bed: she already has one on hers. (Suddenly I hear the bleating of sheep far away: probably being driven somewhere by dogs.)

Adam's A-Level results read:

CHEMISTRY:	DISTINCTION
PHYSICS:	DISTINCTION
MATHS:	DISTINCTION
GENERAL PAPER:	PASS

which shows how good he must be at his own subjects, and also the dangers of starting to specialise at fifteen. We are thinking of putting him in for an Oxford scholarship in December, with a preference for Merton, where there is a closed science scholarship for Etonians as well as open ones. If he got one he could then spend nine months doing some non-scientific subject (probably languages) before going up. He should be in Sixth Form his last two halves.

We have just been out to look at the flock of sheep which are being driven up on to the fell on the other side of the valley. I've had one cheerful letter from Duff, saying that accommodation in Cardiff seems to be plentiful and cheap (he has already been offered a double bed-sitter for 30/- a week) but not describing his work, which I have now asked him to do.

Most poets are shocking readers: Dame Edith is indeed largely inaudible, but Yeats was grand and Dylan Thomas superb. Cecil Day Lewis is also very good, but most of the rest are agony to hear.

How Green gets more and more reproachful on the shelf. Since we got here I have read a new Simenon, John Fothergill's *Innkeeper's Diary* (I find J.F. was a friend of Oscar's and so worth searching) and part of the proofs of an immense (and immensely too long) biography of the Nineties poet Richard Le Gallienne (another friend of O's), kindly lent me by Martin Secker. I am also studying (with the aid of a tiny dictionary) the egregiously full notes to a German edition of *De Profundis*: '*Clapham Junction ist eine der belebtesten Londoner Vorortstationen*' and things like that. If I don't break the back of the Oscar work here, I simply don't know how or when it will be done: here only is peace. Ruth sends much love and says she is already looking forward to seeing you in October.

30 and 31 August 1960   *Grundisburgh*

A blank Tuesday morning post—as of course is apt to happen when you are at Kisdon, so I am writing this at the club in Ipswich where I have finished the papers and am storm-bound by the punctual daily downpour. I do hope you are not getting all this monstrous hysterics of Nature, though it might be all to the benefit of Oscar. I still await some 300 papers from British Guiana, and have a faint hope that they may have been sunk on the journey. *Wednesday.* Still no letter. You are probably cut off from any postal facilities. I shall post this after the second delivery today. The possibility must always be considered that one of the chores which you are delighted to get away from is your weekly letter to G.W.L.

Well now, what is there from Suffolk? Little of interest I fear—and it becomes daily clearer that quite soon there will be as big a gulf between me and what is going on as there was between Abraham and Dives. My attitude to the daily paper is almost Balfourian. It is no good reading about Cuba, the Congo, Ceylon, Algeria etc unless one has followed all the news from the start—and even then! I am *not* excited by a young English girl getting a bronze medal for swimming. And, apropos of the Games, will you kindly tell me what *repêchage* means? French presumably, but it rings no bell, though it is now compulsory in any article about the games. Yesterday I browsed for an hour in the library on *Shakespeare and Company* by Sylvia Beach. Is it very fine? I was handicapped by ignorance of most of her dramatis personae; but to you I suppose Bryher, Djuna Barnes, Adrienne Monnier, Harriet Weaver, Eugene Jolas, George Antheil, Robert

McAlmon, Archibald McLeish, Valery Larbaud and Stuart Gilbert are household names? I have never heard of a single one, and so the lavish praise each gets from Miss Beach leaves me rather cold. There is a tremendously grim and formidable photograph of T.S.E. Am I right in surmising that it was taken just after he read or had been asked his opinion of *Ulysses?* The meeting between Joyce and C.K. Ogden must have been interesting—one wanting enormously to develop and enlarge English vocabulary, the other to reduce it to 500 words. I haven't the smallest interest in either, so write me down an ass and a philistine.

I say, the *Lit. Sup.*!! The two main articles last week were on the Soviet Cinema and the poet John Oldham. Is this remotely sane? It looks as if Pryce-Jones's feelings as he contemplates his successor may be much the same as those of Sin when she first saw her offspring Death.

I was a good deal bored by Swinburne's letters—all that interminable stuff about Hotten and Chatto should surely have been cut down. And I found the informative notes on the origin of such expressions as 'tender mercies' and 'apple of his eye' very irritating. I suppose Yankee editors are like that. S's deep interest in flagellation is very odd to my Victorian mind, and his eulogies of Count de Sade, but I know little about such anfractuosities of the human mind. What I *should* like to know about is his friendship with Jowett, who cannot really have had much in common with de Sade. Where does the story come from of S., staying with J., sitting in a neighbouring room to one where J. was taking a tutorial, and from time to time a high triumphant screech from S. (who was reading some classical researches of J's) 'Another howler, Master, another howler!' and a demure 'Thank you, Algernon' from next door? It is an engaging tale—not, I think, told in these letters.[1]

I like Andrew Young very much, though I don't always follow him. But the proof of how little I know about modern poetry is that the comments and dicta of modern critics on these poems are *completely* mystifying.

[1] But in *The Life of Algernon Charles Swinburne* by Edmund Gosse (1917), p. 213.

Wednesday, second post.

All well; letter on hall-table. Thank you for breakfast menu at Bawtry. I was with you in spirit. Smells. Yes, cut grass is among the best. Almost my favourite is sacks in a coal-cart, especially after rain. Surely with the sheep in the offing you can't be smell-less? Hay-smell of course is superb. My old and very great friend C.D. Fisher (killed in the *Invincible* at Jutland. His brother the Admiral in the *St Vincent* swept into the battle past the wreck) maintained that his favourite smell was the top of a very small baby's head. And—*verb. sap.*—he wasn't far wrong. Gosh how you would have liked C.D.F.

You should surely send Adam in for a scholarship. His father will see to it that he doesn't develop into a Lancelot Hogben.

I have given up all hope about *How Green*. Couldn't you get Ruth to read it while you are at some special proof-reading? Only a few pages are necessary; I would rely on her judgment with entire confidence—so would you. It really is a shame not to read it at Kisdon. It cries to Heaven, as the butler said about what was in Dr Jekyll's room. But I suppose, in fact I am sure, that being a publisher, you are very stubborn.

P.S. No, T.S.E. was sickened not by *Ulysses* but by *Leaves of Grass*.

5 *September 1960*   *Kisdon Lodge*

I was both touched and conscience-stricken to read of your so eagerly awaiting my dull letter and being so often disappointed. I only hope that this week you will have learnt to expect nothing from Kisdon until (with luck) the second post on Wednesday. Your letter flew back and was in my hands by Thursday evening. Why have I not answered before? Because, as I've always found, the less one *has* to do, the less one *does* do, and how enjoyable that is! It has rained every single day since I last wrote, but so far not to-day, and this morning we helped the farmer, his son and daughter-in-law to turn their sodden hay in the field up here, which has lain cut and awash for sixteen days. Saturday too was fine till the evening, and we descended the hill after a solid week up here (our longest unbroken sojourn so far) and drove to a sale in a little village near Thirsk. It proved a total washout—nothing one would have gladly taken as a gift—so we ate our picnic and drove home, doing various shopping at Hawes, Bedale, Thirsk and Ripon—all of which we like.

Oscar is limping on: another three weeks up here and the job would be almost done: as it is, with the piles of proofs, manuscripts and letters which will certainly be waiting, I simply don't know how or when I shall be able to finish. Incidentally I have recently, and quite by chance, acquired a new helper—an O.E. called Henry Maas (aged thirty-one) now schoolmastering in Surrey. His fresh, and extremely perceptive, mind is pointing out many errors and anomalies, asking pertinent questions, and generally improving the book. But it all means more work. Have the British Guiana contingent rolled up yet?

I once had Einstein's theory of Relativity explained to me so lucidly that for an hour or so I completely understood it: now nothing remains. In the same way have I several times been instructed in the meaning—and indeed the *working*—of *repêchage*, but alas! The French word must mean 'fishing up again', and I *think* here refers to some kind of proportional representation in timings—but who cares?

I've no doubt you're right about Sylvia Beach's book, though I must confess that all those names you list are comparatively well known to me—but then I am a literary bloke, immersed in all such nonsense, so take heart. When Richard Le Gallienne, the long-haired poetaster of the Nineties, published a book called *If I were God by Richard Le Gallienne*, some wag commented: 'If I were Richard Le Gallienne by God I'd get my hair cut'.

What you say (rightly) about the note-excesses of Swinburne's American editor makes me ever so slightly shiver in my shoes, for it's much harder than perhaps you think to decide where to draw the line. Young people today seem to know almost nothing. When Oscar wrote to Reggie Turner in 1899 'I hear you joined the Fleet Street Kopje at the Cecil', I feel obliged to explain Kopje *and* Cecil, both of which would be obvious to you.

You have twice referred to Andrew Young as 'modern poetry', but Andrew is 75, and surely his verse is timeless. Or do you see modernity lurking in his landscapes? Ruth is revelling in *Middlemarch* and wants to know whether you have read it lately, so that she can talk to you about it in October.

Duff writes very happily from Cardiff, where he has taken the 30/-

a week bed-sitter and finds the work most congenial. I am going to send him a thriller I've just read called *The Progress of a Crime* by Julian Symons, which is all about a young provincial reporter. I think you might find it enjoyable—or at any rate readable.

We are, alas, driving south on Thursday (leave here 11, picnics on the way, reach Soho 9 p.m.) so write to Bromsden, which I shall reach on Friday evening. The perfect relaxation, deep peace and easy slow rhythm of our life up here make the immediately subsequent days and weeks almost intolerable, and next May or June (when we can hope to return) seems a long way off. *Perhaps* I shall then be able to come without any proofs, with plenty of time for *How Green*—but in fact I daresay poor old Oscar will still be on the stocks. The index alone will take months.

7 September 1960   *Grundisburgh*

Wednesday second post. I was prepared for it this week, and the starting tear called for no drying. You were quite right not to attempt answering my letter before. An answer must be allowed to come to the boil, not forced with a blow-lamp. And how right you are about the ease of doing things when time is ample.

I must tell you that I feel sad this evening—not because of the weather, Lumumba, the end of 1960 cricket or growing consciousness of senility, but with a vicarious sadness about you two leaving Kisdon. Such is the happiness that breathes through your letters from there, and then the return to the great ant-heap. I know how I should loathe it. I was afraid you must be getting a lot of rain. This is a notoriously dry corner of England, but we have had enough to hold up the harvest most days, and—as to-day—though dry, the sky is all over the colour of the belly of a dead fish. No doubt it is no more than we deserve, as an evangelical aunt of mine used to say—and how mealy-mouthed and soft was that generation which did *not* murder her. How right Thomas Hardy was in his remark 'It has been obvious for centuries that the Supreme Mover or Movers, the Prime Force or Forces, must be either limited in power, unknowing or cruel'. Can you see any way out of that?

Maas K.S. must have left about when I did, but I never came across him. I wasn't taking English Extra Studies at the end of my time. He sounds a competent chap.

You make me feel very ignorant, being totally unaware of all those authors mentioned by Miss Beach, whom you know all about. I shall throw up the sponge, and abandon the vain struggle to keep up. Next time we meet I shall babble of Besant and Rice, and Miss Braddon, and Mary Cholmondeley. But one thing makes me strike the stars with uplifted head, and that is that *Middlemarch* has always been my favourite novel. I read it first in 1904 and have read it at least three times since then. I am delighted to hear that Ruth likes it. It is simply crammed full of good stuff of all kinds. I often think of it when they babble (in speech or print) of the 'incomparable' Jane Austen, who just tinkles along in comparison. I could talk about it for hours, so dear Ruth had better look out. And if the British Guiana exam-papers still delay their coming, I may very well read it again. Didn't V. Woolf call it one of the very few really grown-up English novels? Even so one thing is missing, *viz* Dorothea's physical reactions towards her dreadful old husband. I don't want any *Room at the Top* stuff, still less the probing obsessions of Lawrence, but dash it all she must have had the matter much in her mind. I wonder why G.E. called him Casaubon. Could one bring a great sailor into one's novel and call him Nelson? Because the real Casaubon was actually a great scholar.

Richard Le Gallienne. Thank you. A lovely story. How immensely dead many of those chaps are—Stephen Phillips etc. And Vernon Lee —who the devil was she? I know absolutely nix about her.

You needn't surely be nervous about notes to Oscar; you never put a foot wrong with *Hugh Walpole*. But what a lot of incompetence there is about. *Old Mortality*, set for next year's G.C.E., is as you know full of full-blooded Scotticisms. Well, believe it or not, Everyman's edition has a glossary in which words like 'blithe', 'bracken', 'cannily', and 'feckless' are explained, but about 'grane', 'cess', 'tow', 'marts', and many others, no solitary word. I doubt if the Board, which chooses the books, are wise to choose Scott. He is so tremendously long-winded, and half the speeches of his ladies and gentlemen have the air of pieces set to be put into Ciceronian prose. And his young women!

Yes, the young are very ignorant (as I expect they always were) about the generation or two just before their own. Practically no undergraduates remember the declaration of war in 1939. An Oxford don told me recently that not one of the class to which he was lecturing had any idea what *Lebensraum* meant. A good many, of course, just don't read the papers. No one except me in the Ipswich Club ever reads the *Spectator* or *New Statesman*. I expect they regard them as just as devitalising as I find the *Express* and *Mail*. *Punch* seems to me positively abysmal nowadays, but my daughters tell me it is immensely funny, and they don't resent one or two of the pictures being (i) incomprehensible and (ii) not at all funny when explained. Well, Caran d'Ache[1] dispensed with captions or stories, but was surely very much funnier than our modern Johnnies (who, incidentally, don't draw a quarter as well).

I read *The Progress of a Crime* and greatly enjoyed it. Are his others good? Tell me. My bedside book is the new Ngaio Marsh. A prime theatre bitch has just passed out, and no doubt to-night Roderick Alleyn will blow in. She writes well. My nephew Charles says she is charming, and that counts quite a lot. Probably you have known her for years. The library is extraordinarily slow in producing P. Quennell's book, but I fancy nothing at all happens in August when all are on holiday. (Thursday) you are at this moment starting from K.—a horrible moment.

10 September 1960   *Bromsden Farm*

Your letter was waiting faithfully for me yesterday (Friday) evening when I arrived, heavily homesick for Kisdon, missing Ruth, loathing London and all its inhabitants, publishing and all its ways. The rain, which fell pitilessly through our blessed fortnight, cleared off only as we left the cottage, and we got more sun on the drive south than we had had during our whole stay. Yesterday the hot sunshine in London was almost unbearable, but to-day I have relaxed again in the garden here, reading first the weeklies since I left, and then a once-famous play called *Frou-Frou* by Meilhac and Halévy, which Oscar mentions and I couldn't annotate in ignorance. Now, on the same

[1] French caricaturist (1858–1909).

errand, I am reading Part III of Balzac's *Splendeurs et Misères des Courti-
sanes*—good full-blooded stuff.

I think it wonderful that, without having been there, you can so
truly sympathise with, and enter into, our passionate love of Kisdon,
our happiness there, and our ever-increasing sorrow at leaving. Everything you have ever written about it shows that you perfectly understand, whereas most people are perturbed by the thought of its
primitiveness and isolation.

On our last evening at dusk we watched *five* hawks hovering over
the hilltop. Suddenly a huge owl got up, was attacked by the hawks,
and gradually drove them away, one by one. We watched, spellbound,
in the fading light. Stopping the grandfather clock wrings our heart—
but I need say no more—you know it all. London yesterday was unspeakably awful—jostling crowds of hideous people everywhere, stink-
ing cars bumper to bumper, all my dear colleagues full of their own
problems, my office piled high with waiting paper (I counted forty-
two letters that need answering), and at mid-day my beloved friend
Leon Edel, American professor and expert on Henry James, arrived to
stay in the flat for a fortnight. Both Ruth and I love him dearly, but
yesterday it was all we could do to be decently hospitable. I managed
to arrange for him to spend the week-end with a friend in Sussex, thus
gaining a brief respite.

Ruth will be delighted to hear of your love of *Middlemarch*, which
she brought back with her to finish. Her daughter-in-law is now
pregnant, so she will soon have three grandchildren, though I doubt
if she will ever challenge your impressive brood.

I could write you pages about Vernon Lee, the great unread, if not
unreadable, but I will spare you. Stephen Phillips's story was tragic:
from incredible success ('the elder Dumas speaking with the voice of
Milton' was how one of his plays was described) he faded into total
failure, and so far as I know not one of his plays has ever been
revived.

The sort of thing that holds up Oscar interminably is this: a few
months ago I managed to get from Paris photostats of two letters from
Oscar to Mallarmé, the French poet. One is undated, the other clearly
postmarked February 1891. I put them both together, only to be reminded by one of my invaluable helpers that in the Stetson Sale

Catalogue (1920) there is a quotation from a Mallarmé letter to Oscar which is dated 10 Nov 91 and is clearly an answer to my undated letter. This entails moving my letter from February to November and shifting the main Mallarmé footnote to the other letter, which is now the first to him. Multiply this by several hundred and you will see the problem. Many things which I have laboriously read during the last five years (including this catalogue) couldn't then disgorge their full relevance, and there's a limit to what one can keep ready in one's head. I enjoyed the new Ngaio Marsh, and all Julian Symons's thrillers are good or goodish.

Duff writes enthusiastically of Cardiff, and his life and work there. I find I did Adam an injustice, since the only results in the General Paper are Pass or Fail, so in fact he couldn't have done better. At present he is pining for love of the fifteen-year-old daughter of a neighbour, who isn't very nice to him. His appetite, usually immense, has quite disappeared.

Peter can't find a subject for his next book: all I need is time to finish mine, but when shall I get it?

14 September 1960   *Grundisburgh*

How often the Ancient of Days indulges in sardonic humour. That you had ceaseless rain your whole fortnight at Kisdon and golden September days the moment you got back to Soho Square is a fine instance of it. Sheer cussedness! Did you see in to-day's *Times* the definition of a Combination Room—'a strange mixture of vestry and pantry'? My fourth-form mind liked it. Did you know, by the way, that, according to Macaulay, Soho Square in the 1700's was the most fashionable spot in all London? Your front-door bell in fact was the very latest thing in 1670, and people watched those who rang it (as they do me now). I shall be more careful on October 11 (is it?) not to deracinate it.

Fancy your ending up with five hawks and an owl! The sardonic gods again—they wanted to put the last edge on your regrets at leaving. And it is clear that what mainly oppresses you in London is my exact *bête noire* too—that horde of hideous people—mud-coloured, devoid of any sign of interest or intelligence or fun, noticing nothing, that is how they appear, and they are the people on whom democracy stands or falls. It is not hard to see which of the two it is in process of doing at the moment.

Everything is very costive here. My British Guiana papers have not *yet* arrived (is there some hope they can get no transport?) and that infernal library will not produce Quennell's book, though I am sure I am the first applicant for it. (The latest book on the new book-stand is the *History of High Wycombe* in two volumes—also an exciting-looking volume called *Solutions*, which deals however not with mystery-problems but with liquids.) Whenever I ask for the librarian or deputy, or secretary, they are all on holiday.

You must get rid somehow of the good Edel. Very odd people are. Gow used to come and sit in one's room and expect to be talked to between schools in the afternoon. And yet no man ever was quicker to get rid of a visitor when *he* had work on hand. And he was good value when one was not busy—a dry wine, but very palatable, though never quite the 'chatty and confident claret' once advertised in a catalogue, or even from the same place a 'champagne of great wit and repartee', which would no doubt produce the 'sober incalescence and regulated aestuation' approved of by Sir Thomas Browne, followed, you may remember, by his deprecation of any indulgence which leads to 'dementation or sopition of reason'.[1] If you don't know these quotations you will like to meet them; if you do know them, you won't mind being reminded of them (the prize bore's apologia).

I glanced yesterday at *Middlemarch*, and put it to you confidently that the very first three pages have more satisfying food for thought than fifty pages of—but I won't specify! I hope Ruth agrees in loving that charming prig Dorothea. In the story of Mr Casaubon's arid, in-deed bloodless, courtship there is one quite delightful sentence: 'D. said to herself that Mr C. was the most interesting man she had ever seen, not excepting even M. Liret the Vaudois clergyman *who had given conferences on the history of the Waldenses*'. What a lot of the Victorian age, as well as of D., is in that sentence.

Tell me who or what to read about Vernon Lee. I dislike being so wholly ignorant as I am about her; I have never seen anything to do

[1] *Pseudodoxia Epidemica* (1646), book 5, chapter xxxi.

with her, or any kind of picture of her. Does she come into *no-one's* biography? Because I must have read most of them.

Do you know Leonard Woolf, whose reminiscences are interestingly reviewed? It isn't quite easy to take Bloomsbury very seriously in 1960—or the great G.E. Moore, whom I tried many years ago and stuck in irretrievably. Did they, in spite of the good things they wrote, amount to much *collectively*? And isn't the last word on them in Max B's devastating 'From Bloomsbury to Bayswater'?[1] Is anything less attractive than faded arrogance—or more ridiculous? One gets the impression of rather pinchbeck Ozymandiases. I find that much the really best things in Lytton Strachey's writings are those in which he is *not* mocking, however subtly—though these can still amuse when, like e.g. Monsignor Talbot,[2] the victims really were absurd.

I have to write a paper on Gilbert for the Ipswich G. and S. society of which I am President. Yesterday I got Hesketh Pearson's Penguin on G. and S. which is excellent reading. What a good face H.P. has, at least on the back of this volume. I think you once said he was a capital chap—even though he dislikes Mr Gladstone. So did Gilbert, whose dislikes were largely fortuitous. He must on the whole have been a detestable man. His dialogue in the plays (not his lyrics) is dreadful reading now. You will be pleased to know that dear Queen Victoria thought the plot of *The Mikado* 'rather silly'.

18 September 1960   *Bromsden Farm*

I fear you won't get this before Tuesday. My whole week-end was disjointed by yesterday, when we were obliged to drive over to the Victor Gollanczes' new cottage near Marlow and play bridge with them for *six hours*. I am very fond of them both, but as you know I seldom play bridge (or anything else) and have a great deal to do. However, I think Comfort enjoyed it, and we eventually staggered

[1] Published in Max Beerbohm's *Mainly on the Air* (1946).

[2] George Talbot (1816–1886), fifth son of the third Lord Talbot de Malahide. Private Secretary to Pope Pius IX, who helped Manning to become Archbishop of Westminster. He ended in a lunatic asylum. See Strachey's *Eminent Victorians* (1918).

home the richer by 7/6. Now I am trying to cram two days' business into one, and the sun has been seducing me out of doors.

Adam was much pleased and flattered by an extremely nice letter from Birley, congratulating him on his scholarship etc. An excellent gesture, I thought. Apparently a Distinction in A-Level counts as one in Trials, so Adam now has *seven* to his credit.

Last week in London was most exhausting. No one could be a less demanding guest than my dear friend Leon Edel, but Ruth and I have come to depend on the flat for moments of escape and peace—coffee and the crossword at 10.30, often lunch, a quiet whisky-and-soda after the office, and so on—and to find even the nicest of guests always there, having to talk when one longs for quiet, is persistently frustrating. However, the dear fellow flies home next Saturday, and somehow we'll stumble through till then.

My spies tell me (*this is frightfully private*) that the big City investment firm which owns Heinemann (and me along with it) is negotiating to sell the whole caboodle to an American tycoon. Nobody can guess what this would mean, but I don't much like the sound of it. I'll let you know as soon as I know any more.

Where exactly does that splendid bit of Sir Thomas Browne come from? I don't immediately know where you can read about Vernon Lee, though there's certainly a bit about her in Maurice Baring's autobiography, *The Puppet Show of Memory*. I shouldn't bother about Le Gallienne. When he emigrated to America, Max sent him on a postcard:

> Bewitched by American bars,
> Pan whistles you home on his pipes.
> We love you for loving the stars,
> But what can you see in the stripes?

I do indeed know, and like, Leonard Woolf. I have bought his book but haven't yet begun it. Your wise strictures on Bloomsbury sum it all up beautifully, but I'm sure you needn't worry; time winnows away the chaff of arrogance etc, and the grain (of which there surely was some) will remain.

Many Oscar notes still elude me, and the galley-proofs are little nearer completion than they were this time last week. My wild Irish boy, a child-prodigy of research, is with me for another fortnight, adding to the confusion in Soho Square with a powerful gift of the gab. But he is biddable, and I have prepared a long programme for him in Somerset House, British Museum, London Library, Record Office etc.

How dull the papers are without any cricket—and soon the clocks will be altered, and darkness will close in.

Peter is meditating a book on Siberia 1918–1919, Admiral Kolchak, and the Russian civil war—but this too is secret for the moment. His present (Younghusband) book we have postponed till January. Diana's third volume begins in next week's *Sunday Times*, but please don't read it there: I'll soon send you a proper copy. I dined last week with her and her son, and although it was all very nice I didn't enjoy myself much. Maybe I have reached some kind of climacteric or change of life, but I certainly feel ever less social, gregarious and tolerant, and long to do what I want to do in a place of my own choosing. Perhaps one day it will work out that way, and meanwhile I must grit my teeth and carry on. Seeing you on 11 October will be most cheering.

22 September 1960   *Grundisburgh*

Your Duff's article is *excellent* reading; he makes it all very vivid. And what substantial support he brings to that dictum of Oxenstierna's[1] which Dr J. was fond of, saying to a young man: 'You will be surprised to find when you go out into the world, with what little wisdom human affairs are managed'. Not that to my limited and impatient mind the Creator has all that much to boast about. I wish I shared the belief of many that some day we shall know all about it. Meanwhile there is Clough:

> But play no tricks upon thy soul, O man;
> Let fact be fact and life the thing it can.[2]

You really are an amazing man. *Six* hours of bridge with all that mountain of work waiting to be tackled. Do you *always* do what

[1] Count Axel Oxenstierna, Swedish statesman (1583–1654).
[2] 'Dipsychus', part 2, scene ii.

friends want you to do? And then you go and fill another hour with a lovely letter to me. You will get to Abraham's bosom very much sooner than I shall—which I *suppose* is a highly delectable region??

I have at last finished my exam-papers—about three hundred of them from overseas. And am I sick of vague and vapid jaw about Brutus and Cassius, or am I? But they are well up-to-date in British Guiana. One candidate stated that Caesar was a homosexual, the proof being his saying 'Let me have men about me that are fat'— which recalls a scabrous limerick which I found in my psalter in Eton chapel in 1896—which I shall *not* tell you.

Yes, there is a glut of apples here too, which doesn't seem to be doing much good to anybody—too many to gather, and no profit in selling. And this is just the moment when our half-gardener takes his ten days' holiday. But following the old advice to 'count one's blessings', well, of course my chief one is having you as a fairy god-mother—for I go nearly as far as Southey in finding my cheeks 'often bedewed with tears of thoughtful gratitude', whenever I contemplate my revolving bookshelf, *entirely* filled with gifts from R.H-D. And now the beloved Tim has sent me Alan Ross's cricket anthology,[1] which I was on the brink of buying last week at The Ancient House, and was stopped by a spasm of economy. There are splendid things in it, and a good deal I have *not* read, plus old favourites. I wish R. had found room for C.P. Foley's superb account of Alletson's innings in 1911, when he ended his vast innings by getting 139 in half-an-hour, *89 of it in fifteen minutes*. He clearly went quite mad—and remained so, for he never made another run practically, nor even tried to hit, though A.O. Jones told him that if only he would hit he should play in every match, however few runs he made. But of course, half the fun of an anthology is picking holes. This looks a very good one—even though Lyttelton is spelt Lyttleton. I hope *you* foam at the mouth when called Davies? It is almost incredible what a vast percentage of G.C.E. candidates agree that '*Philippi*' is the only incorrect way of spelling the name. By and large 'Philpi' was furthest from the truth, from, I think the same chap who said that Brutus followed the 'sotic' philosophy.

Adam, I hope, had (till last week) his feet on the fender reading

[1] *The Cricketer's Companion* (1960).

non-scientific literature. Warn him that Darwin, when he ultimately found himself at leisure, realised that he had completely lost any taste for literature, especially fiction (not that that matters) and Shakespeare. I wonder why Gilbert disliked S. so much. I have to read a paper some soon day to the Ipswich G.S. Society, and am lazily collecting stuff for it (it is on Gilbert alone) slightly daunted by a feeling of increasing dislike of the man—practically always in a temper when not getting his own way, and with such an obvious relish for bloodshed, torture etc. His famed witticisms (like many of Oscar's?) are pretty flavourless now, less witty than Housman's, and with the same edge of snub and rudeness (though I *do* like—having a vulgar mind— 'Where is Miss X'? 'She's round behind'. 'Yes, I know, but where is she'?). The librettos and dialogue in plays one never saw or heard, and therefore can't call up any tunes, are rather heavy-going, though Hesketh Pearson says that G. never was more brilliant than in *Ruddigore* and *The Mountebanks*. I can't quite see it.

I shall be interested to hear what you make of Leonard Woolf's book. It is on my list, but the library has been very dilatory of late. The reviews stimulate one's curiosity. I rather wish he had avoided the modern fashion of proclaiming his virginity up to such and such an age. Is *anything* of less general interest?

25 September 1960   *Bromsden Farm*

The sun calls me outside, so you will get poor measure to-day, I fear.

After last Saturday's bridge-marathon, I had another long day of frustration yesterday. I brought Leon Edel down here on Friday night, and we set off for London Airport (25 miles) at 11 a.m. yesterday. L.E. is a nervous traveller with ever-mounting gangplank-fever. We got to the airport at 12 and I took him to the huge central section, where 10,000 cars were parked. With some difficulty I found room for ours, lugged his heavy suitcase a long way to the first floor, only to be told that we were in quite the wrong part of the airport. Lugged the suitcase back, de-parked the car, was roundly ticked off by motorised police for going the wrong way (it's very confusing) and drove off to the *right* place. Here we were told that the flight had been postponed

144

from 1 p.m. to 5.30 p.m. It was by now 12.30, the sun was shining hot and strong, and I felt I simply *couldn't* leave the wretched fellow to hang about for five hours. So I put him firmly back into the car and drove off.

Meanwhile, as they say in clumsy old novels, Duff had come over from Cardiff to pick the apples, found there were *far* more than we could use or store, so rang up Julia Coleridge and sold her 200 lbs at threepence a pound.

Meanwhile, again, Adam had telephoned delightedly to announce his election to the Library[1] and to ask for his tape recorder, portable wireless, box of electrical equipment, two spare recording-tapes, some eggs and other food, and (once again) his braces.

So, laden with all this clobber, and the undeparted guest, I drove to Eton. As we reached Fred's Boys' Entrance a boy, twitching and groaning with pain, was carried out on a stretcher and driven off in an ambulance. (It turned out that his name was Romer-Lee and his trouble a slipped disc.) We found Adam, and with some difficulty persuaded the dame to cough up £2. 10. 0. for the apples. Adam and the odd-job-man almost ruptured themselves getting the fruit out of the car. We admired the Chess Cup in the dining-room; Adam said he was playing football at 2.15, so didn't want to come out to lunch. Leon acquiesced in all the hurly-burly—and then I drove him to Monkey Island, which was looking very beautiful, and had a good lunch. I could see that L.E.'s anxiety-neurosis was growing rapidly, but managed to divert his attention by asking him to tell me about the time when he was psycho-analysed. This kept him going happily through a protracted lunch, and at 3 p.m. I suggested that we might examine the secondhand bookshops of Windsor and Eton and then return to the airport at 4.30 as instructed. He said he'd be happier if we rang up the airport for confirmation, so I sat in the sun by the river while he got the necessary pennies. Soon he came disconsolately back to say he'd pressed the wrong button and lost all his pennies, so I got some more, rang up the airport, and was told the flight had again been postponed—till 8.30 p.m.! This news completely shattered him, and I simply didn't know what to do. I could have brought him back here, but he would have hated that as much as anything else. Instead

[1] The boys' governing body of an Eton house.

I drove him to Windsor and we pottered in the bookshops, buying a few odd books. Then he said he must telephone again, so we sweated to the Post Office at the very top of Windsor Hill, and got some more pennies, and the flight was still 8.30.

L.E. was really very touching, saying he realised I was being very kind, and he knew he ought to be enjoying the sunshine and the adventure and the bookshops, but that he simply couldn't control his exasperation, so after giving him a cup of tea I drove him back to the airport and left him there at 5.30, with three hours still to go. I got back here at 6.30 utterly exhausted, having driven eighty miles and spent all the apple-money.

I have got Alan Ross's cricket anthology, but needless to say haven't had time to examine it. I am enjoying Leonard Woolf very much, and I think you will too.

Tomorrow is T.S.E.'s seventy-second birthday, and Ruth and I have been bidden to drinks at 6.15. On Thursday I am to take part in a hideous evening party given by the Society of Authors in (goodness knows why) a room in the House of Commons. An 'informal discussion' is to take place between Compton Mackenzie, Rebecca West, A.P. Herbert and *me*! How on earth did I let myself in for such folly? 'It was an insensate step', as Henry James once said. The full horror shall be reported to you next week. Now I must finish correcting the proofs of the Gissing-Wells letters, and read the Sunday papers and spend a little time with Oscar's dog-eared proofs. I see no daylight at the end of the tunnel: your diagnosis of a surfeit of people is a jolly good one, but what is the cure? My London life is all or nothing: one either participates or withdraws: half-measures simply aren't possible.

Now you've got six pages of complaints and I shall try the sun.

28 September 1960   *Grundisburgh*

'Poor measure indeed' followed by *six* pages of the best! Irony, or litotes (or if you prefer it, meiosis)—of which my favourite example is Swift's reference to the woman who had been flayed alive, 'and you cannot think how much it changed her appearance for the worse'. A blood-freezing man with, as Taine says, 'his terrible wan eyes'. There are some deeply grim stories about him, as you know.

This is the perfect summer-house day—coldish east wind and bright sun, and I as warm as a toast, whatever that may mean. We are beating up for a fine October, which is very common in these regions, though it is rather like the brief heartiness and eupepsia of a septuagenarian, with November in the offing, when 'Not till the spring recapture Joy as it flits along, Shall we regain the rapture Either of scent or song!'.[1]

What a nightmare of a time you and Leon Edel had over that flying. The only faint silver lining was that you sold 200 lbs of apples, which surely no one else has done this year. There seems to be a glut everywhere—and I suppose we are importing millions, or is that potatoes? I met John Hare, recently released from the Board of Agriculture and clearly happy about it, as he said bluntly that three out of four of the problems that come before the Minister are insoluble. I reassured him by saying that *all* government problems are the same in 1960—except of course such perfectly useless ones as hitting the moon. The last word (as so often) was said by Johnson—in *Rasselas*, no doubt—that the scientists had much better busy themselves in discovering a cure for asthma rather than in learning how to fly. You must have been entirely exhausted by the end of the day, but I suspect you very often are (like everybody—not that there are all that many —who does exactly what any friend asks him to do).

I love the refrain of Adam's braces—invariably sent after him with much else. The young are like that. We never have any part of the family here without sending half their wardrobe after them. I have simplified packing by having a list inside my suitcase of everything I could possibly want. It saves a lot of time. Not that I didn't, last winter, carefully pack a hot-water bottle minus its stopper. As Swift might have said, you would be surprised to find how little use it was when I arrived.

I wonder what bookshops you found in Windsor. There used in my day to be—literally—none. Only W.H. Smith, and he didn't go much beyond Penguins etc. Mrs Brown at Eton set up her shop twenty years ago and makes a good thing of it, or used to. I sold her a lot of

[1] Galsworthy, 'November'.

books when I left (*all* of which I have wanted since) and saw some of them in her window priced a good deal higher than what she had paid me, but as she once explained, when you buy a library, you find three-quarters of it practically unsaleable and only a few make the buy worth while.

Alan Ross's anthology has lots of good stuff in it, and—as one might expect—plenty that one could spare. Are you *very* good at the MCC match in *Tom Brown's Schooldays*? I am not, and still less so at Vachell's Eton v. Harrow. In fact, to come out into the open with trailing coat, I am not permanently a-giggle over Macdonell's famous match in *England, their England*. But the explanation of that may be that, as my daughters say when I condemn *Punch*, my sense of humour is going the same way as my hearing, sight, memory etc.

At last the library has coughed up Quennell's book, and I start it this evening. After sampling an odd page or two, I know I shall enjoy it. He seems to think T.S.E.'s appearance is or was, very incongruous after *The Waste Land*. E. Pound looks much more 'agin' everything and everybody. What does T.S.E. really think of E.P.? I think you ought to garner a good deal of interesting stuff from T.S.E.—not necessarily with a view to publication, but, say, to conversation with G.W.L. Does he write any reminiscences? They should be very good. Perhaps, like General Alexander, he is too much of a gentleman.

I get some definite pleasure from the *T.L.S.* reviewer who begins a paragraph about Kingsley Amis's last novel: 'This is a very nasty book'. He is, as you know, one of my steadily lengthening list of *bêtes noires*. A sure sign of old age. I become steadily deafer, the arch of my right foot steadily descends, my shins steadily itch, one deltoid muscle creaks and stiffens. Otherwise, thank you, I am perfectly well, though, as Lord Clive who is no longer alive said, there is a great deal to be said for being dead.

I should like to hear you at the H. of C. with your sparkling party. Rebecca West always strikes me as the cleverest woman in England (as J. Agate maintained) though I haven't read her last one or two. A.P.H.?_Well some don't like him, but *What a Word*, *Topsy* and *Misleading Cases* are frequently at my bedside, and I should like to meet him and tell him how one of his poems 'The farmer will never be happy again, He carries his heart in his boots', etc was regarded as sheer gold by my father-in-law when he was President of the Royal Agricultural Society and recited the poem at at least twenty dinners through the winter instead of a speech and had his audience in fits of delighted laughter. Over and over again they told him that 'For either the rain is destroying his grain, Or the drought is destroying his roots' is not only very funny, but contains in a couplet the *whole* problem of farming. Do hand this on if you get a chance with him.

What line shall I take in my paper on Gilbert to the Ipswich society? It is not easy, I find, to like him. Q.[1] dallies with the problem of the popularity of the tremendously Victorian operettas long after people were turning up their noses at Tennyson and Browning. Fundamentally he has only about three–four plots, and practically all his young women are identical, and all his old ones fat and wrinkled and repellent. I wonder why Q. thought *The Bab Ballads* were better than his lyrics in the plays—'much' better, I think he says. I found the *B.B.* definitely hard to read at all continuously, a few days ago. As to his plays, away from Sullivan, well, in that nice French expression, they do not permit themselves to be read, and the poor man thought so highly of them. And as to Sullivan, have you ever heard his 'Golden Legend' which a critic, after its first performance, said combined the merits of Haydn and Beethoven? It is a very odd story.

Well, my dear R., here are six pages. Too long I know, but you began it. *Vous l'avez voulu, George Dandin*[2] (not that yours were too long for me).

1 *October 1960*   *Bromsden Farm*

Last week's six-sider was a *lusus naturae*, unlikely to recur for ages, but since it drew from you an equally long answer, I may one day be tempted to send you a twelve-sider, just to see how you react.

The coming of winter is depressing enough without this wilful encouragement of darkness by putting back the clock. We still have masses of *strawberries* in the garden, though to-day they are soggy with rain. Squirrels and rooks squabble for the walnuts, though in

---

[1] Sir Arthur Quiller-Couch in his *Studies in Literature, Third Series* (1929).
[2] Molière, *George Dandin, ou Le Mari Confondu* (1668), act I, scene ix.

fact there are plenty for all, and I gathered a large basketful this afternoon. No children here this week-end, and all is peace. I have just read three hundred pages of a draft of my old friend Wyndham Ketton-Cremer's history of Felbrigg, his house in Norfolk. It's not exactly sparkling, but I know the house well, and any competent and documented family history of three hundred years is interesting as a sort of microcosm of history. Before Monday I must also read *six hundred* pages (typescript) of the first volume of Guy Chapman's history of the French Third Republic (1871–1940). Also a French book on the Algerian war, which I fear would be out of date before it could be translated. Also I must cut, edit and partly re-write Jock Dent's sloppy introduction to the Agate anthology I am to bring out next year. And, in case I have time to spare, I have brought along a 300-page (typed) 'extravaganza' by Arnot Robertson. So you will not be surprised to hear that the Oscar galleys are locked in the safe at Soho Square for the week-end: if they were here I couldn't resist fiddling with them.

Mrs Brown now belongs to the ages, but her bookshop goes marching on, and it was one of those we visited last Saturday. Now (long since my day—and yours, I fancy) there are two good secondhand shops just over the bridge, both on the right: one opposite the cinema and the other exactly on the first rounded turning of the road up the hill (used it to be a furniture shop?). Both are well worth a visit, though the first (like so many of its fellows) is gradually surrendering its front room to paperbacks and gramophone-records.

T.S.E.'s birthday party was most touching and enjoyable: just the two of them; her mother (very nice, from Leeds); a dear old friend of T.S.E.'s and mine, called Mary Hutchinson; Ruth and me. A tiny one-candled cake and champagne (which this time I opened without drenching the Epstein bust, as I did two years ago). Tom still looks terribly grey, but better than he did two months ago. We talked of Leonard Woolf, and *Lady Chatterley*, and the theatre, and this and that. I wish I remembered more, or knew shorthand, or didn't always have each episode pushed aside by an immediate successor. I doubt whether he (T.S.E.) is writing anything much now, though I fancy he's continually brooding over a new play—and I wish he wasn't, for his plays aren't getting any better, and he has probably written enough.

Reminiscences—I fear not, though I will try and raise the subject one of these days.

The Society of Authors rout in the H. of C. turned out (as so often happens with something one has long been dreading) to be rather fun. Some two hundred authors were crammed together, each with his (or more often her) name pinned to the lapel. (Most of them seemed to be called Margaret Bulge or some such.) The main attraction was the Brains Trust, which lasted well over an hour, and seemed to give general satisfaction. A.P.H. was on the right wing, then Compton Mackenzie, then the chairman Denzil Batchelor, then Rebecca, then me. I had previously given dinner at the Garrick to Robert Holland, a nice young Lecturer in English from Liverpool, and the drink I had had (two whiskies-and-sodas and one glass of claret) must have been just right, for I suddenly felt on top of the Brains Trust and more than able to cope. The questions were quite sensible, and enabled everyone to speak a little about themselves. A.P.H. actually quoted 'The farmer will never be happy again', to the delight of the massed authors. Rebecca was most amiable, and afterwards her husband (deaf, friendly, hospitable) begged me to drive over and see them.

I am much too ignorant of Gilbert to advise you about your speech, but it seems clear that neither he nor Sullivan was any use without the other, whereas in partnership their complementary second-rateness became in its way first-class. And I *still* haven't seen a single G. and S. opera!

Tommy has great hopes of getting Siegfried Sassoon into the Lit. Soc. and indeed you would find him most congenial—cricket and all. I've told Tommy I'll happily second him, and I fancy T. is planning to bring him as a guest to the November dinner.

I greatly enjoyed Leonard Woolf. He says most things three times, like the Bellman, but one soon forgives that, because most of what he says is interesting. A batch of R.H-D. books should reach you soon, if they haven't already arrived. The list for next year looks pretty thin so far: it's a fearful effort trying to keep up output *and* standard, and I increasingly feel that I've been at it long enough.

I can hear the rain hurtling down outside, the Third Republic is waiting, and it's another six-sider. No precedent, I promise. No need to reciprocate.

P.S. I had a huge plate of fresh ripe strawberries and cream for supper!!

'October *rediit, rediit pars tristior anni*'.[1] Do you remember your
Clivus? O. is very often the best of months in Suffolk, but it has made
—meteorologically—a poor start, though nothing like what it has in
Cornwall, the English Riviera. But all horizons are lightened by a
parcel with a lovely quintette of books from R.H-D., whose generosity
beggars gratitude of any adequate words, for they have all been used.
Talk about fairy godmothers! What a rich feast of reading awaits me!
And I have just finished Quennell's book, a great deal of it with great
pleasure. I found the Prologue and Epilogue a bit dry and difficult,
like—to me—all writing about the principles of art, but whenever he
gets on to people he is fine. 'Camp-followers' is an absorbing chapter.
'Stylists' too, with its visit to old George Moore—and much else. Is
P.Q. bilingual? There is a great deal of quotation from French
writers.

I am all for Siegfried Sassoon. I wonder what Sir Cuthbert would
say about him. You will have to let me off Sir C. on Tuesday week;
the plain truth must be faced, *viz* that I grow steadily deafer. The
National Health hearing-aid is really unwearable—so clumsy and
undiscriminating—you hear your own heart beating, and, much
louder than anything else, your own voice. My cynical Scotch specialist said in answer to such complaints: 'Yes; I suspect half the hearing-
aids in England are put away in cupboards'. But they do improve as
time goes on. Not that at seventy-seven plus there is much of it to
spend waiting.

Have you noticed how putting back the clocks seems to shorten
the day by much more than one hour—or rather bring darkness over
an hour sooner? Partly no doubt because at five the sky is heavily
clouded. But it isn't a conspicuously pleasant time of year, anyway,
after youth. Your strawberries are rather offensive—a second crop!
We rarely have any at all. Pamela discovered (as with fowls too) that
to grow them costs more time—and money as well—than buying

[1] October has returned, a sadder part of the year.

them. And of course mushrooms too. What humbug the advertisements are—pretending that anyone can grow crop after lavish crop with a minimum of trouble. I expect those lessons on how to earn several hundreds a year with short stories are much the same. How, by the way, are Jonah's coming along? You are suspiciously silent about them.

Heavens, the jobs you take on! Six hundred pages on the Third Republic! I thought Brogan had written the last word on that in 1939. I remember being impressed with his certainty that France was about to collapse months before she did. I am surprised at Jock Dent's writing being 'sloppy', because it used not to be. I have a persistent but quite irrational feeling that he has gone downhill these last years. You will probably know for certain. I am glad you were well-primed for that Brains Trust. Did you tell A.P.H. about my father-in-law? Perhaps you didn't get as far as that in my letter. His satisfaction must in his seventies be that he has certainly added to the gaiety of nations.

By the way, Cyril Foley in his excellent account of Fowler's match makes a very grave error of fact in saying that T.O. Jameson was laid out for a bit through being hit 'on the head'. It was really a much more vulnerable place—and a commoner, especially *on a wet wicket with none but slow to medium bowlers.* I met T.O.J. three years ago when he told us in a very husky voice that he had cancer of the throat and would die in six months. He seemed entirely cheerful about it. And in fact he is still alive. I read that old Maugham too contemplates death with perfect calm—what would appal him would be the prospect of eternal life, and how right he is, especially if, as Arthur Benson said, there are many people who appear to think that in the next world they will have a prescriptive right to one's company. The old S.M. is very corrugated now, but after all at eighty-six one has a right to be.

The Quashiboo Rangers. Author totally forgotten. There was an arrogant regiment in India that regarded itself as invincible. Some man with some kind of grudge against them trained an eleven of black men who batted and bowled very sketchily, but could catch literally anything however close to the bat. They made practically no runs, going in first, but the regiment made *none*—all caught *the moment* they hit the ball. The black eleven were named after the twelve apostles. I will try and find out about it. Unluckily Rockley Wilson[1] is dead. He knew everything about cricket history.

I should have liked to hear you and T.S.E. on *Lady Chatterley*. I suspect that the book is one of the very few things we disagree about —I mean its publication unexpurgated. I wonder what the gutter press will make of the trial. A lot will depend on the judge. I am sure my cousin the late Sir George Talbot[2] would have been very fierce about it; so would old Avory[3] but then of course they *were* Victorians. So are most judges. Have you read, shall you read, Kingsley Amis's last? Some man in the *Spectator* says it is his best, in total opposition to the *T.L.S.*

Shall you, by the way, attend the Johnson Club dinner on the 25th? I think I must go, as I have not attended one for a year. But I shall tell the good secretary that I will *not* propose the guests' health. Why should anyone? It is an otiose proceeding.

9 October 1960   *Bromsden Farm*

Is this the second Flood? Have you an arkwright handy? Goodness knows what our rainfall has been to-day alone. Except for stacking a few logs in the woodshed I have stuck to proofs and manuscripts in the library. I am struggling through the birth-pangs of the Third Republic, of which I assure you the good Brogan has scarcely scratched the surface. So glad you have enjoyed Quennell at last: he is not, to my knowledge, bilingual, but is clearly well-read in French lit.

Jonah's short stories are in the printer's hands: the book is to be called *The Bishop's Aunt*, after what I think the best story in it. Last Tuesday I dined alone with Jonah and Evy in their St John's Wood eyrie. They gave me a superb dinner (they have a daily Viennese cook) of smoked salmon, a huge melting *vol-au-vent*, a fine bottle of Mouton Rothschild, and a wonderful *soufflé surprise*, topped up with

[1] E.R. Wilson (1879–1957) played cricket for Rugby, Cambridge and Yorkshire. Assistant Master at Winchester 1903–1946.

[2] Barrister, and judge of the King's Bench Division (1861–1938).

[3] Sir Horace Avory (1851–1935), barrister, and judge of the King's Bench Division.

coffee, liqueur and an excellent Partagas cigar. Afterwards we sat and gossiped most agreeably. Jonah is definitely much better: his breathlessness greatly reduced and his colour better. Jock Dent has indeed deteriorated lately, and his writing has gone soft. I didn't tell A.P.H. about your father-in-law, because I didn't get your letter about it till *after* the Brains Trust.

I *can't* go to the Johnson Club on the 25th, being already bespoke for that evening. It's much more than a year since I attended, so I shouldn't let that worry you. Ruth and I will be waiting for you at six on Tuesday, expecting you to be deaf, breathless and drenched; we will stay you with flagons.

13 October 1960   *Grundisburgh*

On Sunday we go up to Westmorland; Pamela, I really think, enjoys the journey; I rather hate it. Senility of course. I am always convinced the car will cease to function in the middle of some northern moor.

I have just finished Diana Cooper's book. I do hope it will be decently reviewed because it is really a lovely book—all beautifully done and the end *very* moving. Pamela thinks so too (and is a very good judge). My dislike of the *New Statesman* in general and R.H.S. Crossman in particular was strongly reinforced by C's review of Pug Ismay's and Horrocks's books—so sneery and omniscient and entirely blind to the obvious fact that both men are outstandingly good chaps. And then of course he praises the man—name forgotten—who runs down Monty in favour of the Auk. To call, as he does, Churchill 'the little white politician' is schoolboy stuff—and not very high in the school either.

I shall take Druon to the north and send you a report. Is the Wells-Gissing correspondence any good—or was G. too gloomy—admittedly with pretty good reason for most of his life? I address the Leys School sixth form on Saturday. The gist of my address will be that they will get very little education from beaks but a lot by themselves, if they read properly. Half the staff, I believe, are to be there. I also intend to abuse Leavis. Half the staff worship him.

I forget how long you're staying with Roger, but hope this will catch you there. Both Ruth and I thought that on Tuesday, far from being deafer as you announced yourself, you were definitely *less* deaf— so there! Perhaps the contraption in your ear is more use than you think.

So glad you liked Diana's book: she is apprehensive about its reception and refuses to be reassured, even by Evelyn Waugh, who has sent me this for use in advertisements:

> '*Trumpets from the Steep* is as brilliant, diverse and poignant as its two memorable predecessors and triumphantly crowns one of the great autobiographies of the century.'

What more could one ask?

The Wells-Gissing correspondence is pretty small beer, but you shall have it as soon as it's ready, sometime early next year. And I must chase the man who is supposed to be editing the Shaw–Wells volume: it should be the best of the four, but I haven't seen any of it yet.

This week-end I have only a 200-page monograph on Christopher Smart (by Christopher Devlin) to keep me from Oscar.

Everything in the garden is so sodden that we can get the bonfire going only by 'borrowing' some waste-oil from Peter's huge grain-drying machine. P. himself has gone for ten days to Roscommon on what I told him was certainly in every sense a wild-goose chase. He answered an advertisement in *The Times*—'guns wanted' or some such.

Next week *may* see me in the witness-box at the Old Bailey. I've never set foot in the place, have you? Anyhow I'll describe it all for you, despite your disapproval of *Lady Chatterley*.

I long to know whether your drive took you anywhere near Keld or Kisdon. Have a look at a map, and let me know. How I wish I was there now! I have just heard on the telephone that I have to be at a meeting in London at 11.30 tomorrow (Sunday) morning—the usual intrigue and skulduggery of Heinemann's. Twenty-five years ago one of the typists in my office said to another: 'Mr Hart-Davis is very nice as long as his own personal comfort isn't interfered with', and the older I get the truer does that home truth become. All my complicated arrangements depend on my having Sunday clear for reading and writing. Damn them all!

Please give my love to the charming Sibell and to the impish demure and beloved Roger. Is he safe among those schoolgirls, or should you go along to protect him—I mean *them*?

Having made all my arrangements to travel to Rapallo on All Saints Day for the unveiling of the plaque, I now hear from the Consul in Genoa that the ceremony may be postponed for some days. Damn *them* all too! Kisdon Lodge is the place for me.

Forgive all these outbursts and send me cheerful tidings from the north.

19 October 1960   *Barbon Manor*
                                                              Kirkby Lonsdale

Your letter duly arrived, though I had a sudden compunction that I had not given you Roger's address; only second thoughts reassured me that of course you have known it for years. We had an excellent journey from Cambridge on Sunday, and go back next Sunday, having firmly decided that that is the best day for travel—especially if—as we did—one starts at 7.15 a.m. Roger and Sibell are both in excellent form and clearly much pleased by your mention of them. How right was the man—name forgotten—who said that anyone who said he did not like being praised by his fellow-men was either a fool or a liar.

What you and Ruth say about my deafness is really very interesting—because one or two others have said the same, but I myself am conscious of nothing at all except that my worse ear *is* worse, and the other much the same, except that the little contraption makes it continuously tickle; which is tiresome but I suppose I shall ignore it in time. The gadget isn't *supposed* to produce any improvement for at least a fortnight. I shouldn't wonder if faith has a good deal to do with it. We shall see.

It is very pleasant up here and Pamela is having a grand rest from her numberless chores in Grundisburgh, where half the inhabitants' first idea is 'When in doubt about *anything*, send for Mrs L.'. The last before we left was from a woman whose husband had to go to hospital, and *would* dear Pamela just nip over and help to pack his clothes. I imagine this country is very like Kisdon—rolling moorland and vast horizons (usually obscured by cloud) and 'solitude of shepherds, High in the folded hill'.[1] When they come in I will look at a map and see how near we have ever been to Kisdon. The name has never passed my lips to anyone but Pamela. I believe even Ruth's lovely lips would be pursed in censure if it ever did.

You will, I hope, be pleased to hear that both Pamela and Roger greatly like Diana C's book, and both were quite expecting *not* to. I can't believe that any honest and competent reviewer could do anything but praise it—but perhaps those two adjectives are too extravagant? I agree with every word Evelyn Waugh says about it.

R. has many of the latest books and I batten on them. Lloyd George by his son: my Victorian view is that it *may* be interesting, amusing, and important to reveal that a big man's chief relaxation was promiscuous fornication, but that the revelation ought not to be made by his son. R. is a bit cagey about it, but I rather gather that to his cynical, 1960, man-of-the-world eye the bulk of readers may well praise the father's contempt for old-fashioned conventions and the son's courageous frankness. If they do, my conviction of the Gadarene course of all standards will be still further strengthened.

L. Woolf's *Sowing* did not wholly please me, though full of interest. Doesn't he jeer too much at all other views and convictions than those held by the Stracheys and Stephens and Keyneses etc? Do you know all about G.E. Moore and his philosophy? He is, as always, extravagantly lauded in this book—though represented by two curiously dull letters. When I went up (October 1902) I was urged to read his *Principia Ethica*, but I made no more of it than Dr Johnson did of playing the flageolet. But he does appear to have impressed a great many very intelligent people, though for many years his name has very rarely been mentioned, so far as my observation goes. I wish there was a picture of L.W. at twenty-four instead of that very unattractive one of him as a boy. And, Rupert, *surely* nothing flatter than those two imitations or parodies of Henry James on pp. 110–116 has ever been written? They seem to me to bear no relation whatever to

[1] A.E. Housman, 'The Merry Guide'.

H.J. It may, of course, be the same with me as with Hume when he said he had no fear of death. 'Sir, his intellect is disordered'.

I look forward to seeing you reported as an enthusiast for *Lady C's Lover*. Please tell me all about it. It is all a fine piece of fantasy—jurymen all looking like figures drawn by George Morrow, quite clearly mystified, almost certainly shocked, very probably flattered by being told they are men of the world into denying what they *really* think. I wonder who will be the judge. Will passages be read *aloud* in court? Will there be women on the jury? Gosh, how I feel like Housman's Terence: 'I, a stranger and afraid In a world I never made'.[1]

That typist who spoke of your personal comfort. Dash it all, do you *ever* stop putting yourself out for other people? To want your Sunday clear, while bustling about through all the other six days. Well that is very much what the fourth commandment enjoins.

I have been looking at maps. After Doncaster the road here is north-west through places like Skipton and Settle. But I asked about Swaledale and Sibell says we will go there to-morrow, as it is superb. So far the little village of Dent is about the closest to Kisdon, though on a previous visit we went one day to Hawes which I have heard you mention.

Roger to-day is at some function at Giggleswick of which he is a governor. Yesterday S. took me to Sedbergh where Brendan Bracken fitted out for them the nicest library I have ever seen—quite perfect. We talked to a nice prefect. When I told him I was Humphrey's father his jaw fell.

23 October 1960   *Bromsden Farm*

This has been a most tiresome week, beginning with my having to spend five and a quarter hours of last Sunday arguing in London with two Americans called Benjamin and Mannheim. In the middle was a heavy lunch in a private room at the Dorchester—so is big business done—and the best one can say is that our side won a complete victory.

On Wednesday afternoon my old father (eighty-two) fell down in his service-flat in Knightsbridge and broke his femur (hip). Had it not

[1] *Last Poems*, xii.

been for the janitor bringing round the evening papers, the old boy would have lain on the floor in agony till morning. (The whole problem of old people who will insist on living alone is insoluble.) When I went to see him next morning he was not in pain, but grumbling as usual. His doctor told me on the telephone that if they put him to bed for three months and let it mend naturally he thought the old boy would never get up again, so on Friday they operated and inserted a 'pin'—all very successful, but my sister, who visited him yesterday in the London Clinic, reports him as a shocking patient, refusing to try and get up, as they want him to do, and being generally tiresome. I shall have to go and see him once or twice this week.

On Friday about 6 p.m., when Comfort was driving to Henley to meet me at the station, an idiotic little man, coming the other way, suddenly swung across C's bows and she hit him at about 55 m.p.h. That the fault was entirely his is little consolation, and it's a miracle that Comfort wasn't killed or badly hurt. In fact she is only very bruised and shocked. By the time I had been to the hospital, seen the police and collected Bridget from the station it was almost 9 p.m. We put Comfort straight to bed, where she has been ever since. She has a fever each evening, aches all over, and her teeth chatter if she gets out of bed. The doctor says these are all normal shock-reactions, and he thinks she will be all right in a few days. I didn't like the idea of her being alone here at night during the week, so this afternoon I bundled her up and took her over to a friend's where she is now in bed. All yesterday she wanted me to sit by her (very unlike her usual isolation), so one way and another Oscar has once again suffered. The car is a ghastly mess and will take weeks to mend, so I have had to hire a Hillman at huge cost—oh dear!

I couldn't help being a little cheered by this morning's *Sunday Times*, where Leonard Russell (the Literary Editor) writes: 'There are three men on my beat in London whom everyone loves—Sir Compton Mackenzie, Rupert Hart-Davis, and John Betjeman'. Even when such words are spoken in error (as here) they cannot fail to be encouraging.

Lady Chatterley has been adjourned till Thursday. I am apparently still on the short list of thirty defence-witnesses (selected, I am told, from four hundred volunteers), but can hardly think I shall be called. I hope however to see a bit of the fun. The defence were very keen to get some women on the jury, believing them to be more tolerant: please tell Pamela this.

I long to hear of your Swaledale drive. We love Hawes, and shop there, but it's in *Wensleydale*, which we like less than our beloved Swaledale.

27 October 1960   *Grundisburgh*

What a wretched week for you! I *am* sorry. All old men living by themselves have a fall sooner or later—and all men of character are shocking patients, chiefly because they don't really believe in doctors —and indeed there is a dreadful lot that doctors don't know, and the honest ones will admit it. And then Comfort's accident. I am always being horrified to read of accidents where *all* the blame is on one side, and how disturbing that thought is to one like me who always in any case expects the worst. Bed, they tell me, is the only thing for shock, so keep C. there till all symptoms are gone.

Pamela drove me over five hundred miles in all to and from Barbon, and we met no imbecile on the road, and also, which was odd for 1960, only an hour or so of rain altogether. There was quite a lot at Barbon and unluckily the worst day was that on which we meant to go to Swaledale. At Hawes we found ourselves in the middle of a wet dark cloud and could only come home. I wanted to get a picture of S. in my mind. But I suppose it is not very different from the majestic Barbon-dale or even Wensleydale, where we saw several little establishments advertising the famous cheese—but they tell me it isn't so good as it used to be. (But what is?)

I duly noted L. Russell's sentence in the *S.T.* and see no reason at all to doubt its truth. I don't think there will be an angry contradiction next Sunday. I never felt more sure of anything than that *Lady C.* should *not* be published unexpurgated. I hope you won't be summoned as a witness, for, if you are, I can't imagine what answer you will give to the question which any decent counsel must ask, *viz* 'How do these dozen passages lift the book from what it has been for thirty years in its unexpurgated form (which many think dullish) into a work of genius which mankind simply cannot do without?' Surely practically all the *real* reasons for 250,000 copies being printed are pornographic, and the pretence that they aren't is sheer *cant*. An Ipswich lawyer told me yesterday that the jury will condemn it, but I gather his prophecies in the past have nearly always been wrong.

The last book I read at Roger's was the life of Dr Arnold. I found myself hating him. That episode of his giving *eighteen* blows to a boy for lying merely shows him up as foully cruel and dreadfully stupid and impatient and self-assured; he made no attempt to find out if the boy might be telling the truth (which he was). And when the boy stayed out for two days the egregious old ass was convinced he was malingering. He should have been sacked after that caning—and nowadays, would be. It is clear Strachey didn't know about it. I wish he had. What portentous prigs Arnold's sixth-form boys were when they went to Oxford. The uncle in Clough's 'Dipsychus' described them very well.

29 *October 1960*   *Bromsden Farm*

I was disappointed to hear that you had missed Swaledale, for Wensleydale isn't a patch on it. Never mind—next time you visit Roger you must insist on going to Keld.

I'm happy to say that my old father is fast recovering, and Comfort is up and about again, still a little groggy but determined to resume her teaching on Monday. The car is still a crumpled ruin.

Your insistence on the suppression of *Lady Chatterley* is the only symptom of age that you have ever shown me, and I realise that the longer a tabu has been cherished, the harder it is to eradicate. Surely if you remove words from smoking-room stories and lavatory walls, and allow them to be printed in their proper context and meaning, they cease to be obscene and become ordinary—not in a moment, but in the course of time. As far as *Lady C.* is concerned, the expurgated passages seem to me the whole point of the book—but you will have read the evidence in *The Times*, and indeed I shall be thankful when the trial is over, for (being readily accessible by telephone) I have become a sort of Perpetual Twelfth Man for the defence witnesses. They never know whether any particular person is going to be five minutes in the box (E.M. Forster) or an hour and a half (Hough and Hoggart), so they keep having too few or too many witnesses waiting. At lunchtime on Thursday they thought they were going to run out, so sent out a three-line whip, as a result of which I sat from 2 till 4 gossiping with Tony Powell and Anne Scott-James. Asked to reappear at 10 a.m. on Friday, I found *fifteen* waiting. I sent in a message to the solicitor, saying that there were more than eleven waiting to bat, and if we had a batting-order, some of us could fall out. On this I escaped, but was urgently recalled for 2.30, when I probably *should* have been called if a legal argument had not occupied an hour and three-quarters. As it was, I talked to Dilys Powell, and for a short time watched Mr Justice Maude dealing with a teddy-boy knife-slasher in the next court. Now Dilys and I are both called for 10.30 on Monday. It must end soon.

In the middle of all that I attended a two-hour meeting, outspoken and acrimonious, about the direction of the Heinemann group, which, with two dinner-parties, produced such a rushed and exhausting week that I began to lose the power of sleep. However, ten hours last night helped a lot. Did I tell you (I'm sure I repeat myself much more than you do) that I am travelling to Rapallo next Thursday to attend the unveiling of a plaque on Max Beerbohm's Villino? It will mean forty-eight hours' travelling and ten hours there, but it will be a good change, and I look forward to the meals on the trains. You shall hear of it next week. I should get back here on Saturday night. I shall take Oscar with me: the Rome Express seems just the place for his letters to be corrected.

There seems to be a chance of Andrew Young's *Collected Poems* getting the Duff Cooper Prize this year, but it's not certain, so mum's the word. I should be delighted if it happened, for A.Y. is seventy-five and pretty hard up. The prize is worth only £150, but that's tax-free, and the publicity is bound to sell some copies of the book.

The Durrell book (*Zoo in my Luggage*) has gone off with such a bang that the first edition of *25,000* copies is almost exhausted: another 10,000 will be ready on November 18. A few more winners like that, and publishing would be a lot easier. Have you looked at *Hired to Kill*[1] yet? As usual, I can foresee *no* selling books for 1961, except Oscar if

[1] By John Morris (1960).

I can get him out, but perhaps something will turn up. Oh yes—yesterday I talked to Bernard Levin in the Old Bailey. He looks about *sixteen*, and at first I thought he was someone's little boy brought along to see the fun—very Jewish, with wavy fairish hair, very intelligent and agreeable to talk to. I imagine he is 'covering' the trial for the *Spectator*. Look out for it.

Yes—old, narrow-minded, prim, stubborn—the perfect square in fact. That is what I mainly am, as you have spotted. *Lady C*'s jury must be much the same, but I suspect the temptation to show that they are not may sway them—though the first part of the judge's summing-up looks this morning to be rather against *Lady C*. I don't think the prosecutor was very forceful, but he was no doubt handicapped by the odd legal ruling about witnesses for the prosecution *not* to be asked about the book's decency. The rock I founder on is this. No doubt all those high-minded experts were quite sincere in their views about D.H.L.'s loftiness of aim, his support of marriage, and hatred of promiscuity, the book being an allegory etc etc, but how many of the 200,000 new readers will take it like that? Some day, you say, the essential beauty of all that frankness will be seen. A devilish long time, surely, before the giggle will be taken out of sex?

You weren't called, I gather. As you say, it was odd to see how differently witnesses were treated. One thought E.M. Forster would be a star witness, and he was in the box for five minutes, while e.g. Hoggart was a good deal badgered. (By the way, might not the absence of witnesses agin the book be owing to so few common readers having read the unexpurgated book? I wonder if there is anyone on the jury who holds firmly the old advice: 'Always consult experts, and always distrust them'.)

You *very rarely* repeat yourself—and your journey to Rapallo is new to me. So you won't get this till when—Sunday? Like old Shaw, you do a lot of work in the train. Good for Oscar. And what excellent news about the Durrell book. P. is enthralled in it at the moment. That *must* surely mean a few more bobs in the R.H-D. kitty, though according to A.P.H. no money is to be made out of books now. You ask about *Hired to Kill*, but, my dear R., I have never yet seen it. An intriguing (a banned word?) looking book about Tibet awaits me, from my ever-generous fairy godmother; and I have just—shuddering —finished *The She-Wolf of France*. What an almost appalling amount Druon knows about French history. There are so many characters that they close in on one like a jungle now and then. But I have discovered that to be a *little* hazy about all the relationships doesn't really matter and the story is very gripping. I looked up the further history of Mortimer in the *D.N.B.* and find he had the same end which he had inflicted on the younger Despenser—*not* a very kindly one. No doubt Dr Arnold would have approved—as indeed Queen Isabella did, with relish, in the front row of the stalls. And it gave a gust to her reception of Mortimer that night. Another *Lady C.*?

I am rather coming round to Bernard Levin—so long as he keeps off party-politics; his comments on things are full of point and wit. I never see his dramatic criticisms. Is he good at them? His fellows in it seem to me very capricious and untrustworthy. I see Doris Lessing thinks the end-pages of D. Cooper's book are artificial and so fail. She is, I need hardly say, quite wrong. Was it in the *T.L.S.* that I read a really first-class review of the book, and do you know who wrote it? Out of sight more understanding than any other I have seen. I think you will have to read Christopher Hollis's history of Eton, just out. As he says, much of it is based on Maxwell Lyte,[1] but M.L. had nothing about the last 96 years, and, even on ground common to both, H. is much the livelier. How Eton survived rapacious and hostile kings, the ineptitude and brutality of some of her headmasters, and her own fantastic and ridiculous ways down the centuries, is a mystery just as 'spirit-searching, light-abandoned' as any mentioned by the literary ladies of America to Martin Chuzzlewit. Hollis is excellent on my uncle Edward. The book is dedicated, if you please, to *me*—odd that the only error I found in a proof he sent me has been left uncorrected, viz that E.L. captained the last Cambridge side to beat the Australians, when of course everyone knows they did so again in 1882 —after which one of their genial toughs said to a Cambridge man: 'In

[1] Sir Henry Churchill Maxwell Lyte (1848–1940), deputy keeper of the public records, published in 1875 *A History of Eton College 1440–1875*.

future you'll only have to hold up a light-blue cap and we'll run'. They have never run since.

The only other Australian dictum I know is, I think, Noble's (as good a judge of the game as ever was) after playing v. the Universities, that Oxford were so superior that it really was a pity the match should be played. The match was won by Cambridge (experts again!).

Thursday.

Well, so *Lady C.* won. The judge, surely, really summed up against it, but the jury, as I thought they would be, were either intimidated by that highbrow phalanx, or resolved to show that they were as jolly broad-minded as anyone. And I remain in (I suppose) a small minority —with however the brother and nephew of D.H.L. (his sister hails the verdict with rapture, but her face in the *Daily Telegraph* rouses a strong suspicion of insanity). I see that lofty moralist Sir Allen Lane hopes to publish a further 300,000—making half-a-million. What an unsuspected love of culture the public are showing! It is all very odd. And now we shall see what we shall see. I shall be surprised if we like it much.

Love to R. of course. See you both on Wed. *Lady C.* shall not be mentioned!

6 November 1960   *Bromsden Farm*

I got here exhausted late last night, so didn't read your letter till this morning. Don't be depressed about *Lady C.* See the last words of the full-page review in the *T.L.S.*: 'Young persons of either sex are the last out of whose hands anybody should think of keeping this book. The worst it could do to them would be to make them a little over-solemn'. See also Levin in the *Spectator*, and a splendid article by Ken Tynan in today's *Observer*. Anyhow that beastly Archbishop is on your side!

As you surmised, I was told on Monday morning that I wouldn't after all be called, so Ruth and I spent the morning in court as spectators and then went back to work. Everyone seems agreed that Richard Hoggart was the star-witness. I honestly don't foresee any evil consequences to this trial: pornography can still be prosecuted, and if a wedge has been driven between it and literature, as I think, *tant mieux*.

On Monday night Ruth and I were taken to *The Playboy of the Western World*, which I last saw in Dublin thirty years ago. I enjoyed it all over again, but shan't mind if I don't see it again for some time. By the end of the evening that poetic idiom of speech begins to sound like a trick, which is only *just* strong enough to support the Irish-whimsy anecdote. On Tuesday, agog, we go to *The Importance of Being Oscar*.[1]

Adam is home for Long Leave. He reports South Meadow totally flooded and Bud Hill's (once Piggy Hill's) garden awash. I was asked to review Hollis's *Eton* for the *T.L.S.*, but simply hadn't the time. Had I known that it is dedicated to you, I should have felt obliged to squeeze it in somehow.

I can't think why you haven't had *Hired to Kill*: it shall set off to waterlogged Suffolk tomorrow. The *T.L.S.* review of Diana was written by Alan Pryce-Jones: naturally it delighted Diana, as it did you and me.

Now for my journey. Ruth saw me off at Victoria at 9.30 a.m. on Thursday. A gale was raging in the Channel, but with the aid of two Kwells pills and a large brandy-and-soda I survived unsick in an arm-chair in the bar, and was able to do full justice to a wildly expensive but wholly delicious lunch on the Paris train. Altogether I ate five huge meals (four on trains and one at Rapallo), each of five courses and a half-bottle of wine, and felt all the better for it. I got to Paris at 5 p.m. (6 p.m. by French time), transferred my bags to the Rome Express, and strolled round the Gare du Nord till 7. A superb dinner (soup, a trout cooked with almonds, chicken, cheese and ice-cream), an hour's work on Oscar and a pretty good night in my sleeper. Got out at Rapallo at 10 a.m. A grey day, no sun but warm and dry. The little town put on all it knew for my benefit: first a fine funeral with purple-robed priests and much ornament, then banners bridging every street in honour of forthcoming elections: VOTA COMMUNISTA, DEMOCRAZIA CRISTIANA and so on. I had scarcely had a bath and

---

[1] A one-man performance by Micheál MacLiammóir, Irish actor, writer, painter and linguist (1899–1978).

changed when, right outside my window on the sea (by which open horse-carriages ply for hire under the palm-trees) an Armistice Day procession (the Italian armistice with Austria was on 4 November 1918) marched up with wreaths, bands, veterans and much fancy dress. Half an hour later when I went out for a walk I saw them all returning in a huge motor-boat—where from? I had some delicious coffee in a café, made a few purchases, and then worked on Oscar in my very comfortable hotel-room until 1.30, when I descended for the luncheon-party, twenty-two strong, given for the Ambassador (Ashley Clarke) by the Consul General from Genoa. I was between the retired C.G. (a Scotswoman called Fowler) and a writer called Cecil Roberts, a tolerably agreeable old queer. The lunch was Italian—shellfish (assorted), ravioli, *fritto misto* of local fish (so good that I had a second helping), excellent cheese and a fine chestnut pudding. Local wines, white and red. At 3 p.m. we were conveyed in three cars to the Villino, where a small crowd was waiting. As the Ambassador's Rolls pulled up opposite the house, the police stopped the traffic both ways on the narrow steep crowded road. The local mayor read out a speech in Italian, which I naturally couldn't understand. Then H.E. spoke (also in Italian) about Max, and I could follow most of it. By the time he pulled the cord which released British and Italian flags from the plaque, the traffic-jam stretched for several miles in both directions, with every horn hooting. Nevertheless there was just time for a last look at the terrace and garden, all very desolate and wintry, with house and study shuttered. Ichabod! As I was driven back to my hotel, infuriated motorists were still hooting, bumper to bumper, for miles.

I then had a nap and worked on Oscar till it was time to catch the Rome Express at 7 p.m. Another good dinner (Italian—the restaurant-car changes over at the frontier), more Oscar and another goodish night. At 8.30 a.m. yesterday I had *brioche* and *café-au-lait* in the dining-car and then settled down to a couple of hours of Oscar while the train first waited in the Gare de Lyon and then trundled round the *ceinture* to the Gard du Nord. Altogether I corrected more than a hundred galley-pages of Oscar, the longest consecutive stretch I've managed since Kisdon.

After putting my things in the Calais train I had an agreeable hour strolling round in the sun, examining a bookshop and having a drink in a café. A last delicious lunch on the Calais train, a smooth crossing, tea in the London train, a blissful reunion with Ruth at Soho Square, and down here by the 9.30 p.m. train. The whole thing was rather fun, and any guilty feelings of truancy were obliterated by such splendid progress with Oscar. Another such journey or two, and the back of the work would be broken!

The Heinemann business is dragging on, but there's little more I can do, so I refuse to let it worry me. My old father has now left the London Clinic and is back in his flat with day and night nurses in attendance, but my sister and I simply don't know what to try and arrange for his future. He has no constructive idea of any kind.

13 November 1960   *Bromsden Farm*

No letter this week, as arranged, but here, instead, is a one-question exam-paper. *Who* wrote this and *when*?

If I am right it will be a slow business for our people to reach rational views, assuming that we are allowed to work peacefully to that end. But as I grow older I grow calm. If I feel what are perhaps an old man's apprehensions, that competition from new races will cut deeper than working men's disputes and will test whether we can hang together and can fight; if I fear that we are running through the world's resources at a pace that we cannot keep; I do not lose my hopes. I do not pin my dreams for the future to my country or even to my race. I think it probable that civilization somehow will last as long as I care to look ahead—perhaps with smaller numbers, but perhaps also bred to greatness and splendour by science. I think it not improbable that man, like the grub that prepares a chamber for the winged thing it never has seen but is to be—that man may have cosmic destinies that he does not understand. And so beyond the vision of battling races and an impoverished earth I catch a dreaming glimpse of peace.

The other day my dream was pictured to my mind. I was walking homeward on Pennsylvania Avenue near the Treasury, and as I looked beyond Sherman's Statue to the west the sky was aflame with scarlet and crimson from the setting sun. But, like the note of downfall in Wagner's opera, below the skyline there came from little globes the pallid discord of the electric lights. And I thought to myself the *Götterdämmerung* will end, and from those globes clustered like evil eggs will come the new masters of the sky. It is like the time in which we live. But then I remembered the faith that I partly have expressed, faith in a universe not measured by our fears, a universe that has thought and more than thought inside of it, and as I gazed, after the sunset and above the electric lights, there shone the stars.

You shall have the answer next week.

16 November 1960   *Grundisburgh*

Thank you for that very fine passage. It might well have been written by Judge Holmes, a very great man. In his letters there is often that deep bourdon note—he often looks at things *sub specie aeternitatis*, but not, of course, usually for as long a spell as this. Tell me all about it next week. G.K.C. sometimes strikes this note, e.g. in the account of the Battle of the Marne, Shaw never except in one tiny sentence about Ellen Terry. There was of course something rather shallow about him. He saw and knew that some Shakespeare passages were tremendous, but I don't think he *felt* them.

Hired to Kill has arrived and I start it to-night. What a memory you have for kind actions—I mean for *doing* them.

I have just been to the oculist—five guineas and new bi-focals which will cost about £10. Am trying a hearing-aid which is modestly priced at £63. I hear with it everything I don't want to hear much more clearly, voices only a little. Last Sunday I wore it till the first hymn in which the organ, plus a handful of now stentorian voices, nearly blew me from my seat. On the whole I hate it, but whether I shall be brave enough to tell Mr Plume so on Saturday, I gravely doubt. But £63!

I had a good crack with Roger and then Jonah on Wednesday, and Ivor Brown joined us. Lift home with R. and Roy Jenkins, clearly an excellent chap. How bad of Betjeman to shirk and leave an empty place next to his old tutor. Old Cuthbert was merely one protracted smile; I think being next to the most distinguished guest pleased him. Very natural.

I am writing 500-word biographies of sixteenth- and seventeenth-century literary men for Dick Routh. How *devilish* difficult it is to be brief and not dull. I told every new division at Eton of Wellington's apology for the length of his despatches from Spain: 'I had not time to make them shorter', which I suspect may be as *'crambe repetita'*[1] to you as Habakkuk. But there it is. I am sure Johnson has somewhere a majestic defence of repeated stories etc, but all I remember is a rather slighting reference to it as a habit of Swift. But he hated Swift and was as unfair about him as—comparing small with great—I am about Lawrence. Levin, by the way, begged too many questions; it is a little schoolboyish to overpraise all who take one view and sneer at all who take the opposite one. How hard our journalists find it to make *balanced* comment.

I suppose you don't yet loathe the winter as much as I do—more every year. It rains every night—not very much but enough to keep everything dank. Indoors is pleasant of course and would be even more so if coal cost the pound a ton that it used to. But let us count our blessings. Books are much easier to handle, print is better, and e.g. the Pastoral Symphony, now playing on a long record, is better than my aunt Sybil's piano-playing and Jack Talbot's throaty rendering of Maude Valerie White's 'Devout Lover'—'It is not mine to sing the stately grace, The great soul beaming in my lady's face' etc. The second line rather puts the lady with Mrs Wititterley who, you remember, suffered from being 'all soul'.[2]

Have you read Hollis's *Eton* yet? It is in many ways very good but a bit uneven, and oddly careless in places. Anyone who writes of Eton should not call *Wasey* Sterry *Walter*, or write *'on* the bill' instead of *'in* the bill'. I am glad he pillories Dr Goodall simply as 'that wicked man'. He wouldn't have *anything* changed, though he knew perfectly well that the conditions in College were sheer disgrace and that the Fellows were barefaced robbers. Eton in the first half of the nineteenth century was a ridiculously bad school. I can't think how it survived. I am glad too that Hollis—not *too* strongly—shows up the snobbish

[1] 'Cabbage hashed and rehashed.' Juvenal *Satires*, vii, 154.
[2] In *Nicholas Nickleby*.

arrogance of Julian Grenfell and co at Oxford; they were as bad as the segregationists of Louisiana and Milton's 'sons of Belial flown with insolence and wine'. Eddie Marsh loved them, but also hints at this unlovable trait in his autobiography. Still there remains 'The naked earth . . .'[1] and their deaths. *Per contra* Sir Philip Sidney wrote 'With how sad steps . . .' and 'Fool said my Muse; look in thy heart and write', and was loved by *everybody*. Would Julian Grenfell have given his water-bottle to a wounded Philip Sassoon? Did you know that Sidney, going into battle with a friend, found that the friend had left off some of his armour, and Sidney, therefore, doffed his own greaves that he should be at no advantage. So he was hit in the leg and subsequently died. Pamela's comment on this ultra-Quixotic heroism was, 'I think he must have been a bit dotty'. *We*, my dear Rupert, are the romantics. Women are delightfully matter-of-fact. Will dear Ruth corroborate this?

We shall see you this day week; we go to Diana's on Friday. I believe you will meet my two favourite nieces, both very good fun. Lavinia Dénnys has the most impregnable derision for the game of cricket, thereby, considering the age-long atmosphere of Hagley, showing a considerable strength of mind. She was in the W.A.A.F.'s or A.T.S. in the war, and you cannot tell *her* anything she doesn't know about words of many letters or few. And the knowledge never did her a moment's harm (one for you and *Lady C.*!). The other, Anne Riddell, helped to run the Oxford University Registry and then, I gather, completely ran the University of Khartoum. Unmarried and apparently quite content. I accused her once of misanthropy. She denied this warmly, but added that the trouble was that all the men she most liked were middle-aged and happily married. That was at Oxford. In Khartoum she says that on the whole the Egyptian young men she meets are more civilised, intelligent, courteous, and generally nicer than the British—but you can't marry an Egyptian. So what?

[1] In Julian Grenfell's poem 'Into Battle'.

Sorry this paper has turned blue: it was the only colour Ruth could find. Full marks for your test-question. Those words *were* by Judge Holmes, and the astonishing thing is that they were spoken at a Harvard Law School dinner in New York on 15 February *1913*. Look at them again, and marvel at the old boy's foresight and perspicacity. When you've got your new spectacles and a £63 hearing-aid, there'll be no more mobbing in div.[1]

I fear T.S.E. will haunt the Lit. Soc. no more, after an evening with Cuthbert on one side and vacancy on the other. Leslie Hartley sent an abject apology next day, but Betjeman has made no sign. I now think I should have bullied you or Ivor into moving over to the other side of the table, but I couldn't believe that *two* people would default without notice. Jonah was in goodish form: you should have discussed *Lady C.* with him, for he seemed to share your views. I am in the middle of correcting the proofs of his stories, which read a little better in print (most things do), but are unlikely to set the smallest stream on fire, I fear.

The Duke of Wellington's admirable remark about brevity in writing was quite new to me—so there! And I'm prepared to bet that I *do* hate the winter as much as you do. Hibernation or Jamaica seem the only tolerable cures. I haven't yet read Hollis's *Eton*, and don't know who took my place as *T.L.S.* reviewer. If you haven't already done so, *do* write Frank Swinnerton a fan-letter. He's a pet, and his address is *Old Tokefield, Cranleigh, Surrey.*

You seem to think Diana's dinner-party is on Wednesday, but I have *Thursday* down in my book. I much look forward to meeting your favourite nieces, cricketing or otherwise.

Last Tuesday I attended the sixtieth birthday celebrations of my old friend Hamish Hamilton, the publisher, who first insinuated me into the lamentable trade. The proceedings began with a gala performance of *Romeo and Juliet* at the Old Vic, which I thoroughly enjoyed. Wonderful scenery, and every word audible—and *what* words! I know the play so well that I was outraged by a number of pointless cuts, and the Mercutio ruined the Queen Mab speech by trying to

[1] i.e. ragging in school.

make it funny instead of allowing the poetry to carry it through, but on the whole it was pure pleasure.

Then back to the Hamiltons' house in St John's Wood, where at midnight we sat down eleven strong to a sumptuous dinner (bortsch, pheasant, and a superb Italian sweet—Mrs H. is Italian—good white and red wine, champagne and brandy). I was blissfully placed between Lady Drogheda (an angel and old friend) and no less a person than the Duchess of Kent, for whom I fell hook, line and sinker. Very attractive, intelligent, charming and cultivated. Her sister, Princess Paul of Yugoslavia, to whom I talked after dinner, is another charmer. She speaks countless languages, including Yugoslav and Swahili. I said 'I'm sure your sister can't speak them', and she said 'But, you see, she's much younger than me', which I thought delightful. Altogether the evening, which I had been dreading for weeks, was pure joy.

I had sent my host, as a birthday present, a fountain pen, which I knew he wanted, and in an accompanying note I described him as 'just the man to put the sex into sexagenarian', which seemed to please him.

How soon is your *Times* cast away? Duff had an article in last Thursday's (November 17) on the court page, anonymous and called 'Mysterious Altercation'. Do look at it. He is now film critic of the *Western Mail*, has had two articles on Welsh spas accepted for the leader page, and is to broadcast from Cardiff!

26 November 1960   *Bromsden Farm*

Habit dies hard, but this won't be a letter, just a tiny snack between meals. And talking of meals, that was a delightful dinner at Diana's, and I was so happy to be between her and Pamela. I thought your two nieces charming, and only wished I had had more opportunity of talking to the married one. The male American must surely be one of the stupidest men at liberty? He seemed to be suffering from concussion, I thought.

On the way to dinner I had paid a brief visit to my old father, and couldn't help being moved by the pathos and irony of two excellent women (nurse and physiotherapist) *forcing* the old boy to walk again, when he has nowhere to walk to, and no desire to move.

Adam has just rung up to say he will be home for next week-end, on his way to his scholarship-exam at Oxford, and that he will be bringing a boy called Fitzhugh with him. It could scarcely be less convenient, as Comfort will have all her own exam-papers to correct.

I am once again deep in Oscar, pausing only to read through the *Satires* of Juvenal in search of a quotation (if I ever achieve retirement I shall try to regain a little Latin through the excellent Loeb Classical Library) or to seek for French Anarchists in the *Encyclopaedia Britannica*. Jonah's proofs must be finished by Monday, but I have had enough of those stories. I am reading countless books (mostly bad) about the 1890s, and am slowly coming to know quite a lot about that maligned decade.

The oak-tree in front of this window is still clinging to some of its leaves, and there are almost always a couple of cock-pheasants eating underneath it: do they particularly like acorns? The nuthatches are back at the bird-table, but today they gave place to a spotted woodpecker. The world is so full of a number of things . . .

I should have liked to attend D. Somervell's funeral, but it was in the country and I couldn't, as they say, make it.

St Andrew's Day 1960   *Grundisburgh*

Thank God I am not playing at the Wall to-day. It is anyhow an immensely absurd game, but in mud—well, there aren't any adjectives. Glance at Hollis's *Eton*, where there is a picture of it—in mud!—which in a sane society would kill it. But then of course a sane society would kill county and test cricket too. And if it comes to that a *perfectly* sane man wouldn't have written to me last Sunday. On the whole I am glad we *don't* live in a completely sane world—partly of course because that is what E. Summerskill and others of her kidney would like (how nauseating to think of E.S.'s kidney!).

I knew you would like whichever niece you had a crack with. Alexander and Diana always like *large* parties. The American mainly talked finance with Alexander. I gave him a widish berth. We saw

Anne Riddell again on Sunday. She confided to us that R.H-D. was simply 'it'. I knew she would. Of course she ought to be married—she is thirty-five, *but* I live in hope. Diana married at thirty-seven, and nothing can be happier than *that*.

Your old father. Yes, there is something immensely pitiful about old age when, basically, the wish is to be left to pass quietly away—but they never let one do that—excepting of course such benefactors as good Dr Bodkin Adams (bad luck for him that he should have the *face* of a murderer!).

We called on the Cranworths yesterday. He has (*aetat* eighty-three) also taken to a hearing-aid—of the type that *my* good man said was *not* now regarded as satisfactory. He doesn't like it (Lord C.) any more than I do mine, but I handed on, to his comfort, the unanimous testimony to the good results of use and patience. At present if anyone drops a pen I am deafened by the din, but hear much less well the human voice. However *my* comfort is that Pamela definitely says she no longer 'has to bellow like a bull' (wives *do* exaggerate you know) at our *tête-à-tête* meals, so all is not lost. Poor old Cranworth seemed to me to hear no better than before (such was his belief too) but I fear that often his brain was not taking much in. There would surely be literally nothing to be said against euthanasia if it wasn't for nears and dears. I like the story of the old Roman who lay in a hot bath with a vein open, chatting with his friends, and plugged the vein whenever the talk was interesting, and removed it when the interest faded. The Yank's talk you met at the Hoods' would have led to no plugging of *your* veins, I opine (such a good word. I haven't used it for years).

I had an excellent evening with Jonah *tête-à-tête*—a delicious dinner which he said was *exactly* the same as the one he gave you—just as it should be. I can never see that the old boy is at all a bore, as I believe some still find him. He was full of good observations—humorous, pertinent, percipient. His deep affection for the Lit. Soc. is very pleasant.

Do you ever dine at *Prunier's*? That is where Alexander took us on his cook's night-off. Marvellous food, and gosh! the fistful of notes which A. disbursed at the end. If he was anyone else, how abashed we should feel at the fare he gets here—e.g. soup, scrambled eggs and cheese—but he takes it in his placid and amiable stride.

I have just been listening to Mahler's Second Symphony on the radio—did you hear it? I enjoyed it enormously, and all the more in contrast to Alban Berg's opera *Wozzeck*, which I heard last night at Covent Garden. It is based on a German Expressionist play (someone in the interval said it was like *Carmen* written by Freud) and is written in what I believe is called atonal music. To a non-musical novice this seems like a free-for-all in the orchestra-pit, with distressing results. Nevertheless I found it all interesting, and the Droghedas' box (which is really two boxes) is attached to a private dining-room in which an excellent dinner is served *seriatim* during the intervals. The French Ambassador was of the party but consumed only a glass of water.

On Thursday I was summoned to a drink at Kensington Palace, to tell Princess Alexandra the drill for the Duff Cooper Prize, which she is to bestow next Wednesday. I thought her enchanting—infinitely easy to talk to, intelligent, and very attractive, with pale chestnut hair and a lovely skin. Her photographers don't do her justice. The Duchess of Kent was there, and their nice secretary Philip Hay—all very enjoyable.

On Wednesday I went to Cambridge and spent the night with Madeline House. We both dined with Graham Storey in his rooms in Trinity Hall and talked about the Dickens Letters, which they are jointly editing.

On Monday (sorry to work backwards so relentlessly) I dined very cosily with Joyce Grenfell and her husband (very old friends) in their flat. Joyce has promised to write a book (autobiographical) for me to publish.

Yesterday, before the opera, I had a feverish two-hour session on the Oscar proofs with the excellent Henry Maas, who is helping enormously.

Adam is home, en route for Oxford, and is even now playing bridge with Comfort, his friend Fitzhugh, and a neighbour. His Second Five side was beaten in the final, but he still has a chance of getting his House Colours, since Fred's are in the final of the House Cup, and their regular Goals is a doubtful starter. A. is in the semi-final of the Chess Cup.

Duff may have the chance of a job on the new *Sunday Telegraph* in London in February. He saw the editor in London yesterday and will know the result on Monday. If he gets it, he will speedily get married, and since Bridget looks like getting her chap to the altar in August, I shall spend next year in and out of Moss Bros.

Jonah's proofs are still with me. I went through them with him on Thursday, but his writing is so illegible that I must transfer all the corrections on to a clean set of proofs before sending them back to the printer.

I wonder how your deaf-aid responded to Gilbert and Sullivan. I'm sure you ought to persevere with it, and I assure you it doesn't *show* at all.

I have only once or twice flown as high as Prunier's, when it was quite first-rate.

On Monday Ruth and I are giving the Eliots dinner at the Garrick, on Tuesday we trek to Twickenham for The Match, and afterwards dine with Max's sister-in-law. Wednesday is the Prize-giving—and so it goes on.

I read nothing but memoirs of the 80's and 90's, though I have ordered Betjeman.[1] The wind is wailing, the rain lashing. I shan't go out tomorrow if I can help it. The library is warm and cosy. Please give my love to Pamela—and to yourself.

7 December 1960   *Grundisburgh*

I like paper which turns blue—light blue of course, which reminds me that you saw a fine Cambridge victory at Twitnam. My blood-thirsty soul wishes they had topped twenty points in the second half. They seem to have been a pretty hot side. Scotland of course is a bit of a genius; the first try reads finely in both *Times* and *Telegraph*. (I see the blue paper was your November 19 letter: I am an incurable leaver-about.)

Mahler. You are, *pace* your declaration, a higher-browed music-lover than I—but I don't really know Mahler and didn't hear his symphony. Encouraged by you I will try him next time he is on. I

[1] *Summoned By Bells* (1960).

178

have heard a bit of *Wozzeck*, and like the stuffiest of Victorians (which I fundamentally am) I find it hard to believe anyone who says he enjoys it. I would as soon listen to the road-drillers (who I see have been afflicting Dame Edith Sitwell). 'Atonal' frankly means 'cacophonous'. I wonder what 'interested' you in it. My tastes are very mild and old-fashioned. I don't really stretch much above Beethoven's Pastoral Symphony. Summing up, I enjoy quite a lot, but I don't think I understand very much. You can probably follow the plan of a symphony and have a notion of its structure. I don't and haven't. Drogheda's box sounds all right, but really the French Ambassador and his glass of water! Like Edward VIII when Prince of Wales being lunched by the Harlech golf-club, which scoured the principality for viands and vintages—and he asked for rice-pudding and lime-juice, neither of which they had. But that was either bad manners, or bad organisation by his major-domo. However we were still eating the lunch meant for him weeks afterwards, so good came out of evil.

Did you realise that Reggie Grenfell was a cousin of mine—and also a pupil at Eton? I have never heard you mention him. I have met Joyce only once or twice, and—like everybody else—liked her immensely. Keep her up to that book. Where is their flat? I must call on them.

The news of your family sounds good. I suppose A. has the Chess Cup in his pocket—or is there some morbid K.S. who has played since he was two? Duff seems to have his foot firmly on the ladder. Are you happy about his marrying so young? There is no general rule about such things. Circumstances alter cases. But the chap who said 'A young man married is a young man marred' wasn't talking 100% rubbish. I still have wedding-garments—about thirty years out of fashion, and as a brilliant daughter put it, more Moth Bros than Moss ditto—and relish the feeling that I shall never wear them again; I would give them to Humphrey, if he ever wore anything but sacking.

We will aim at a Monday for our annual—and invariably delightful —luncheon *chez vous*. The mud round about you will not actually engulf us I, presume? My exam-papers start piling up on Saturday and I must miss the Lit. Soc. next week. Please tell me all about it. Jonah's writing is baffling, though I know worse. I have no sympathy with the really illegible, though I suppose some cannot really help it, however hard that is to believe.

We went to *The Mikado* last week, myself well furnished with hearing-aid, which, *more suo*, was fairly good at the voices but made the trombone etc deafening. But I shall, they tell me, learn to discriminate.

Talking of criticism, how bad Sir Charles Petrie is in the *Illustrated London News* on Behrman's Max book. Who *is* Sir C.P. and why should anyone suppose he is capable of appreciating Max? He says that M.B. liked the Paddington Hotel perhaps because a royalty died in it. Evidence? I hate writing like that, and so many indulge in it.

I have just written biographies of Spenser, Sidney and Marlowe for some venture of Dick Routh's. To get any of 'em into 550 words and be interesting—well how the devil is it done? I wonder if I have sufficiently concealed my opinion that *The Faery Queene* is unreadable. Columbia University in their rather disgraceful plebiscite on 'the ten most boring classics' had it second to *Pilgrim's Progress*. *Paradise Lost* was third or fourth and later in the list came *Silas Marner*, *Ivanhoe*, and *Boswell's Life of Johnson*!! All of which makes me very dubious about alliance with America in spite of Abe Lincoln and Stonewall Jackson— oh yes and *certainly* Judge Holmes, as great as any. I must go and hew wood, but *not*, you will be surprised to hear, draw water. Really the rain!

Love to Ruth. You didn't send me hers in your last letter. I grieve —but understand!

10 December 1960   *Bromsden Farm*

This afternoon I drove through snow and icy wind to Oxford and fetched home Adam after his week of scholarship-papers. To-morrow he returns for two interviews, and on Monday a Chemistry Practical (how many marks should *we* score in that, dear George?), so we should know the result pretty soon. He thinks he did pretty well, but we shall see. It is now certain that he is to play in the final of the House Cup on Wednesday, so his House Colours seem assured. The Chess Cup is still in the semi-final stage, but Friday is the beginning of the holidays.

Duff has apparently heard no more of his London job: at least we've heard nothing from *him*.

I certainly can't follow the plan of a symphony or any other musical work, but I can get lots of pleasure out of it. Do try Mahler: he is very lyrical and romantic, and several of his symphonies introduce singers. He is nothing like *Wozzeck*. Nor is Sibelius, that doom-laden Finn, whose Second Symphony I enjoyed this evening. Try him again too.

I certainly didn't realise that Reggie Grenfell was a cousin of yours, though from his niceness I might have guessed. Their address is Flat 8, 34 Elm Park Gardens. It's between the Fulham and King's Roads and would be handy from Chelsea Square. Reggie and Joyce have been dear friends since 1927, though I don't see them as often as I'd like.

Duff's marriage? Since I was first married at twenty-two, and again at twenty-six, I am not in a strong position to tell him he is too young at twenty-four and a half. In any case marriage is surely partly a matter of luck—whether you grow at the same pace in the same direction, and things like that—and, though wisdom of a sort comes with age, luck is impartial.

Sir Charles Petrie is a bearded DUD. On no account read anything he writes. I'm sure Max stayed at railway hotels because (1) they were comfortable (2) he was unlikely to be bothered by anybody he knew (3) the child in him responded to the romance of trains leaving for distant places.

I shall attend the Max Beerbohm sale at Sotheby's on Monday, Tuesday and Wednesday, and have agreed to be interviewed by the B.B.C. Television on Monday morning, though goodness knows what I'm supposed to say. Last week Ruth and I spent two lunch-times examining the stuff that is to be sold—and we did a lot of other things too.

On Monday we finally penetrated the fastnesses of the Home Office and were allowed to examine and check Oscar's prison-petitions and other documents—very interesting and touching. That evening we dined very agreeably with the Eliots at the Garrick. T.S.E. seemed unmoved by his exposure to Cuthbert, and was altogether more robust than he was in the summer, though his lungs and heart (his wife told me privately) are still as dicky as could be, so that he might pop off at any moment.

On Tuesday the rain miraculously held off for Twickenham, and our corner seats turned out splendidly, for all the scoring—and

Dawkins's terrific last-minute efforts for Oxford—took place right in front of us. Cambridge were infinitely superior, and the great Sharp was made to look paralytic.

That night we had a terrific German dinner with Elisabeth Beerbohm's sister and brother-in-law—a wonderful fish-dish of sole in a sort of bun, flooded with a delicious sauce of lobster and shrimps; very good pheasant with sour cream sauce, cherry jam, potatoes and sauerkraut; a superb almond cream sweet, and a heavenly Riesling (two bottles among four). We both felt stupefied afterwards but thoroughly enjoyed it all.

On Wednesday was the unveiling of the Duff Cooper plaque in the crypt of St Paul's—very well handled by the Dean and Harold Nicolson. On in a hired car to Hyde Park Gate, where Princess Alexandra very charmingly gave the Duff Cooper Prize to my poet Andrew Young.

From your silence about *Hired to Kill* I imagine you hated it.

Oh yes—in one of George Moore's books Max wrote:

ELEGY ON ANY LADY
by G.M.

That she adored me as the most
Adorable of males
I think I may securely boast . . .
Dead women tell no tales.

Max's books are full of delicious little *jeux* like that. I only wish I could afford to buy a few, but I expect they'll fetch thousands.

14 December 1960   *Grundisburgh*

It has rained all day. The glass is rather high, the forecast said there was an anti-cyclone over England. Such are the facts. I make no comment or complaint; only an occasional question like Sam Weller's crosses my mind, 'Ain't somebody going to be whipped for this 'ere?' Incidentally this is the driest region in England.

Your letter arrived yesterday just as I was going into Ipswich—in a black tie, of course, as no doubt you were, it being the day of the month on which Dr Johnson died. Quite a good day to choose. I always thought the period between St Andrew's Day and Christmas Day the gloomiest stretch of the year. Pitch-dark, dank, thoroughly sulky, no character. But don't forget next Saturday p.m. is *one* minute longer than it was last Saturday.

I expect you may have had news of Adam's venture by now. I do hope it was successful. You are right about my knowledge of chemistry. One thing alone I retain from Tubby Porter, viz that 'a body immersed in liquid loses in weight the weight of the liquid displaced'. I have found it most useful in life. For the rest I am incurably non-scientific, and full of pro-humanity saws like Dr J's 'We are perpetually moralists, but we are geometricians only by chance'.[1]

Anyway warmest congratulations to him on his House Colours. Let us hope he won't emulate the boy spoken of by a preacher at Eton (oh yes, *Crum*). The boy's *one* ambition was to play goals for his house in the final, and so after many vicissitudes he did—the day of his life. All his family came to watch and hoped he would distinguish himself. And so he did—by putting the ball through his own goal.

Stupid of me not to have looked up the Grenfells before. I somehow thought they didn't live in London. Her father Paul Phipps was a delightful man. I remember a nice simple witticism of his. My sister on the way to church with large party said: 'I do hope the hymn books won't run out'. To which P.P. said 'If they do, I'll run after them'.

I love asking you about X. and Y. Your replies are so direct and have an air of rightness—no doubt partly because they so often corroborate a suspicion of my own. I pay no more attention to the bearded Dud. Max's sale seems to have made a mort of money. I hope you are pleased? I have a feeling that the *sneerers* are soon to have a go at him—as they will too at Betjeman.

What did you say on TV? The hour is surely nearing when we shall have to get a TV. Not *quite* yet. Sixty guineas for a hearing-aid and a cool million on the roof has temporarily put me back a bit.

I am interested in your saying Sharp was obliterated in the O. and C. match. It proves that though in the first class he is not yet at its

[1] *Life of Milton.*

top. You couldn't obliterate Stoop or Monro or Davies in old days. Like Hitler's their motto was '*So—oder so*', i.e. 'If not in this way, then in that'. But someone told me weeks ago that the Cambridge forwards were tremendous.

I have been reading *The Duke's Children*. I forget whether you are a Trollope fan. I love him—and am maddened by him. The snobbery thick—a slab of the times and circles he wrote about, and those infuriatingly virginal young women. They all need a soupçon of *Lady C.*! Apropos of which I see Sir Allen Lane, contemplating the sales of one and a half million of 'em, expressed distress that many people had bought them from the wrong motives! I suppose that the tiniest whisper of 'humbug' would have made R. West, Joan Bennett, that bishop, K. Tynan, B. Levin (and R.H-D.?) red with indignation??

Oh dear, I thought I had told you how much I liked *Hired to Kill* at least a fortnight ago—and certainly Young's poems two months ago. Forgive apparent gracelessness. But *H to K* also humiliated me— not that I didn't know it already—by proving what a rotten critic I am. I liked the book very much, but couldn't for the life of me say why. The only silver lining was that a good many of the reviewers suffered from the same disability. He is a delightfully *honest* writer. Perhaps honesty is as rare in literature as in life.

How good you are about menus. I share your gulosity at secondhand. That embunned sole and its sauce! It added a relish to Pamela's kedgeree, which, I may say, is by no means to be despised.

Thank you for M.B. on G. Moore. Delicious. I should like to see his jottings on A.C. Benson's *Beside Still Waters*, one of those sweet spinsterish books he used to pour out like Tupper.[1] I have heard M.B.'s parody of A.C.B. in *A Christmas Garland* called very cruel, but that seems to me rot. The smallest exaggeration made A.C.B.'s stuff *wholly* absurd. Was that M.B.'s fault? But he was wrong about Kipling. I suppose his nausea at K's bounce and noise and vulgarity blinded him to the tremendous merits of K's best.

---

[1] Martin Tupper, poet and inventor (1810–1889). His versified *Proverbial Philosophy* sold many editions.

Ten million cheers! I haven't been so pleased for years! I have sent Adam congratulations, but doubt if they will get to him till Monday. I should have rung you up, but for believing that Friday sees you *en route* for B.F. It really is quite splendid.

This has been an exciting week. On Tuesday night we heard (as you have probably since read) that Adam had been awarded an Open Scholarship (or, as they call it, Postmastership) at Merton, having apparently been placed top of all the scientific candidates! Much jubilation at Eton, as you can imagine.

Next day A. played (as substitute Goals) in the final of the House Cup, the only player on either side in a white shirt. It was *bitterly* cold, with ankle-deep mud. I went down by train to Slough, thence by taxi. It was an exciting fast game, but I walked round a good bit, trying to keep warm, and talked to the Coleridges, the Headmaster, Van Oss, and one or two friends (Kenneth Wagg, Michael Astor) who had boys engaged. Two-all at full time. Ten minutes extra each way. Still two-all. Darkness falling rapidly. After a lengthy consultation in midfield they agreed to play five more minutes each way. After some three minutes a boy called Perkins got the ball through Snow's goal, and Coleridge's had won for the first time, after four previous failures in the final (including Duff's year). Adam was given his House Colours on the field, and I almost wept with pride and joy. He hadn't had much to do (having Lumley, the Field Long, in front of him), but he did it adequately. I wonder if he'll ever have two such exciting days again?

Meanwhile Duff has finally clinched the job on the new *Sunday Telegraph* in London, and is to start work there on January 9 at £18. 10. a week. This means he can get married, since his girl (Phyllida Barstow) already has a similar job in London. Easter week is being considered as a suitable time. The wedding will be at her home in Wales. When they all arrived this morning (after a dance in London last night) we cracked a bottle of champagne in general congratulation. (Adam is in the final of the Chess Cup—to be played off next half.)

The Beerbohm sale was fun, with high prices. My television interview about Max was conducted at Sotheby's at 10 a.m. in riotous confusion, and was shown in the news at 10 p.m.—not, thank goodness, to me.

Ruth had a beastly cold and cough on Monday, so I put her to bed in the spare room in the flat and nursed her whenever I could. She slept a lot and went home yesterday much rested and improved.

The Lit. Soc. was ruined for me by that ghastly Lockhart, who sat (as usual) next to me, with (as usual) an empty chair on his other side, and talked of the sales-figures of his own books. We had fillets of sole, saddle of mutton and vanilla soufflé *or* mushrooms on toast. All quite good.

I say, what about that Test Match in Australia! If only that tempo and spirit could be preserved into 1961! I think Sharp's chief trouble in the U.M. was that his scrum-half was so slow in getting the ball to him, and the Cambridge forwards were so quick, that they were always on top of him before he could pass or even kick.

Adam is to spend his last two halves doing German and French with Van Oss. Since he will be in Sixth Form and will presumably have no exams, he should have a good time. At the moment he is concerned only with his Driving Test, which takes place on Thursday. Sorry there's so much family in this letter, but it has been rather a family week. I have done *nothing* so far about Christmas presents—oh dear!—and this week I have to lunch with the editor of *The Times* and go to another opera. When do you go to Eton? And what address there? Oscar, as you can imagine, lingers in galley-proof. I fear you will be sick of hearing about those letters long before you see them. And there are moments when I despair of finality. At the Max sale I saw S.C. Roberts, who reported a good Johnson Club evening (with himself as speaker). Shall we ever go again?

This is rather a hectic affair after a perfect day's journeying from Grundisburgh, except for the too-dazzling sun in P's eyes (December 22!) and an occasional patch of ice or muddy grease. Whereas in Suffolk every road was as dry as a D.H. Lawrence novel.

I did send you a card and the Postmaster a word of congratulation the moment I saw the great news, but I fear it didn't reach either before Monday. It was a magnificent achievement, and already I gather the science staff here are walking about looking several inches taller, as Mr Shandy said all women look after producing a baby (and every right they have to do so). You too should be what one can only call cock-a-hoop—in fact I *think* your letter shows signs of it. After all it really *was* a week for you. Duff's weekly wage sounds very handsome. In my day it would have been £4. Wage-earners of all kinds, grave and gay, are, roughly, the new well-to-do. The poor old *rentier*'s number is up—those who live on their savings and investments. No doubt we have had our day, and anyway there is nothing we can do about it.

You are too kind about Lockhart, and ought firmly to plant him next e.g. to Jonah or Harold Nicolson; both of whom, in their different ways, would deal with him faithfully. Last Lit. Soc. sounds a good party—good fare too. I share the Forsyte view of saddle of mutton. In the pre-pre-war Simpson days no man of taste had anything else for lunch (second help—or should I say 'additional portion'?—*free*!). Total cost—with cut of Stilton—four shillings. Have you read Harold N's last book?[1] As a worker, he looks to be in the R.H-D. class. But I was sorry to read that one reviewer thinks H.N. 'doesn't much like Dr Johnson'. That would be a grave failing in an otherwise good man. I shall tackle him at the next Lit. Soc.

We have in mind and joyful hope coming to you for lunch on Sunday week. How does that strike you? Pamela pessimistically thinks the track to Bromsden Farm from the road must surely be impassable with mud. I—never having had much opinion of Nature's common

[1] *The Age Of Reason* (1960).

sense—have a notion that the track is for some reason just as stolchy (Suffolk) in dry weather as in wet.

Adam was particularly delighted by your letter, and it was charmingly thoughtful of you to write. A letter from the Headmaster announces his award of O.S.[1]—which nicely matches Duff's. I do indeed feel very cock-a-hoop about the boys and their satisfactoriness. I'm glad to say they'll both be here next Sunday, when we shall expect you about 12.45. Does Pamela remember the way? If not, telephone and I'll remind you.

So far our Christmas has passed off peacefully. I have had a number of 'useful and acceptable' presents, including a superb case of Riesling from Max's sister-in-law, but the one which pleased me and Ruth most was two home-made cakes from our Kisdon farmer and his family. How I wish we were there now, with perhaps some of that snow on high ground of which the radio-announcer so fruitily speaks.

It isn't a question of my being *kind* to Lockhart, but rather of my failing to take adequately defensive measures by inviting two others to sit beside me. Harold N., who was responsible for introducing this giant bore to the assembly, always takes good care to sit far away from him. I don't think I shall bother with H.N.'s latest: it sounds an unnecessary book, and he is clearly past his best. Poor Geoffrey Faber, I hear, has had another stroke and is pretty well unconscious, having to be fed through the nose. One can't wish him long continuance of such horrors.

Last week, in the intervals of frantic, and largely abortive, last-minute shopping, I lunched with Sir William Haley at the Athenaeum (potted shrimps, liver and bacon, treacle tart—all of which would have been good if they hadn't been luke-warm). W.H. neither drinks nor smokes, but graciously joined me in a half-pint of rather good cider, which he apparently (and quite wrongly) considers non-alcoholic.

On Thursday Ruth and I were taken to yet another opera,

[1] Oppidan Scholar.

Donizetti's *Lucia di Lammermoor*, a splendid rip-roaring piece based on Scott's novel and wonderfully sung by Joan Sutherland: very enjoyable, but like most operas a little too long.

I have brought the tattered galley-proofs of Oscar down with me (I've been carrying them about and tinkering with them since *May*!) hoping once again that I may at last get a glimpse of finality.

By the way, have you ever read Geoffrey Faber's *Oxford Apostles*? I simply can't put it down, and I only took it up to supply a footnote for Oscar. Do try it if you don't know it. The whole matter seems at once so remote and so compelling. Ivor Brown has sent me the typescript of his new word-book, which I think I must publish. I'm also reading a new French novel and a manuscript about an eighteenth-century quack, so you see I'm not exactly as idle as I could wish.

INDEX

Achurch, Janet, 119
Adam, *see* Hart-Davis
Adams, Dr Bodkin, 176
Adeane, Michael, 62
Adeane, Robert, 88
Agar, Herbert, 62
Agate, James, 25, 67, 77, 96, 148, 150
Alexander, General, 148
Alexandra, Princess, 177, 182
Alington, C. A., 6
Alington, Hester, 95
Allen, G. O., 45
Alletson, E. B., 143
Allingham, William, 82
Alma Tadema, Lawrence, 88
Altham, H. S., 96
Amis, Kingsley, 3, 148, 154
Anatomy of a Murder, 21, 43, 45
Armstrong-Jones, Anthony, 69
Arnold, Matthew, 33, 125
Arnold, Dr Thomas, 162
Ashcroft, Peggy, 111
Astor, Michael, 185
Auden, W. H., 109
Austen, Jane, 7, 29, 31, 73, 135
Avory, Sir Horace, 154

Bacon, Francis, 48, 50
Baines, Jocelyn, 20, 39
Baker, H. T. (Bluey), 115
Baldwin, A. W. (Bloggs), 50
Balfour, Arthur, 13
Balzac, 137
Baring, Maurice, 141
Baring, Rose, 36
Barrie, J. M., 77, 96
Barrington, Patrick, 81, 83
Barstow, Phyllida, 185
Batchelor, Denzil, 151
Battie, Dr, 45
Beach, Sylvia, 130, 131, 133, 135
Beaverbrook, Lord, 10, 11, 12, 18, 36, 84, 85

Beddoes, T. L., 57
Beerbohm, Elisabeth, 73
Beerbohm, Max, 15, 17, 19, 54, 57, 58, 66, 70, 118, 119, 120, 121, 123, 124, 140, 141, 163, 168, 180, 181, 182, 183, 184, 186
Beethoven, 149, 179
Behrman, S. N., 118, 120, 180
Bembo, Cardinal, 101
Bennett, Arnold, 53, 67, 95
Bennett, Joan, 184
Bennett, Stanley, 2
Benson, A. C., 94, 95, 153, 184
Bentley, E. C., 25, 26
Bentley, Nicolas, 25, 26, 33
Berg, Alban, 177
Berlioz, Hector, 69
Besant, Annie, 20
Betjeman, John, 160, 170, 173, 178, 183
Bevir, Anthony, 102
Birkett, Lord, 55
Birley, Robert, 18, 87, 141, 185, 188
Birrell, Augustine, 6, 20
Blake, Admiral, 60
Blake, William, 83
Blunden, Edmund, 16, 18, 79, 87
Blunt, Wilfrid, 72
Blunt, Wilfrid Scawen, 7
Boll, Theophilus, 39, 41
Boswell, James, 52, 60, 77, 180
Bott, Josephine, 26
Bourne, Bobby, 102, 115
Bourne, Rose, 114
Bracken, Brendan, 159
Bradman, Don, 52
Bratby, John, 53
Bridge of San Luis Rey, The, 10, 58, 60
Bridget, *see* Hart-Davis
Brien, Alan, 14
Bristowe, Rowley, 95
Brogan, Denis, 153, 154
Brown, Ivor, 21, 91, 106, 108, 116, 119, 170, 189

Browne, Sir Thomas, 139, 141
Browning, Robert, 149
Bryson, John, 92
Buchan, John, 74
Bugga, St, 120
Burns, Robert, 63
Butler, J. R. M., 63
Butterwick, Cyril, 119, 123
Byron, Lord, 15, 68, 71

Calvert, Phyllis, 55
Campbell, Mrs Patrick, 117, 118
Campbell-Gray, Diana, 111
Cape, Jonathan, 23, 24, 25, 26, 27, 47
Caran d'Ache, 136
Cardus, Neville, 113
Carlyle, Jane, 58, 63
Carlyle, Thomas, 11, 17, 28, 30, 31, 32,
    35, 39, 52, 54, 55, 56, 58, 59, 60, 61, 63,
    64, 66, 67, 68, 71, 74, 77, 80, 93, 98,
    103, 107, 114, 116
Carr Bosanquet, R., 115, 118
Casanova, 41
Casaubon, Isaac, 135
Casey, 'Skin the Goat', 40
Castle, Barbara, 52
Catullus, 33
Cavendish, Lady Frederick, 40, 42
Cazalet, Thelma, 62
Cecil, Lord David, 31, 120
Chandler, Raymond, 41
Chaplin, Charlie, 95
Chaplin, Oona, 95, 96
Chapman, Guy, 150
Chapman, R. W., 64, 65
Charteris, Martin, 21, 37
Chessman, Caryl, 41
Chesterton, G. K., 170
Christie, Agatha, 57, 60
Christie, John, 46, 98, 107
Church, Richard, 27
Churchill, Winston, 24, 32, 40, 45, 54,
    69, 115, 155
Clarke, Ashley, 168
Clough, A. H., 142, 162
Cocteau, Jean, 40, 41, 44
Coleridge, F. J. R. (Fred), 100, 177, 185
Coleridge, Julia, 145, 185
Coleridge, S. T., 11, 15, 16, 109
Colman, Geoffrey, 44
Colman, Lettice, 40, 42, 44, 84
Colvin, Sidney, 48, 49
Comfort, see Hart-Davis

Compton, Fay, 11
Coningsby, 1, 3
Connolly, Cyril, 67, 109
Conrad, Joseph, 7, 20, 39, 41
Cooke, Alistair, 70
Cooper, Diana, 5, 23, 35, 54, 82, 86, 118,
    120, 142, 155, 156, 158, 165, 167
Cooper, Duff, 5, 32, 42, 44, 182
Cowdrey, Colin, 45
Crace, J. F., 54, 56, 71
Cranworth, Lord, 3, 176
Creevey, Thomas, 67
Croker, J. W., 52
Crossman, R. H. S., 155

Daman, Rev. H., 88
Darwin, Bernard, 25
Darwin, Charles, 144
Davies, Peter, 54, 57
Day Lewis, Cecil, 86, 129
De Havilland, R. S., 102
De la Mare, Walter, 8
Dehn, Paul, 94, 96
Dennys, Lavinia, 172
Dent, Alan (Jock), 66, 150, 153, 155
Devlin, Christopher, 5, 6, 7, 8, 22, 51,
    156
Devlin, Madeleine, 5, 51, 117, 118
Devlin, Patrick, 5, 22, 51, 68, 117, 118,
    120
Dickens, Charles, 26, 29, 31, 165, 171,
    182
Dickson, Dorothy, 94, 95, 96
Disraeli, 52
Donaldson, Rev. P. A., 109
Donizetti, Gaetano, 189
Douglas, Lord Alfred, 104
Drogheda, Garrett, 69, 177, 179
Drogheda, Joan, 174
Druon, Maurice, 95, 102, 104, 105, 116,
    118, 119, 155, 165
Duff, see Hart-Davis
Durrell, Gerald, 163, 164

Earlham (by Percy Lubbock), 23, 24, 40
Edel, Leon, 137, 139, 141, 144–146, 147
Eden, Anthony, 9, 11, 16
Edward II, King, 105
Edward VII, King, 102
Edward VIII, King, 179
Egerton, Alfred, 126
Egoist, The, 20
Einstein, 133

191

Eliot, George, 135
Eliot, T. S., 12, 15, 16, 18, 30, 31, 56, 60,
    61, 63, 87, 97, 108, 109, 110, 111, 112,
    113, 114, 131, 132, 146, 148, 150, 154,
    173, 178, 181
Eliot, Valerie, 12, 15, 16, 97, 150, 178,
    181
Epstein, Jacob, 5, 7, 150
Evans, Edith, 12, 13, 122, 127, 129
Expresso Bongo, 2, 4

Faber, Geoffrey, 125, 188, 189
Fergusson, Bernard, 89
Fisher, C. D., 132
Fisher, K., 46
FitzGerald, Edward, 12, 14, 15, 16, 18,
    19, 48
Flash Harry, *see* Sargent
Flower, Sir Fordham, 62
Fleming, Ian, 33, 51, 59
Fleming, Peter, 21, 22, 38, 42, 50, 54, 70,
    89, 106, 109, 119, 121, 138, 142, 156
Foley, C. P., 143, 153
Foote, Samuel, 40
Forster, E. M., 23, 30, 31, 97, 111, 113,
    127, 163, 164
Fothergill, John, 129
Foyle, Christina, 26
Francis, Alfred, 62
Francis, F. C., 9
Freud, Sigmund, 47, 177
Froude, J. A., 17, 52, 63, 103
Fry, C. B., 115
Fulford, Roger, 36, 37, 65, 72, 84, 85, 86,
    87, 156, 157, 158, 159, 162, 170
Fulford, Sibell, 40, 85, 157, 159
Fuller, Margaret, 52

Gaitskell, Hugh, 71
Galsworthy, John, 102, 147
Galt, John, 186, 187, 189
Garnett, Edward, 100, 102
Gaukrodger, G., 70
Gerhardi, William, 14, 16
Gide, André, 59
Gielgud, John, 12, 65, 66
Gilbert, W. S., 140, 144, 149, 178
Gissing, George, 146, 155, 156
Gladstone, W. E., 52, 140
Glyn, Anthony, 56
Glyn, Susan, 56
Goldsmith, Oliver, 34
Gollancz, Ruth & Victor, 140

Gordon Cumming, Sir William, 22, 23,
    25
Gore, S. W., 85
Gosse, Edmund, 131
Gow, A. S. F. (Granny), 119, 122, 124,
    127, 139
Grace, W. G., 45
Greene, Hugh, 62
Grenfell, Joyce, 177, 181, 183
Grenfell, Julian, 172
Grenfell, Reggie, 177, 179, 181, 183
Grimond, Jo, 22
Guinness, Alec, 108

Habakkuk, 19, 171
Haig Thomas, Peter, 102
Haley, Sir William, 30, 188
Hamilton, Hamish, 173–174
Hammond, Walter, 70
Harcourt, Sir William, 67
Hardy, Thomas, 134
Hare, John, 147
Harrer, Heinrich, 7
Hart-Davis, Adam, 1, 2, 5, 8, 9, 10, 11,
    15, 17, 19, 32, 36, 38, 43, 46, 49, 50, 54,
    59, 68, 70, 86, 87, 100, 101, 104, 115,
    117, 124, 126, 132, 138, 141, 143, 145,
    147, 167, 175, 177, 179, 180, 183, 185,
    186, 188
Hart-Davis, Bridget, 29, 38, 43, 59, 160
Hart-Davis, Comfort, 5, 8, 29, 42, 59, 62,
    86, 87, 93, 98, 114, 117, 121, 124, 140,
    160, 161, 175, 177
Hart-Davis, Duff, 6, 22, 42, 47, 50, 57,
    59, 87, 89, 90, 114, 115, 118, 121, 124,
    126, 129, 133, 138, 142, 145, 174, 178,
    179, 180, 181, 185, 187, 188
Hart-Davis, Richard, 159–160, 169
Hartley, L. P., 108, 173
Hassan, 13
Hay, Philip, 177
Haydn, 149
Headlam, Cuthbert, 3, 37, 38, 58, 60, 64,
    80, 91, 13, 104, 106, 108, 109, 111, 152,
    170, 173, 181
Headlam, G. W. (Tuppy), 45
Heinemann, William, Ltd, 4, 6, 141, 169
Henry II, King, 45
Herbert, A. P., 146, 148, 151, 153, 165
Herodotus, 110, 112
Hesketh, Phoebe, 62
Hill, M. D., 10, 59
Hobbs, J. B., 102

192

Hogben, Lancelot, 49, 132
Hoggart, Richard, 163, 164, 166
Holland, H. Scott, 76
Holland, Robert, 151
Holland, Thelma, 66, 69
Holland, Vyvyan, 9, 66, 67, 69, 86, 88, 90, 92
Hollis, Christopher, 165, 171, 173, 175
Holmes, Mr Justice, 169, 170, 173, 180
Hood, Alexander, 175, 176
Hood, Diana, 12, 172, 173, 174, 175, 176
Hopkins, Gerard Manley, 5
Hotson, Leslie, 1, 3, 14
Hough, Graham, 109, 163
House, Humphry, 5, 42
House, Madeline, 20, 177
Housman, A. E., 7, 24, 56, 63, 102, 115, 119, 120, 158, 159
How Green was my Valley, 39, 67, 69, 74, 76, 79, 80, 129, 132, 134
Howard, G. Wren, 26
Hugh Walpole, 36, 38, 59, 135
Hugo, Victor, 83
Hulme, T. E., 110, 112
Hulton, Nika, 8
Hunt, Leigh, 90
Hutchinson, Mary, 150
Hyson, Dot, 96

Importance of Being Earnest, The, 9, 11, 13, 122, 123, 124
Innes, Michael, *see* Stewart, J. I. M.
Irving, Edward, 58, 61
Ivor, *see* Brown

Jackson, Stonewall, 180
James, Henry, 58, 85, 86, 103, 105, 107, 137, 158, 159
Jameson, T. O., 153
Jardine, D. R., 46, 52
Jenkins, Roy, 170
Jepson, Selwyn, 91, 98
Johnson, Doctor, 3, 6, 7, 8, 10, 40, 60, 63, 71, 72, 76, 110, 113, 142, 147, 158, 180, 183, 187
Jonah, *see* Jones, L. E.
Jones, A. O., 143
Jones, Lady Evelyn (Evy), 154
Jones, L. E. (Jonah), 12, 91, 108, 154, 155, 170, 175, 178, 179, 187
Jowett, Benjamin, 131
Joyce, James, 131

Kaye, Danny, 7
Keats, John, 19, 48
Keele, C. A., 6
Kent, Marina, Duchess of, 174, 177
Keown, Eric, 67
Ketton-Cremer, Wyndham, 150
King Lear, 40
Kinglake, A. W., 95
Kingsley, Charles, 76
Kipling, Rudyard, 41, 56, 184
Lady Chatterley's Lover, 36, 77, 123, 124, 126, 127, 150, 154, 156, 159, 160, 162, 164, 166, 173
Lamb, Charles, 83
Lancaster, Osbert, 16
Landor, W. S., 31, 33, 35, 83
Lane, Allen, 166, 184
Lane, Margaret, 9, 94
Larwood, Harold, 46
Lascelles, Sir Alan (Tommy), 151
Laver, James, 66, 90, 93
Lawrence, D. H., 29, 77, 99, 123, 127, 135, 164, 166, 171, 187
Lawrence, T. E., 97, 108
Le Gallienne, Richard, 130, 133, 135, 141
Leavis, F. R., 3, 88, 90, 123, 155
Lee, Vernon, 135, 137, 139, 141
Lehmann, John, 89
Lehmann, Rosamond, 50
Lessing, Doris, 165
Lettice, *see* Colman
Leverson, Ada, 23
Levin, Bernard, 164, 165, 166, 184
Lincoln, Abraham, 180
Livingstone, R. W., 10, 59, 61, 63
Lloyd George, D., 158
Lockhart, R. Bruce, 80, 91, 186, 187, 188
London Library, The, 35, 43, 48, 50, 51, 54, 62, 64, 67, 87, 97, 98, 100
Lubbock, Percy, 103
Lyte, H. C. Maxwell, 165
Lyttelton, Edward, 165
Lyttelton, Humphrey, 116, 122, 159, 179
Lyttelton, Lord, 65, 66
Lyttelton, Oliver, 118
Lyttelton, Pamela, 1, 14, 21, 22, 39, 40, 46, 49, 56, 71, 72, 76, 81, 88, 91, 109, 152, 155, 157, 158, 161, 174, 176, 178, 184, 187, 188

Maas, Henry, 133, 135, 177
Macaulay, Lord, 29, 51, 55, 138
MacCarthy, Desmond, 19

Mackenzie, Compton, 146, 151, 160
Macleod, K. G., 80
MacLiammóir, Micheál, 167
Macnaghten, H., 17, 88
Madan, Geoffrey, 39
Madeline, see Wigan
Mahler, Gustav, 177, 178, 181
Mallarmé, Stephane, 137–138
Mankowitz, Wolf, 2
Manning, Cardinal, 76
Mansfield, Katherine, 19, 99
Margaret, Princess, 69
Marsden, H. K., 99
Marsh, Eddie, 172
Martin Chuzzlewit, 165
Martineau, Richard, 67
Mary, see Stewart Cox
Masefield, John, 16, 29–30, 31
Mason, James, 70, 72
Masterman, J. C., 9
Maude, Mr Justice, 163
Maugham, W. S., 43, 59, 97, 126, 153
McTaggart, J. M. E., 85
Mencken, H. L., 33
Menuhin, Yehudi, 65
Meredith, George, 20, 66
Middlemarch, 133, 135, 137, 139
Milton, John, 32, 33, 40, 84, 103, 126, 172
Mitford, Nancy, 43
Molière, 149
Monkhouse, Allan, 44, 107
Montagu of Beaulieu, Lord, 94
Montague, C. E., 126
Moore, George, 152, 182, 184
Moore, G. E., 140, 158
Morrow, George, 127, 159
Mortimer, Raymond, 1, 105
Murray, Gilbert, 85
Murray, John, 68, 71
Murry, J. Middleton, 18, 19, 119, 123
Mynors, Lavinia, 87
Mynors, Roger, 87, 88

Naipaul, V. S., 24
Napoleon, 89
Naylor, John, 89
Nelson, Horatio, 5, 135
Nevinson, H. W., 126
Newman, Cardinal, 76
Ney, Marshal, 89
Nicholas Nickleby, 171
Nicolson, Harold, 27, 28, 30, 32, 37, 62,

63, 100, 111, 113, 182, 187, 188
Noble, M. A., 52, 166
Nowell-Smith, Simon, 103
Nugent, Tim, 21, 89, 106, 109

Ogden, C. K., 131
O'Neill, Eugene, 17, 92, 95, 96, 98, 99, 101
Ordish, George, 71
Osborne, John, 10
Oscar, see Wilde
Oxenstierna, Axel, 142

Paradise Lost, 40, 84
Peacock, T. L., 41
Pearson, Hesketh, 140, 144
Peter, see Fleming
Petrie, Sir Charles, 80, 83, 85, 180, 181
Phillips, Stephen, 135, 137
Phipps, Paul, 183
Picasso, Pablo, 88
Pickwick Papers, 2
Piper, John, 16
Playboy of the Western World, The, 167
Plomer, William, 47
Pope, Alexander, 113
Porter, Dr, 46, 183
Pound, Ezra, 15, 16, 17, 19, 60, 61, 63, 71, 109, 112, 148
Powell, Anthony, 22, 38, 106, 108, 163
Powell, Dilys, 163
Prescot, H. J., 17
Pride and Prejudice, 29, 31
Priestley, J. B., 1, 23, 25, 27, 29, 33, 34, 53, 54, 56, 58, 59, 60, 106
Pryce-Jones, Alan, 67, 131, 167

Quashiboo Rangers, The, 153
Quayle, Anthony, 97
Queensberry, Lord, 105
Quennell, Peter, 98, 106, 110, 112, 113, 116, 136, 139, 148, 152, 154
Quiller-Couch, A., 149

Ransome, Arthur, 5, 97, 99, 101
Rattigan, Terence, 87
Raymond, John, 73
Regler, Gustav, 3
Reichmann, Eva, 54, 122, 124, 178, 182, 188
Rendall, Monty, 57
Rhodes, Cecil, 54
Rhondda, Lady, 38

Richards, Gordon, 102
Richardson, Joanna, 12
Riddell, Anne, 172, 176
Ridler, Vivian, 89
Roberts, Cecil, 168
Roberts, S. C., 186
Roger, *see* Fulford
Ross, Alan, 143, 146, 148
Ross, Robbie, 104
Routh, C. R. N. (Dick), 171, 180
Ruskin, John, 33, 80
Russell, Bertrand, 13
Russell, Leonard, 42–43, 67, 69, 160, 161
Ruth, *see* Simon
Rutherford, Margaret, 123

Sade, Marquis de, 83, 131
Saintsbury, George, 88
Sargent, Malcolm, 92, 102
Sassoon, Siegfried, 151, 152
Savile, Sir Henry, 60
Scott, C. P., 113
Scott-James, Anne, 163
Secker, Martin, 130
Shakespeare, 1, 67, 95, 144
Shaw, Bernard, 21, 52, 53, 97, 99, 102,
    117, 118, 119, 120, 156, 170
Shelley, 6, 83
Sibelius, Jan, 181
Sibell, *see* Fulford
Sidney, Sir Philip, 172
Simmons, Jack, 31
Simon, Ruth, *passim*
Simon, Timothy, 35, 37, 41, 42, 47, 49,
    51, 54, 55, 61, 86
Sitwell, Edith, 33, 127, 179
Smart, Christopher, 50, 156
Smith, Logan Pearsall, 13
'Sohrab and Rustum', 40
Somervell, Donald, 50, 53, 91, 107, 108,
    109, 175
Somerville, E. Œ., 75
Southey, Robert, 28, 31, 33, 35
Spanoghe, Pam, 107, 108
Sparrow, John, 5, 6, 9, 58, 61, 63, 92, 93
St Joan, 37, 38
Stanley, H. M., 116, 119
Stevenson, R. L., 50, 77, 103, 105
Stewart Cox, Mary, 3, 7
Stewart, J. I. M., 5, 6, 9, 11, 106
Stone, Christopher, 3
Stone, Reynolds, 5
Storey, Graham, 20, 177

Strachey, James, 43, 47
Strachey, Lytton, 33, 43, 47, 48, 97, 114,
    140, 162
Sullivan, Arthur, 149, 178
Summerskill, Edith, 175
Swift, Jonathan, 146, 171
Swinburne, A. C., 74, 78, 83, 131
Swinnerton, Frank, 90, 173
Symons, Julian, 134, 136, 138

Talbot, Sir George, 154
Talbot, Monsignor, 140
Tennyson, Alfred, 54, 80, 149
Terry, Ellen, 53
Tess of the D'Urbervilles, 103
Thomas, Dylan, 127, 129
Thomas, John, 29
Thomson, Roy, 30, 114
Tim, *see* Nugent
Tommy, *see* Lascelles
Trevelyan, G. M., 19, 63
Trevelyan, George Otto, 40
Trollope, Anthony, 3, 4, 21, 184
Trumper, Victor, 70
Tupper, Martin, 184
Tuppy, *see* Headlam
Turner, Reggie, 133
Tutin, Dorothy, 122, 124, 127
Tynan, Ken, 166, 184

Van Oss, Audrey, 45, 67, 69
Van Oss, Oliver, 14, 18, 33, 185, 186
Van Thal, Bertie, 41, 66, 67
Veale, Sir Douglas, 87
Victoria, Queen, 21, 140
Vile Bodies, 37
Virgil, 99

Wagg, Kenneth, 185
Wain, John, 1
Walkley, A. B., 31
Wallace, W. H., 25
Walpole, Dorothy, 118
Walpole, Hugh, 97
Walpole, Robin, 119, 121
Warre, Edmond, 59
Watts, G. F., 88
Waugh, Evelyn, 37, 106, 110, 156
Wedgwood, Veronica, 114
Weller, Sam, 182
Wellington, First Duke of, 5, 89, 90, 91,
    171, 173
Wellington, Seventh Duke of, 36, 90

Wells, C. M., 45, 96
Wells, H. G., 95, 113, 146, 155, 156
West, Rebecca, 146, 148, 151, 184
What Happens in 'Hamlet', 48, 53
Wigan, Madeline, 40, 45
Wigwam, Dr Virgil, 41
Wilde, Oscar, *passim*
Wilkinson, C. H., 11, 122
Williams, Sir Griffith, 19
Wilson, Angus, 106
Wilson, Colin, 41
Wilson, E. R., 154
Wilson, J. Dover, 48, 50
Wise, T. J., 25
Witch, The, 8, 11, 24, 26
Woodham Smith, Mrs, 47
Woodruff, Douglas, 178
Woolf, Leonard, 19, 140, 141, 144, 150, 151, 158

Woolf, Virginia, 135
Wordsworth, William, 11, 14, 31, 32, 35, 97, 99, 109
Wozzeck, 177, 179, 181
Wright, Aldis, 14, 16, 48
Wrong Box, The, 17
Wuthering Heights, 59, 61
Wyndham, Francis, 21, 22

XYZ, 8, 10, 14, 15, 18, 24

Yeats, W. B., 34, 112, 129
Young, Andrew, 116, 118, 131, 133, 163, 182, 184
Yugoslavia, Princess Paul of, 174

Zuckerman, Sir Solly, 69